The
Long Nights
of
Mourning

A Journey with Grief after

Sudden Loss

by

Janis Ost Ford

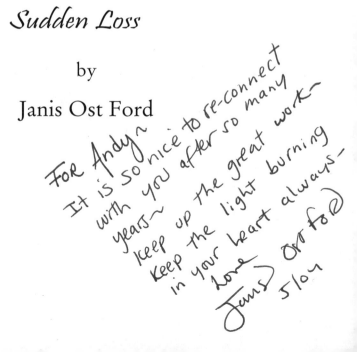

For Andy~
It is so nice to re-connect
with you after so many
years~ keep up the great work~
keep the light burning
in your heart always~
Love, Janis Orford
5/04

Janis Ost Ford
P.O. Box 5332
Santa Cruz, California 95063-5332
Bromador@aol.com

First Edition

Front Cover Photo: Kevin Sheahan
Author's Photo: Gayle Mitchell
Copyediting and Editorial Assistance:
        by Jessica Baron Turner and Jon Akeman
Cover Design and Typography: Karas Technical Services

Library of Congress Control Number: 2003094445

The Long Nights Of Mourning / Janis Ost Ford – 1st ed.
ISBN 0-9742358-0-6

Dedication

"The Long Nights Of Mourning" is dedicated to the memories of the 88 beautiful souls aboard Alaskan Airlines Flight # 261 on January 31, 2000. This flight was returning from Puerta Vallarta, Mexico, bound for San Francisco, California and ultimately Seattle, Washington.

This book is for my brother's amazing children, Ashley and Axel Ost.

This book is also dedicated to the other families and friends of these innocent passengers, with every ounce of heart felt love and solidarity. Some of these people have become special friends, JoVanna, Claire, Paige, Earlene, and Fred.

My words and experiences are written for the comfort of anybody who is experiencing the sudden loss of loved ones. This book is also for the compassionate ones who will befriend the families and loved ones left behind.

I need to thank so many people for helping to bring The Long Nights Of Mourning into fruition. I thank my daughter Carina for being so independent and helping out with her little brother. I thank Greg for keeping things quiet and giving me the space to write, feel, and remember.

I thank Cody for taking naps. I thank my friends for their support. I thank my father Arthur for making me laugh during these past three years.

I thank Jamie Lebovitz for his steadfast commitment and kindness. I thank Jan Rilovich, Dr. Craig Eyemann, Dr. Michael Caulsen, Dr. Nancy Thorner, my acupuncturist Phil Caylor, and elder Laynee Bluebird for helping me to heal.

I thank Diane Pallante, Paula Gomez, Heather Stiles, Kathi Gelini, Stoney Godot and Ventura León for their kindness and help.

I thank Jessica Baron Turner, my dear friend and professional editor who worked like a mad woman with a purple pen, getting things ready for print. I also thank Jon Akeman, another great writer who helped edit as well. A big hug for Ellen Bass, Carter Wilson, Dan Eres, Jan Marquart, Dina Hoffman, Tom Crain and Charles Capone, who saw the beginning of this project and helped to get it off the ground.

I thank my book designer Deborah Karas, and Keith Greeninger, Jessica Baron Turner, (a writer/editor who sings beautifully) and Niki Leeman for their amazing and healing music on the back of this book.

In loving memory of
my mother,
Jean Permison,
her companion Charles Russell,
my awesome brother Bob,
my sister-in-law Ileana Ost and
my beautiful four month old niece Emily Ost

Until we meet again
on the other side,
I shall love, honor, and miss you
each and everyday.

**25% proceeds of this book
go directly to
NADA/F
(National Air Disaster Alliance/Foundation)
www.PlaneSafe.org**

The National Air Disaster Alliance & Foundation was incorporated in 1995 by air crash survivors and family members of victims. It aims to address the long-term and short-term challenges faced by all who have been affected by devastating air tragedies.

NADA/F works with survivors, family members of victims, aviation professionals, government agencies, Congress, social service agencies, the news media and others. At times they are the only aviation safety group on record opposing unsafe practices.

NADA/F's Family Support Team provides trained volunteer personnel to help survivors and victims' families short-term and long-term after an air disaster.

Table of Contents

2003

Forward

On January 31, 2000, the lives of eighty-eight vacationing airplane passengers and their loved ones awaiting their safe return home were forever shattered. The mothers, fathers, children, grandchildren, siblings, spouses and friends of those tragically and inexcusably killed on Alaska Airlines flight # 261 came face to face with the horrible aftermath of an airplane crash; Confronting such chilling details like dental records, DNA, blood tests, memorial services and ultimately funerals.

The joys of life, the laughter, the celebration, the unfulfilled dreams of the future are no more; having been replaced by tears, shock, despair, anger, emptiness and profound sadness.

Five members of a loving and happy family are gone in an instant, leaving behind their bereaved survivors. Now when Janis Ost Ford sets the Thanksgiving day table there are five empty places. Janis lost her mother, her mother's companion, brother, sister-in-law and four month old baby niece in the crash of flight #261. How can a family survive this horrific and sudden destruction of human life?

Janis Ost Ford gives you, the reader, a rare glimpse into a family's struggle to survive – to "go on" with life. Not surprisingly there is no way possible to "go on" and return to a state of normalcy. Survive – yes. But never as before.

When a part of one's heart is torn away it is impossible to be the same. This is a story of a family trying to return to some semblance of normalcy under the most tragic of circumstances one could every possible imagine.

For over twenty years, I have represented families who have lost loved ones in airplane disasters. No words can completely describe the devastation that overcomes a family who suddenly and without any warning learn that their spouse, parent, child, grandchild, sibling or friend will never come home, will never be heard laughing, will never be there to hug, will never be there to cherish.

Aircrash disasters happen not because of some "plan" or "Act of God" – they happen solely because of misconduct on the part of airlines, airplane manufacturers and others. And most often, the causes are multiple in origin – careless maintenance; poorly and inadequately trained flight crews; defective design of systems which are supposed to protect passengers from in flight component failures; failure of the government agencies to enforce rules and regulations intended to keep the skies safe and prevent airlines and others in the air transportation business from putting profits ahead of flight safety.

Fortunately, for families such as Janis', there is a Civil Justice system in the United States, unlike other countries, which allow families to hire lawyers, like myself, to expose the wrongdoings of airlines, airplane manufacturers and others and to hold them accountable to those who bear the consequences of their misdeeds. As a lawyer committed to bringing justice to families of aircrash disasters, it is my hope that with perseverance, persistence and patience, I , along with those I am privileged to represent, can influence airlines and airplane manufacturers in the way they do "business" and force the industry to do everything that is humanly and technically feasible to make absolutely certain that similar tragedies never happen again.

The loss of human life is intolerable. Misconduct on the part of airlines and airplane manufacturers can not and will not be tolerated. We must never lose sight of the fact that the citizens of the United States have the absolute right through our system of justice to make a difference that will benefit the lives and safety of all people.

Janis' hope for those who have also experienced sudden loss is that you will discover peace from the memories, and solace knowing you are not alone.

Jamie Robert Lebovitz, esquire
aviation attorney, Cleveland, Ohio

Newspaper Clippings

Hope dims for survivors

The Associated Press

An unidentified woman stands on the beach before dawn next to a memorial at La Janelle Park in Oxnard.

Beach memorials erected along coastline

By CHRISTINE HANLEY
The Associated Press

PORT HUENEME — Two sisters walked to the end of the pier, threw a dozen red carnations into the cold Pacific water and offered their prayers Tuesday to 88 people lost in a jetliner crash that brought tragedy to this beachside community.

"We're going to say a prayer that they're in God's hands," said Victoria Arjaev, a Port Hueneme resident with her sister, JoAnne Frank. "And maybe for a miracle, that there's some survivor out there. You never know."

The crash of Alaska Airlines Flight 261 drew a few dozen people to Port Hueneme Beach under a cloudless sky, some mournful, some curious.

For a handful, the pier had become a scene of pilgrimage.

Dozens left flowers and pictures around a makeshift cross. One of them, Janelle Davis, lay down a white candle and a pink, blue and purple bouquet. She kneeled before the cross, then sobbed into her hands for a relative she said was on board the plane.

A police sport utility vehicle drove along the beach, looking for wreckage that had washed ashore from the crash site, about 10 miles away. Vessels involved in the recovery moved in and out of view.

"You don't realize when you put someone on a plane and give them a hug that you might not see them again," said Diane Adams, 39, who had

come to the pier.

"It just feels so good to stand out here and pray. It sort of cleanses you out," she said.

The memorials were repeated elsewhere in Port Hueneme, a town of 22,500 and home to a major naval base and a commercial shipping harbor.

On Silver Strand beach, a local artist erected a seven-foot wooden cross festooned with flowers. A white plastic angel sat at the base with a candle blowing in a jar. Through the day, residents delivered bouquets and lit candles.

April Salas, an Oxnard resident, brought a sign that read, "May God bless all the family members who lost their loved ones."

"It's support for the families," she said.

1

Air crash victim was known on Coastside

Ost remembered in Butano

By DEIRDRE PETTIT
Half Moon Bay Review

Coastside residents fondly remember former Pescaderan Bob Ost who, along with four members of his family, was killed on Jan. 31 in the crash of Alaska Airline Flight 261.

Ost, a Butano Canyon resident until he moved over the hill to San Bruno four years ago, was remembered by longtime friend and Half Moon Bay resident Ed Capitanich as a likable, cheerful and caring person who liked to lend a helping hand.

"When something happened in the canyon, he would show up to help," he said. "He was really, really loved."

Ost was born in New Jersey, but was raised in the Bay Area and graduated from Hillsdale High School in San Mateo in 1978.

Ost, his wife Ileana and their 4-month-old daughter Emily, his mother Jean Permison and stepfather Charles Russell were killed in the airplane crash.

A 15-year-veteran of the South San Francisco Fire Department, friends also recalled Ost as an adventurer with a great wit.

"He was dedicated to his job and was a man with a great sense of humor," recalled friend Greg Ford, who is married to Ost's sister Janis Ost Ford. The Fords live in Santa Cruz.

"He was almost a comedian."

"I met Bob almost 15 years ago," said Pacifica resident and fellow

See OST, Page 9A

Ost

Continued from Page 1A

firefighter Brian Young. "My first impression was that he was quiet, unassuming and confident. I liked him from the beginning.

"He was a wild man, although you would never know it by looking at him," he added.

Young said he and Ost were partners in mountain climbing, which along with hang gliding was one of his favorite sports.

"He was a pioneer in that area," Young said of hang gliding.

Ost started a hang-gliding instruction company called Black Wings to introduce people to the sport, according to Young. He traveled extensively and wrote about the sport for several publications.

Although Ost liked to push the limits, Young said he was "one of the safest men I've ever known.

"He didn't do anything without providing for safety," Young said. "So it's doubly tragic he died this way."

Spending time both on and off

> ## "He didnt do anything without providing for safety."
>
> ### Brian Young,
> ### victim's friend

the job with Ost was never boring.

"He had a wit and humor that covered everything from black to white. When he took his uniform off, it was like going into the hills with Woody Allen," Young remembered.

Along with most firefighters, Young said Ost was driven to help people.

"That was a great need of his. A lot of people have Bob to thank for saving them from hurt and sometimes saving their lives."

"Our family is proud that he has been there for other people," Ford said.

Courtesy of Greg Ford

Bob Ost, pictured with wife Ileana and 4-month-old daughter Emily, lived in Butano Canyon until four years ago.

2

County residents on jetliner that crashed

By Michele R. Marcucci, Rebecca Wallace
and Richard Saskal
STAFF WRITERS

At least four County residents were passengers on Alaska Airlines' ill-fated Flight 261 Monday.

Other victims came from Oakland, San Francisco, Corte Madera and many other Northern California cities.

The flight from Puerto Vallarta, Mexico, to San Francisco, with 88 persons aboard, crashed into the Pacific Ocean off Point Mugu in Ventura County.

By late this morning, searchers had found no survivors.

The passengers included Ileana Ost of San Bruno, an Alaska Airlines ticket agent, her husband Bob Ost, a South San Francisco firefighter, and their infant daughter, Emily.

A Belmont woman named Joan Smith was also on Flight 261, according to a passenger list

Bob Ost

The San Bruno resident, along with his wife and their infant daughter, were among the passengers on Flight 261.

Continued from NEWS-1

Alaska released late this morning. Nothing more was known about Smith Tuesday morning.

As of this morning, the airline had identified the hometowns of about half the passengers on the flight.

Bob Ost's father, Arthur Ost of San Mateo, said his son has lived life to the fullest.

Ost, 38, has survived nearly 15 years as a South San Francisco firefighter. He has survived mountain climbing expeditions. He has paraglided, even jumped out of airplanes, and survived.

"Strangely, my son was a daredevil," his father, Arthur Ost, said.

Ost's family and friends are hoping that he and family members traveling with him — who included Bob Ost's mother Jean Permison of Santa Cruz; and Permison's as-yet unidentified traveling companion — survived Monday's crash of Alaska Airlines flight 261. But, they said, it doesn't sound good.

"From what I read, they're almost giving up. It's cold, and they haven't found anybody," said Arthur Ost. "Except my son is such a fighter. Maybe he did survive."

The Ost family was part of a group of Alaska Airlines employees, family and friends together for a weekend in Puerto Vallarta. His wife has been a customer service agent for since November 1996.

A longtime Delta Airlines pilot from Fremont, who didn't want his name used, said airline employees commonly use their free-flight privileges, especially in the winter when more seats are available on planes.

"Each airline is different, but every employee can travel as much as they want for free, as long as they fly on standby," he said. "You go to the gate, and if seats are left after boarding you get on board."

Many carriers charge employees a nominal service charge, perhaps about $10 per flight, he said.

A situation such as that on Flight 261, where the passengers included seven employees of Alaska and its sister airline Horizon Air, and 23 of their friends and relatives, is not unusual, he said.

"It's a slow travel season and Mexico is a nice place to be in the winter," he said. "A lot of people take airline jobs just for the travel privileges."

Arthur Ost said his son and Ileana Ost have been married for three years. Daughter Emily was born three months ago. Bob Ost also has two children from a previous marriage, he said.

In November, Bob Ost was promoted from his job as a fire truck driver to a regular, 40-hour-a-week daytime job as a building inspector, South San Francisco Fire Chief Russ Lee said.

"He was really excited about that, having a lot of fun with it," Lee said.

The couple has been building an addition on their Santa Lucia Avenue home, Lee and Arthur Ost said.

"I'm holding up. I don't know how," Arthur Ost said. "I'm feeling a little numb because it's hard to believe (this happened)."

It could now be up to the 81-year-old Ost to handle his son's affairs, a daunting task, he said.

"I don't know what to do," he said.

Arthur Ost only family now is a daughter in Santa Cruz who is headed to Los Angeles to meet with officials there.

"My poor daughter has lost her mother, her brother, everyone. She's grieving," Ost said.

Firefighters at South City's fire department are shocked over the possible loss of a respected, well-liked colleague, Lee said.

The mood at the department is somber, he said. But there is some hope for the Ost family.

"Certainly, there's always hope a miracle could occur," Lee said. "Periodically, these things do happen."

Also on the flight was Cynthia Oti, the host of a radio talk show on financial issues on 560 AM KSFO. Oti was in Mexico for a brief vacation.

The radio station has been flooded with calls and e-mail messages from listeners who will miss her program, which aired every weeknight from 7 to 8 p.m. for five years.

"I think she was universally liked," KSFO marketing and public relations director Greg Raab said. "She was a bull in relation to the market. She also suggested reasonable strategies for people's life situations."

Oti was a perfect host for the show because, unlike hosts of national shows, she knew what her listeners were experiencing living in the Bay Area. "She knew saving for a down payment on a house didn't mean twenty grand," Raab said.

Oti, 43, was a practicing investment broker and a senior vice president at First Union Securities in San Francisco. She lived in Oakland, according to the Alaska Airlines passenger manifest.

"She's been an absolutely magnificent employee for us," First Union Securities branch manager Anthony Cameron said Monday night.

After working at First Union during the day, she headed to KSFO for her show. Station employees will be hit hard by her loss when Oti doesn't show up at 6:15 p.m. today, Raab said.

Oti's radio audience ranged in age and financial security, from young workers to retirees, from investing novices to millionaires.

The only complaint the radio station received about her was that she was too light-hearted, Raab said.

Two area residents on board Alaska Airlines Flight 261

By DONNA KIMURA
Sentinel staff writer

SCOTTS VALLEY — Grief draped the tight-knit seniors' community of Montevalle as word spread Tuesday that two popular residents were aboard the Alaska Airlines flight that plunged into the Pacific Ocean.

Jean Permison, 73, and long-time companion Charles Russell were among the 88 people on the Puerto Vallarta-to-San Francisco flight that went down Monday afternoon near Oxnard.

Also on board were Permison's son, South San Francisco fire inspector Bob Ost, his wife, Alaska Airlines employee Ileana Ost, and their 4-month old daughter, Emily.

At Montevalle, a still flag was at half-staff Tuesday. The devel-

Choate
Former Santa Cruz resident lost in crash — **Page A4**

opment on Bean Creek Road is a tidy community of 220 homes restricted to people 55 and older.

"They will be sorely missed," said Patricia Nicholas, who lives two houses down from the home that Permison and Russell shared.

"Part of me doesn't want to accept that they are gone," Nicholas said.

When news of the crash hit the

Please see RESIDENTS — PAGE A4

Please see RESIDENTS — PAGE A4

More inside

■ Many N. Californians among victims; complete passenger manifest
— **Page A4**

■ Alaska Airlines employees mourn as an 'extended family'
— **Page A5**

■ Crash at sea brings up obstacles in courtroom compensation battles
— **Page A5**

■ High tech enters search scene — **Page A5**

Friends bid pair farewell

By DONNA KIMURA
Sentinel staff writer

SANTA CRUZ — Family and friends made their way through a gentle rain Thursday to bid farewell to two local residents killed in last week's Alaska Airlines crash.

They came to say goodbye to Jean Permison, 73, and Charlie Russell, 70, of Scotts Valley.

"Jean and Charlie chose life," Pastor Rebecca Irelan began.

The couple's love of life was a theme echoed throughout the hour-long funeral at First United Methodist Church in Santa Cruz.

About 200 people attended the services. As mourners entered the church, they were given buttons bearing a photo of Permison and Russell.

Permison's son, Bob Ost, his wife Iliana and their 4-month-old daughter, Emily, were also killed in the crash. The group was returning from a vacation in Puerto Vallarta, where they celebrated Permison's birthday.

She was remembered as a New Yorker who still had her accent.

He was a Midwesterner from Missouri who had a taste for real butter and real meat.

She was the source of inspiration

Continues next page

Charles Russell and Jean Permison celebrate New Year's Eve, Jan. 1, 2000, in this photo supplied by neighbors of the pair, who lived in a Scotts Valley mobile home park. Both Russell and Permison are confirmed to have been aboard Alaska Airlines Flight 261.

Mourners enter First United Methodist Church in Santa Cruz Thursday to attend funeral services for Jean Permison and Charlie Russell, victims of the Alaska Airlines crash.

Dan Coyro/Sentinel

4

FAREWELL

while he provided direction in their partnership.

The two were longtime companions, who shared a home at the Montevalle senior citizens community.

When asked why they never married, Russell would joke, "Why ruin a perfect friendship?" friends recalled.

Both were remembered as loving parents.

"I am shattered, but still whole," said Janis Ost Ford, Permison's daughter.

Ford, a Santa Cruz resident, recalled regular visits with her mother. They also frequently talked on the telephone, often as Ford relaxed in the bathtub.

Permison would always worry that Ford would be electrocuted.

Russell, a retired engineer, was remembered for spicy jokes and his love for cooking.

Irelan quoted one of Russell's neighbors, saying, "I don't know what his face looked like without a smile."

It was not God's will that they died in the crash, Irelan said.

God's will is in their spirit, she said.

When people stepped out of the church, the rain had stopped and patches of pale blue could be seen between the clouds.

San Bruno family aboard ill-fated flight

Osts remembered as loving and devoted parents

By Michelle O'Donnell
and Jennifer Pearson Bonnett
Independent Newspapers

The house on Santa Lucia Avenue and Anza Way stands half-done, swathed in chicken wire like an unfrosted cake, waiting for its owner to slather on layers of stucco in a do-it-yourself home improvement project that removed the front stairs and pushed the corner home's ceiling skyward.

Instead of a garden, which went to seed during the remodeling, cut flowers, a rosary and candles cover the cement porch. Carnations. White lilies. A funeral wreath signed "The Hoy family."

On Monday, San Bruno residents Robert "Bob" and Ileana Ost and their 4-month-old daughter, Emily, were killed on their way home from a vacation in Mexico when Alaska Airlines Flight 261 plummeted into the Pacific Ocean off the Southern California coast.

All 88 people aboard died.

Instead of handymen, cameramen now flock to the home to shoot memorial tributes to the young family.

"Vultures, vultures all of them," says Robert's father, Arthur Ost of San Mateo, shaking his head, after allowing a Los Angeles television crew to tape him in front of the house.

"Once in a while [Bob would] get a colleague to help him with something. Essentially it was his project," Ost said of the reworked home. "I think they were anticipating the baby and wanted a bigger house."

He stands in the sunny backyard amid the comfortable debris of family life: buckets of building supplies, new double-paned windows awaiting installation, an empty Tony & Alba pizza box, Cherry Coke cans in a recycling bin.

"I'm in a fog. Everyone else has collapsed," Ost said. The crash that took the life of his son, daughter-in-law and infant granddaughter also killed his former wife, Jean Permison of Santa Cruz, and her companion, Charles Russell of Scotts Valley.

Ost, his daughter, Janis Ost Ford of Santa Cruz, and Robert's children from a previous marriage, Ashley, 11, and Axel, 9, are trying to cope with the tragedy the best they can, he said. "Janis is destroyed. Absolutely destroyed. She lost her mother and her brother."

Ileana's mother flew to the Bay Area from her native Mexico to be with her daughter, Bernice Kolber, of San Carlos.

"I feel so bad for her," he said in a stunned voice. "She was just here for Christmas, and now she's back for this."

Ost said he moved here with his former wife and children from Teaneck, N.J., about 35 years ago. Bob, 39, graduated from Hillsdale High School and joined the South San Francisco Fire Department 15 years ago. His colleagues said he was respected and well-loved.

"He was an all around good guy with a great sense of humor," said department spokesperson Susan Kennedy, who knew him for nine years.

"I think of him with sort of a glint in his eye, that the wheels were always turning. He was always somebody who not just wanted to do his job but do it well."

Ost said he visited the fire department where flags across the city

FLIGHT *page 3A*

5

FLIGHT: Residents in mourning

Continued from 1A

flew at half staff, but is still in too much shock to plan a memorial service and will leave it in the hands of his son's colleagues instead.

These past few months had been good to the young couple. Last November, shortly after Ileana gave birth to Emily, Bob was promoted to fire inspector.

Just before their trip to Mexico, Ileana, a Mexico native, returned from maternity leave to her position as a customer service employee at the Alaska Airlines counter.

Despite Bob's reputation as a competent and collected firefighter, fighting fires wasn't the only thing that he was known for around the department.

Kennedy said he was an accomplished mountain and rock climber, who'd been honing his skill since the age of 15.

"As a matter of fact, he was the first person up several ascents in Yosemite which are listed in the park's guidebook."

In addition, Bob surfed, scaled walls and parasailed, according to Kennedy. He also owned a parasailing instruction company called "Blackwing."

It seems easy for the elder Ost to chat about his son and daughter-in-law, as if they're not really gone. He seems at home in front of their house, filling in the details of the young family's life that convey two loving and devoted parents: baby Emily's recent christening, Ileana's regular attendance at Spanish-language Mass at St.

SUSAN GARRISON

South San Francisco firefighters placed a mini-memorial and flew flags at half-staff as a tribute to Robert Ost.

Bruno's Church, trying to arrange the new mother's work hours around Bob's firefighter schedule.

But when asked about his infant granddaughter, Ost eyes fill up and he stumbles away down the driveway. "All babies are cute. But this one was exceptional. There was nothing like her."

A trust fund for Robert Ost's children Ashley and Axel has been established by the South San Francisco Fire Department. Donations can be sent to: The Bob Ost Memorial Fund, c/o First National Bank, 211 Airport Blvd., South San Francisco, 94080. For more information, call (650) 873-0211.

Alaska Airlines mechanics allege push to cut corners

The Associated Press

SEATTLE — Sixty-four mechanics at Alaska Airline's Seattle maintenance hangar told company officials they'd been "pressured, threatened and intimidated" to cut corners on repairs, prompting the airline to put a top manager on leave while it investigates.

Federal Aviation Administration and airline officials began interviewing the mechanics after the airline told the agency about the complaints, which came in a letter delivered to the carrier on Thursday.

Alaska Airlines also notified federal prosecutors and the National Transportation Safety Board, which is probing the Jan. 31 crash of Alaska Flight 261 off the California coast in which 88 people died.

NTSB Chairman Jim Hall said in a statement nearly all major components of the MD-80's tail section have been recovered and the agency announced the completion of its field study.

Hall also said investigators had found no grease on a crucial portion of the jackscrew that helped control the movement of Flight 261's horizontal tail stabilizer, long a focus of the crash probe.

A spokesman for the plane's manufacturer said the part normally should be lubricated, but he refused to speculate about what the NTSB finding might mean.

The Seattle Times reported on its Web site Friday that the mechanics' letter was triggered by concerns over a recent repair to the horizontal stabilizer and jackscrew assembly on an Alaska MD-80 jetliner.

The mechanics allege the plane was fixed properly only after heated discussions.

FAA spokesman Mitch Barker said the agency was aware there had been recent "debate" at Alaska Airlines over a horizontal stabilizer repair. He said the plane was returned to service in proper condition.

A draft of the letter by 64 mechanics quoted by the Times said workers were "directed ... to do things specifically contradicting" federal aviation regulations, and alleged they had been "pressured, threatened and intimidated ... in the daily performance of our work."

In a statement, Alaska Airlines said about 12 mechanics had been interviewed and that it would immediately ground any planes found to be potentially unsafe.

Robert Falla, the leader of the airline's Seattle maintenance base, was placed on administrative leave, the airline said. He could not be reached by telephone. His lawyer predicted he would be exonerated.

"Robert Falla has never knowingly allowed any aircraft to go into service that was not airworthy or (that) failed any safety standard," said a statement from his lawyer, Scott J. Engelhard.

The airline is already the subject of a criminal investigation over alleged maintenance violations at its Oakland, Calif., maintenance base.

A grand jury in San Francisco is investigating whether supervisors signed for repairs that weren't done or that they weren't authorized to approve.

Criminal probe targets airline's maintenance of the MD-80s

By SCOTT SUNDE
Seattle Post-Intelligencer

Associated Press photos

Eric Hermann, a rescue crew member, pulls a piece of fuselage from the water.

SEATTLE — The MD-80 series of airplanes has been a workhorse of Alaska Airlines' fleet, taking the carrier's passengers up and down the West Coast for years. It also has been at the center of a criminal investigation into Alaska Airlines maintenance and a long-running controversy over fumes in the passenger cabin.

Monday, one of Alaska's MD-80s crashed off the coast of California with 88 people aboard. The maintenance of planes like the one that crashed has been the subject of the federal criminal investigation.

John Liotine, an Alaska lead mechanic in Oakland, Calif., set the criminal investigation into motion in October 1998 when he contacted an inspector with the Federal Aviation Administration.

7

A Week Later, Another Goodbye

Grieving families gather at Bay Meadows

By Jonathan Curiel
CHRONICLE STAFF WRITER

Photos by Associated Press

F amily, friends and co-workers of the 88 victims of Alaska Airlines Flight 261 sought solace and comfort at a memorial service yesterday, marking the week anniversary of the plane's crash into the Pacific Ocean.

Inside a large, white tent erected on a parking lot at Bay Meadows racetrack in San Mateo, about 700 people grieved and listened to religious leaders, Red Cross officials and Alaska Airline representatives, who tried to bring closure to the tragedy.

"We are still reeling from disbelief," said Rabbi David Teitelbaum, executive director of the Board of Rabbis of Northern California. "We didn't even have the chance to say goodbye (to the victims). . . . Let us pause now in the reality of here and now and, in a moment of silence, say goodbye."

The silence was interrupted by sobs, then a few moments later by the voice of Teitelbaum, who asked the people in attendance to "find strength in love and support of the families and friends" of the victims.

Symbols and metaphors were an important part of the service. After Teitelbaum and others spoke, people moved outside the tent and formed a circle, then released 88 Monarch butterflies into the air at 4:26 p.m., marking the time of the crash.

"Each butterfly is a symbol of those we remember," said Lanny Pinola, a Miwok Indian and spiritual guidance counselor from Marin County, who helped lead the service outside the tent. "It is their journey to a new place. If you hold a secret wish, then wish upon the wings of a butterfly. Butterflies cannot speak, so your wish will always be safe with them as they take it up to the heavens."

As the butterflies fluttered into the air, the mourners watched from their self-enclosed "Circle of Care." Forty people related to the plane crash victims stood at the center of the circle, surrounded by everyone else who attended the service.

The family members did not speak to the media, who were asked by Red Cross officials to respect the privacy of those in attendance.

Arthur Ost, the father of Flight 261 passenger Robert Ost, was among those who attended yesterday's hourlong memorial. About 30 members of the South San Francisco Fire Department, where Robert Ost was a 15-year veteran, also gathered at Bay Meadows. A group of South San Francisco firefighters drove a fire truck to the service, then draped Ost's fire jacket on the back of it in remembrance of their friend and colleague. They also placed a pair of Ost's boots on the back of the truck.

Every person who entered the tent service was given a long-stemmed white carnation. Flowers draped the speakers' table that anchored the front of the tent. Small spotlights illuminated red and yellow circles on the ceiling of the tent, and images of six Monarch butterflies were also displayed.

Cliff Argue, a vice president with Alaska Airlines, told the mourners that,

"Like all of you, we've spent the last week in grief. For everyone of us involved, it has been an experience that has changed our lives forever."

When the service was over, everyone placed their carnations into two wicker baskets, which Coast Guard members walked over to a vehicle that transported them to a waiting helicopter. The Coast Guard copter then flew over the circle of people, before flying on to San Francisco International Airport. Fog prevented the helicopter pilot from going to the Pacific Ocean and dropping the flowers into the Pacific Ocean as planned. The flowers, said Red Cross officials, will be dropped into the water today.

Above: Lanny Pinola, right, a Miwok Indian guidance counselor from Petaluma, and Sacheen Littlefeather, an Apache Indian led a spiritual service at yesterday's memorial in San Mateo for the passengers of Flight 261.

At left: Two Alaska Airlines employees embraced as the service concluded.

8

Weeping Sky
We bring the Sun
To make you glad
And fill you with the Day.

Quiet Tree
We have the Wind
To Make you dance
And fill you with our Play.

And You shall come
To hear our song
And learn its tune
Before it fades away.

African Folk Song

2000

Running In Slow Motion

January 31, 2000

Running in slow motion, I tried to avoid the huge waves crashing over my head. I gasped for air, something from deep within informed me that this was panic. The survival instinct kicked in, I would do everything in my power to stay above water. I was sinking. My head pounded, my heart raced, I froze. With one limp hand, holding a black telephone, I scooted closer to the television. There, in my face, a large mass of water was shown. Newscasters came on and off the screen, holding microphones, returning faithfully to a piece of the Pacific Ocean. Helicopters flew overhead. Words I couldn't read scrolling on the bottom of the dusty screen.

My Mother's best friend, also named Jean, had sounded so calm, yet disturbed when she called. I kept going over and over her words, "I don't want to worry you dear, BUT a plane just crashed, and your mom is due back today… The plane was traveling from Mexico…"

She asked me to confirm which airline my sister-in-law worked for. "Alaskan Airlines" I told her automatically. There was a pause, we told one another we'd keep the other one posted. We both had to sound optimistic; it seemed bad practice or manners to get worked up over the possibility of something this horrid being true. Neither of us sounded reassured hanging up, I could just tell. We were controlling the rising hysteria.

Jeanette and Dan, my good friends, were in the next room. I considered not mentioning anything to them, but in the next second I was trying to accurately remember when my family's flight was coming in on this day. My nervous brain quickly scanned a mental picture of the five of them sitting on the plane, coming home. I walked into the kitchen, as Jeanette was preparing dinner.

I could tell from Jeanette's expressions that my face looked worried. I had nothing to compare this phone call, this premature possible warning with. Generally speaking, I don't think bad things happen often, and my late night worrying consists of being overly concerned about people's feelings and situations, which can't be changed. A fatalist I am not, and this phone call was like riding the roller coaster. My heart was in my mouth. "This can't be happening," I thought as I sat transfixed in front of the T.V. for another half hour or so.

I thought about calling my dad, but felt uneasy about causing unfounded worry.

I quickly went over the events of the day. I had called in sick, something I rarely do. I woke up feeling very strange. I told Jeanette, who reminded me later, that I said my body felt twisted as if I had no neck. I told her I felt like Raggedy Ann.

Greg, my husband, is a firefighter and was working a 24-hour shift that day. It was typical for me to get together with friends and make dinner when he was on work duty. Life had been really great lately. I loved my new job, and had just started the Master's program at San Jose State. I was fascinated with the cutting edge theories of learning disabilities, and I was eager to become an expert. I had recently re-found optimism for changing the world just a little, fighting for the underdogs. Christmas break was nice and relaxing, and my new job teaching in Watsonville had given me a four week vacation. My family was healthy; we had just celebrated my mom's 73rd birthday. These thoughts were firing through my brain as I watched the Channel 7 News say that there was no further news on the crash, other than it was an Alaskan Airlines plane.

I called my Mom and Charlie. The number hadn't changed in 16 years. It was the number I called more than any other number. Her cute, infamous New York accent just as it always sounded on the machine. I suddenly felt awkward leaving a message, because I didn't know what to say.

I finally called my dad, an 81-year-old eccentric but very kind hearted man. He spends most of his retirement hours writing letters to the paper, denouncing bad government policies and all that is wrong, in his old eyes, with politics these days. He claims that he gets a lot of prank phone calls, due to his radical ink pen, thus he never sounds too chipper when answering the phone. He has answered my calls to "What do you want you pathetic bastard?" on several occasions. He then gets a little bit embarrassed, and tells me that somebody has been calling him, saying nothing. My brother and I used to think that this was so funny, and that our dear father, was perhaps getting more liberal with age, even though it's supposed to be the contrary. On this Monday evening however, a big lump of fear was lodged in my throat and my only mission was to get my dad on the phone. He lived closer to my brother, and was in touch constantly. His routine had been to come over every Sunday and play with his new Granddaughter Emily. He answered the phone abruptly, as he was also watching the news. He knew about this plane crash, but was confused about what time they were due back.

We made a pact to call Alaskan Airlines and get some answers. I wanted him to reassure me, and he didn't. I think I felt worse after I called him.

I remember leaning against the bookshelf, feeling very weak in the knees and hating the adrenaline rushing from my head to my feet. Dan was also cooking in the kitchen, Jeanette's two kids Regina and Julian were over. Dan didn't have any kids, and was known for keeping things light and funny. He joked about everything, ate all of the time, went to the movies several times a week, and seemed to look at life as entertainment. He was preparing rice and chicken, avoiding my presence. He said not to worry that it would-n't do any good. Jeanette, on the other hand, looked at me, studied me, as if she were searching my face for a leading clue. She has these penetrating, all knowing dark brown eyes, framed by beautiful Latina/Native American features. It felt comforting, but eerie having a stare down with her. Jeanette is my wise woman friend. I started picking at a fingernail, and then looked at her earrings, needing an immediate place to put my focus. We love going to Native American Pow Wows together, and these earrings were a gift from me from years past. Our bond was thick as a mountain range, and her parents were very close with my mom and Charlie. If I had to read into it, I saw the doom in her eyes, as she saw it in mine. We both teared up. "I am scared Jeanetty" I offered meekly.

"I know Osti, I know" she replied. She threw herself on me at that moment, her earrings, twisted in her long, wavy thick mane scratched me, sobering me up in an instant to keep moving, to problem solve, to be a good teacher and mother. I had to do something. I couldn't just sit still. There was no way my family could be on this doomed plane, and yet, I had this nagging, impending knowing that they were.

Confirmation

My nerves were shot, so Jeanette called Alaskan Airlines. The line was busy for a long time. Finally she got through, and asked for names on the flight that crashed. She gave them the information they asked for, and told them who she was and how she was related. She told them she was calling on my behalf, and gave them the names of our family members. They promised to call back.

I sat next to the fireplace, feeling cold, scared, and helpless. My dad called, only repeating to me the same thing they had just told him. He sounded very nervous and agitated.

I told my daughter Carina how serious this could be. She was with her friend, busy with a school project. They were making a poster. Carina was in the eighth grade. She looked concerned, but doubted it was the same plane. Everybody ate dinner in the kitchen, I listened to their voices as I collected my thoughts, at the same spot in front of the fire. Dan asked me (again) to come eat. I felt irritable and grossed out by food. Nothing about relaxing sounded appealing to me. Ben, my stepson came home and immediately picked up on something very scary going on in the house. Like Carina, he doubted that my family was on this plane. As time went on, Ben knew my stubbornness and realized I wasn't moving from my spot. He called his dad

(Greg) at the Fire Station. He took the phone in the other room, as I imagined he thought I was over reacting, that I was being paranoid. For the first time in my life, I felt a bit crazy. It was a mixture of being paralyzed and having fear shoot throughout my body. I was shivering. I was aware of only what was immediately in front of me. I felt like a blind woman at a zoo. I was not attached to my environment. I was tiny and insignificant to the giant beasts. I would leave them alone if they left me alone.

Many hours later, my father called. He was matter of fact, solemn, flat. "It's confirmed, they were on the flight, all of them."

I hated the phone; I hated my dad. I thought he was jumping to conclusions and above all, senile. At this precise and deafening moment, I would call him old, confused, demented, and thinking the worst. He had to be wrong, or superstitious, or something. Anything, but correct. I got a taste in my mouth of when people automatically say, "No, no, no, this can't be…" when they are told that somebody has just died. I flashed for a milli-second on the family of four I grew up with. Two adults, two children. A family ending in divorce like so many, but we were still four parts, one whole. Bob and my sweet mother together, just falling from the sky. My aging socialist father and I just getting word that our family's other half was absolutely involved in a horrible plane crash. My mind raced to the consideration of calling 911. Could a policeman help? A sudden murder was committed, or so it felt like. I was standing in a white sterile corridor with no doors, no options, I hated the help-lessness.

The airlines called a few minutes later, had me identify myself, and a lady whose voice was cracking, repeated my father's words. It was confirmed. My mom, Jean Permison, her boyfriend Charlie Russell, whom I loved like a step-father, my only sibling Bob Ost, his wife Ileana Ost, and their four-month old daughter Emily Ost were all aboard this plane. This plane, which had just plunged into the ocean on this Monday afternoon, was carrying my family. It was cruel, definite, cold, mean, and brutal. I felt chilled, nauseated, clammy and sweaty.

Dan walked outside with his cell phone. I was in the bedroom, lying on the floor screaming. People started walking in, I felt claustrophobic. I felt as if somebody slugged me in the chest with full force. It felt both foreign and premature to have these people grabbing me and saying "No, no, no". I was drenched with sweat, tears, and other people's tears. Charlie's daughter and Granddaughter were next to me. Greg, the stoic firefighter left work, and came walking through the bedroom door in full uniform. I never saw him cry before. We were all wailing, as time seemed to be suspended in the air. The phone was ringing off the hook.

Somebody passed me the phone. A lady from Alaskan Airline's care team told me I wouldn't remember her name, but that we were invited to fly through American Airlines the next day to be near the crash site, and she would be there in L.A. to greet us. There was a Search and Rescue in full force going on. Family members would need to be there, if at all possible.

Ben went home to his mother's house. I don't remember saying goodbye to him. I guess the crowd dispersed. My friend Liz made phone calls. Jeanette took my Principal's phone number. Carina hid in her room. The house smelled like chicken and the heater kicking on at the same time.

A controlled moment slivered through my insides. I had an I.E.P. meeting the next day. This is an Individualized Educational Plan in which I meet with the student's parents to discuss a plan for the student enrolled in the special education program. I called my co-teacher Lori. I didn't know I was in shock. She told me later how calm I sounded. I just told her that my family was involved in a plane crash in Southern California, and I would like her to take over this meeting tomorrow at 1:00. We hung up. I thought about my comment to Jeanette, about the Raggedy Ann feeling, and figured I would add that my heart and neck were now fully detached.

February 1, 2000

I called the Jewish, New York relatives and heard screaming. Aunt Ruthie, who had always been my favorite, made me repeat myself. I recall not having the muscle to hold the receiver of the phone. It was too difficult to dial a number, wait for a response, and begin to tell the party on the other line that their relatives were probably dead. I could literally feel a slurring sensation in my speech, and my back wouldn't support my body when I would stand. I was chilled to the bone, and figured I'd get under the blankets for a while. I knew I couldn't sleep, but getting warm and keeping my mind occupied by doing things seemed like the right thing to do. When I tried to lay down, my mind, now in serious shock, refused to let me waste a second. Everything had to be immediate, although when I look back on this early morning, my reality was in slow motion. I couldn't eat. I showered late at night, but people kept showing up in the living room. I stayed in the shower, listening to voices from the other room. I needed a wall to lean on without anybody touching me.

I made a call to a friend I worked with, briefly stating I wouldn't be in, and to let my teaching aides know. I called Kim and Bob in Oregon. They hadn't heard the news yet. More crying, terror sizzling through the phone lines. I called my cousin and couldn't get through. I thought of the five of them, zooming in on their separate selves, and then how they were all a family with me. I asked God for a sign. I looked at my Native American art in my bedroom. Everything felt so still, so ordinary and unchanged. I thought of any Hebrew I might have remembered for prayers. Were they trying to tell me anything? Were they holding on? Were they dead? What did they want me to know? I looked at different scenarios from inside tired and confused eyes. It was now sunrise. I hadn't slept. Greg was on the phone, writing down our flight number. I had to keep busy. I called another teacher friend, Laura. She was getting ready for work. I don't recall the way I told her, only that my voice was stuck for a minute. She knew it was me, and told me in her first grade teacher voice "What are you telling me?" She said what a lot of people would later say, "You're kidding." In the next breath, she lost it, saying this couldn't be true. I needed a jump-start. There was nothing left in me. I almost had to hear myself say aloud that I was heading to Los Angeles to see if there were survivors, just to believe this was reality. Laura adored my mom; it felt absolutely wicked to begin the day upsetting others. I looked up after completing this quick phone call, and my teacher friends from across the street where I had first taught were now standing in my bedroom. Jeanette reappeared. She looked in my closet and threw some clothes in a suitcase. I had that inner panic running through my bones, like a frightened mouse scattering about while being chased by something huge.

I needed my family, the ones I began with. It was a very primal urge. It scared the hell out of me to stop myself in my tracks, as I realized I could not call my mom or brother. They were the clear thinkers, the movers and shakers. I knew I should check in with my dad, but I was afraid that his voice would remind me that I had to make the decisions. I dialed his number. Again, he sounded abrupt and yet confused. The Press had already called him. He refused to go to Los Angeles with us. I think he just couldn't move. As he mumbled something about people pestering him on the phone, I found myself in a trance. My poor 81-year-old father confessed that he couldn't bring himself to call his Grandkids in Connecticut. The painting I was staring at was a Native American Chief, wrapped up in a ceremonial blanket, holding a pipe. There is a look of courage on his long face, as he is looking into the sky. He is not smiling, nor is he exhibiting any kind of social gesture, he is merely saluting the energy above him. I have moved in and out of so many houses with this painting, and it continues to bring me peace. My father sounded very high pitched and yet angry and frustrated. "You must call them, Janis, I tried to last night, and I, uh, just couldn't, I stared at their number written down and chickened out."

The Chief in this favorite painting told me I had to be the brave one now. I hadn't spoken to my brother's ex-wife Lisa in years and years. She answered on the second ring. They were three hours ahead in Bolton, Connecticut. The kids were at school. Lisa listened to me as I mustered up the words. I told her I was flying out to the crash site in an hour or so, that we would keep her posted. The shock in her voice electrocuted my shock through the phone wire. She had me repeat myself, just like Aunt Ruthie. She asked me if I was telling her that Bob was dead? Those words hung on me; they stung my spine and sliced me in half. I wanted to reassure her, and I knew nothing. Very calmly, she asked me what she should do. I suggested picking up the kids, before the news came out as they could possibly hear it from the office at school. "They need you to tell them," I remembered saying. I pictured my laughing niece and nephew. My brother and I never had much cash on us, so we typically took our young children to Taco Bell. It sort of agreed with everyone. They always had beans sticking out of their braces, as they would have belly laughs over something silly. We all picked on my dad when we were together. He was the butt of our jokes, and loved being the funny old man. I didn't want to imagine Lisa driving out in the rain and telling her children that their father, mother in law, new baby sister, Grandma, and Charlie were in the middle of the Pacific Ocean in a broken airplane. I had never called anybody with this kind of news, and for a second, I worried that I could have caused an accident. I thought of Lisa putting her other two young children in the car, and heading out to Ashley and Axel's school in a blizzard, crying, confused, not knowing how to tell the kids about the crash... Lisa would be going over her life with Bob, the birth of the kids, their divorce, and she hits a car coming from the other direction... My over active imagination stopped, as I pulled the big emergency break, and calmly drove – with shock inside of me – for the next period of time. This was the hardest phone call I EVER made in my life.

Carina packed for the trip. Through tears, she told me that she had an image of the movie, "The Titanic". She figured we would be seeing bodies on the water, and we could help rescue them.

Jeanette would watch the house and take care of the cat. We were ready to leave. I looked at my Mom's picture hanging in the closet, wondering what had possessed me to hang it there a few weeks earlier. One day, out of the blue, I placed a big picture of my mom inside of the closet. That steady gaze from her eyes would follow me peacefully every time I'd enter. I would play my guitar inside the closet; this small place I used as a refuge. I don't have the words to explain why I chose to hang it there and why I felt good looking at it, but it just worked well for me. It cheered me up. I felt it almost talking to me, as I would try clothes on, especially if I was being critical after putting an outfit on. She would almost tell me to wear something with my head held high, or to just focus on being comfortable. I stared at this picture for a long time before leaving to Los Angeles. I saw her as a little girl I needed to protect. She almost transformed herself onto a milk carton. I would have to find her. She would be stuck in between rocks and sea moss. She would be cold and scared and bruised, but she would be okay. I would carry her to safety. I felt a big lump in my throat as an exhausted but mature tear slid down my cheek. I threw my Ugg boots in the travel bag, looked at her sweet picture and said "Don't worry, little mama, I am coming." as I closed the closet door and walked bravely to the waiting car in the driveway.

It was a quiet drive to the airport. Greg, Carina, and I, all on this mission to see who would make it, who would survive this crash. My dear friend Lisa, who was also my former neighbor from high school drove us. She looked so scared as she walked us inside the airport. I was told to simply give my name to the American Airline clerk when we approached the ticket line. The response was incredible; I was immediately treated with the utmost honor and privilege, as if I were a celebrity. There were no lines to wait in; somebody was always touching my arm, nodding, or escorting us in and out of rooms. We were ushered into this conference room in the airport. I was pressing my fingernails into my forehead and keeping my face buried in my hands. Everything looked so bright and surreal and I didn't want to call attention to how feeble I felt.

My daughter told me weeks later that she fell asleep immediately that night. People were walking in and out of our house and the crying and yelling overwhelmed her. She cried until she collapsed on her bed, wishing the commotion would cease. When she awoke, she thought she had a bad dream, as I was screaming on the top of my lungs. This was precisely the time I saw my brother and Ileana's faces on the morning news, under the heading of passengers aboard the plane that had crashed. It felt like such a violation seeing my family's faces on the morning news.

I missed my Dad, it felt wrong leaving him alone in his

apartment. He was adamant about not going, so I left it alone. Somebody in the conference room gave me directions about a special van picking us up at the airport in L.A., and that a Karolee would be assigned to help us with everything. I wanted to tell her that I wasn't the one who needed help, as I wasn't aboard the plane, now in pieces in the Pacific Ocean.

I took my one and only First Class plane trip. Like untamable, continual hiccuping completely out of my control, I could not refrain from crying my eyes out all the way there. I do not remember anything else of the hour trip. Businessmen stared at me; a few of them folded newspapers in front of their faces. I didn't blame them, as for the first time; I would be one of the walking wounded. I wouldn't want to look either. I was shaking like mad as well. I was freezing, and weeping loudly somehow propelled me to feel warmer. I was feeling stranger and stranger, scarier and scarier, and making noise would ultimately make me as haunted as I felt.

A man whisked us off the plane as soon as it landed. I gave him the names and ages of our family. A very tall and pretty flight attendant by the name of Karolee appeared. She was polite and respectful wearing a nametag, which read "Family Care Team" on the top and then her full name on the bottom. She assured me that her job was to help us in any way possible, and that she felt terrible about the crash. I suddenly remembered speaking with her the night before; I think she told me she would be looking for me. I felt safe with her right away. We put our bags in the room. I noticed a lot of media around the hotel, but we were told that they wouldn't approach us unless we wanted to talk to them. Karolee met us down in the lobby, and introduced us to Beverly, another volunteer/employee from the airlines. Beverly was "assigned" to Carina, and they ended up spending a lot of time together. I usually study people's faces as soon as I see them, but the only physical memories I have of Beverly were her tights and tennis shoes. Maybe my head was down a lot. She had a fast walk and magically took care of Carina's concerns.

There were status reports from the National Transportation Safety Board located in this hotel lobby twice a day. Beverly asked me if she could take Carina out for a while, to ease her tension a bit. They went to the Santa Monica Pier, and shopping a few times. Carina seemed impressed with the knowledge Beverly possessed from being a flight attendant. I liked that Carina could be spared from these meetings. Beverly had told her that the G-Force would have knocked them out immediately. Although this was promising news, it seemed so premature, so matter of fact, but removed from my reality. I had trouble coming to terms that there were any problems on this flight let alone a crash. I would learn very quickly that I possess strange coping mechanisms. I literally had to look at the unfolding of the past 24 hours at an arm's length. If I got too close with the sobering facts, it caused me to tap into the wild imagination I was born with. What did it look like, on the plane? Who was knocked out first? Did they have time to say goodbye to one another? Where were they now? All that we were told was that the Coastguard and dozens of fisherman were sorting through the debris and pulling "stuff" out of the ocean. This stuff didn't include any bodies.

I was sitting on a couch in the lobby by myself. I had an idea that this was it, they were gone. It was as if a mature, rational voice told me this, the same voice that told me they were in the wrong place at the wrong time, before the airlines confirmed they were on this flight. I nervously tapped my feet on the polished floor, and chose one finger to pick at. I had some old reddish polish on, and it peeled off easily. I accidentally pulled off a little piece of my skin as I looked at a big bouquet of flowers on the table. Next to this fancy spray were a lamp and a telephone. I imagined I was in a hospital waiting room, anticipating news from the crash survivors. The mere thought of my mother with bruises or broken bones on her tiny frame caused instant anxiety. I picked some more at my fingernails. I had stopped biting them in high school, but there was a sense of gratification from pulling a tiny piece of skin and feeling the hurt rush to my head. My head began to throb, but I was also removed from my body at the same time. I wanted to use the phone, but the one person I would call in this twilight zone was my mother. I used to imagine what it would be like to lose her when I was little. I was a super sensitive kid in that way, realizing at a very tender age that all that we love, would be dust one day. I would grow up believing in modern science and honoring my mother's healthy life style. She would live a long time, and if she were in the hospital for some reason in her 90's, a kind doctor would take care of her. I figured this was how life would unfold. Bob would take care of himself and God forbid if he died, it would be from a freak mountain climbing or paragliding accident. He had climbed Mt. Whitney and was known internationally for his epic climbs. I thought of my mom and brother's both funny and poignant lives, and how happy they both were at Christmas. It felt confusing and impossible that they would be unlucky enough to board this plane. I yawned, and felt drugged. I had images of baby Emily and Charlie and Ileana, and while looking at the dim light from this table lamp, I realized that I would never be in a hospital, waiting for news of their recovery. This waiting room in this strange hotel would be the place to hear the horrifying news. I just knew that to be true at that moment, the very second of staring deeply at these flowers. The next thing I knew I was screaming my head off and Karolee was talking to a Doctor about getting me a sedative.

There was a meeting room established in this hotel. Karolee told me that more family members would be arriving, and that there would be status meetings for families only. There was a terribly unsettling feeling, everybody and everything felt uneasy, rude and combative. We were allowed to ask questions to the spokesperson, but no question seemed to be answered directly. I watched people show up with big jackets with the letters N.T.S.B. on the back. They assured us that crews were on the scene and nobody was giving up. Apparently, some news leaked out that a fisherman found one dead male body. They would-n't really elaborate on any more, just that this was the only body found. Karolee found me after a break from this meeting, promising that my Aunt Ruthie was on her way, and that my cousins would be flying in shortly after. I had-n't seen Ruthie since my Uncle Milty died in 1987, but the thought of holding her kept me feeling a tiny bit sane. I desperately needed someone who knew my family well to be here.

Some hours later, my tall, dark, Israeli looking heroine with raven black hair burst into this meeting room. It seemed to be in slow motion, even though this native New York woman moves like the southbound A train. I grabbed on to her and wouldn't let go. Her New York accent and energy was so familiar and warm. She was crying, but she stared right in my eyes and told me that she had taken the first plane out of New York to be here with me. She assured me that her sons Fred and David were coming, and that my other two cousins from my mother's side, Marty and Norman, would also be here soon. Whatever the Doctor had given me was making my eyes close.

I have wracked my brain trying to establish the time sequence with the following vignettes or memories, often relying on other's recollections in order to piece things together. Here are a few:

• Everybody's picture were taken and laminated on a card with their name, and the family member lost. These were worn around the neck and security was tight. Only people wearing these necklaces were allowed in the morning and evening briefings.

• We changed hotels after the first night, as herds of people began to show up. There were information centers set up in the hotels, where volunteers were calling and arranging vic-tim's families to fly out. The Red Cross and clergy were also present.

• I spoke with CNN news after we arrived. I have a copy of the tape but remember almost nothing but bright lights.

• There were two briefings a day. During one of the first, a very upset Uncle kept enthusiastic hopes that his nephew could possibly be alive, as he knew children could survive colder climates than adults. It was very moving. I was ready to jump in the water and look for his baby nephew. He made me want to believe in the impossible.

• During the second day in L.A. the medical examiner announced that officially circumstances had changed from "Search and Rescue" to "Search and Recovery". It was a very grim, startling, maddening, shocking, and plummeting remark.

• It was like a very unhappy, yet popular party. Every hour more people with wet faces and boxes of Kleenex came.

• There were buffet breakfasts, lunches, and dinners each day for us, the confused families. I would brush my teeth, trying to get rid of the wretched taste in my mouth, but it didn't go away. It was as if acid was burning in my stomach. I am not sure how long my unplanned hunger strike went on, but Karolee bought a blender for me and I was able to drink some protein with fruit juice. The amount of food around me, strangers with the same look of disbelief and horror as me on their faces within inches of me, the clatter-ing of dishes, the smells of turkey and gravy and white toast made me feel sick to my stomach. It was the one time in my life where my Jewish mothering smoldered out like an old candle. I felt no need to feed somebody and listen to his or her troubles. I felt like a disturbed little orphan kid with old clothes on, swimming in a dirty and crowded pool. In this pool there were hundreds of bodies and quicksand was pulling me under. I felt nauseous under the water as well as on the surface. The only image that seemed agreeable to me was my mother finding me, handing me a warm towel and getting me out of this horrible place.

• Towards the end of the week, they had a make shift police station where we were asked to give completely accurate descriptions of our lost ones. When the last questions of facial hair, ring sizes, and amount of fillings in the mouth were asked, I was giving DNA samples for the forensic team. It was a moment of feeling tall and patriotic, like my presence could actually fill a purpose. I was so tired of crying, it felt suddenly hopeful to offer blood and knowledge of my tribe.

• I was so touched that my whole family (with the exception of my Dad) was able to fly out so that we could be united. Jeanette arrived the next day with Greg's mother and Lisa. Tori also flew out. Kim and Bob, my dearest friends now living in Oregon were suddenly in this cafeteria in the hotel. Karolee found that my favorite food in the whole world is sushi. She and Lisa brought more sushi into my hotel room than I had ever seen. Okay, the picture is getting clearer. I think this was on Friday night. I hadn't been outside; I smelled like death, I looked like death. I would put a brush through my hair, and go into town with Karolee and Lisa and choose sushi for everyone. We were all to meet in my room later that evening. I was coming to terms with early signs of not wanting to be around a lot of people. This was new to me, startling, but ever present. It wasn't so much the people, as it was the over stimulation, the having to stay focused for everyone. I would learn how death, a tiny bit like a wedding or the birth of a baby, brings forth such intense feelings and bizarre emotions. The way in which people process these life-altering events are about as polar as blazing hot understanding ice cold. There is not a lot of middle ground. Hurt feelings are running rampant. Some say nothing and want to make it all better; others depend on religion and don't want to discuss it further. Nobody understands why some make a big deal out of nothing, while others are flipping out about how untouched other people appear. Sudden death scenarios are the student teachers of human psychology. It's a stuffed monkey puppet show party. Bring your present and be on time. It's a set table with innocent and slow characters, props, and no scripts. Come see how human and plastic we all can be. It's a freak show, yet it's all-real. We are falling off of our platform shoes, our lipstick doesn't stay on, and we want so badly to be held as we run as far as we can from one another, not wanting to connect.

I walked out of the lobby with Lisa and Karolee, took one look at strangers walking down the street and taxis going by, and I knew immediately I needed to be lying down, in the safety of my hotel bed. I quickly rode the elevator back to my room.

• We were shuttled to Port Hueneme, the closest we all could get to the crash site, on several tour busses. The Police Force had actually blocked off the L.A. Expressway so that we could pass. My cousin Norman, who is very religious, wanted to have a Rabbi to do a prayer. The sense of family coming together rings so loudly to me. My cousin Fred was so amazingly loving and solid. He knew how to be present. That stands out the most for me.

• There was a multi-denominational memorial service at Pepperdine University. 88 candles were lit, and at the end of the ceremony, 88 doves were released.

• My friends and relatives flew back home

• I learned it was okay to lose control. I learned well that your good friends would comfort you, catch you, and can be counted on. The most intense suffering one will ever go through, however, will be, and has to be done alone. Ultimately you can talk about the process, journey, and eventual burial with your friends, but it will be shared like two people comparing notes about a disturbing movie. It's as if a large, indifferent hand throws you off of a diving board with blindfolds on. One day, you can talk to somebody who loves you who genuinely wants to know what it was like, but when you first hit the cold water, nobody is allowed to hear you or comfort you. I don't know why this is so.

Cousin Fred Ost with pictures of Jean, Charlie, Bob, Ileana & Emily at Pepperdine University Memorial Service February 5, 2000.

Jessica Ost, Carina Ost, Fred Ost, Janis Ost Ford, Harriet Ost at a ritual service we had on the beach near the crash site.

Coming Home From The Crash Site

I felt fairly numb for the duration of the flight. I thought a lot about where they sat, the screeching noises they'd probably heard. Leaving the hotel had seemed like a good idea, but now going home and facing people didn't. I felt like I had lost a very important contest, or I had flunked a test I'd needed very badly to pass. My head was downer than down. I was aware of my bad breath, even though nobody mentioned it to me. I wasn't eating; I still wasn't sleeping for more than hour or so at a time.

Karolee flew home with us, and then drove us back to Santa Cruz in a rental car. When we pulled into the driveway, I wanted to disappear more than anything. I sat in the car for a while. Then I noticed my old friend Dan (not the same person who was at my house when I got the news) sitting in his car. I didn't want to see anybody, just recognizing a friend in our quiet little cul-de-sac reminded me of the aversion I had recently developed. I didn't want to be noticed. I didn't want to look at familiar faces and have to focus on what had happened. My soul felt punctured, wounded. I didn't want to go backward and I couldn't go forward, but I hated being idle. It was nerve wracking having to face people. I couldn't and didn't recognize myself. I never had known the world to be so devastating. Seeing my mother and brother's pictures on the front pages of the newspapers and on the news made me feel suddenly public. It was almost as if I were in a freak show, and people could and would look at me gasping, holding their faces. Seeing Dan as soon as I returned from the airport made me realize that something bigger than me had sent him, and I wasn't ready to deal. I had met Dan in the most unusual way I had ever met anyone. He is one of my biggest heroes. I will talk about him later, as he has influenced me so much with his courage.

My house looked like The Japanese Tea Garden in San Francisco. There was a quiet holiness about it, surrounded by flowers and plants and plush greenery. I was struck by the colors, the rich hues cascading through the fireplace. Ned and Jeanette were there, cleaning up, collecting mail. Ned gave us big hugs, his eyes looking watery and blood-shot. I don't recall if I said anything to him about it, but I thought back to 1997 when he suddenly lost his sister to a deadly heart condition. She was fine until she had a horrible pain and died almost instantly. I didn't really know what to say to Ned at the time, and now I was in that same lost sibling land, the abandoned valley.

I am not sure how long Karolee stayed. I do remember sitting by her and telling her I needed Keith Greeninger's music. We were on the couch, looking at the fireplace. The phone was ringing and ringing. Tears were flowing evenly down both of my cheeks, and I told Karolee that I bought this CD after seeing Keith (A local singer/songwriter in Santa Cruz), and couldn't stop playing it. The first song starts out with very melodic piano, and just hearing it, put me over the edge. Karolee put her hands over her face. She seemed to have the same reaction from the music – moved to tears.

I looked at Karolee, and suddenly felt guilty. She volunteered for this thankless job, to hold victim's family's hands through the worst time, and here she was, complete-ly enveloped inside my family. It must have felt like a black hole. She always had her lip liner on so perfectly, but at this moment there was no color to her lips. She just looked like a tall, pretty saint with no color in her face. I was making her listen to sad music, and she was missing her daughters at home for sure – but she was sworn to be our "Jesus", taking it all in and not taking any of it personally. I felt sorry for her.

After she left I was alone. She had done as much as anyone could. In retrospect, I thank my lucky stars that the lousy airlines did offer recruitment and intense training for tender hearts like Karolee, to assist families during airline catastrophes.

It rained a lot. The phone rang off the hook. I started a list of the people asking me to call back. Many people told me not to call back, but just to know I was in their prayers. Some messages were unintelligible muffled screams and cries.

Plates of food started arriving the day we came home, Sunday the 6th of February. I mostly wanted to stay in the living room and watch the fire. The fireplace was a gas one, and I could turn the flame on high or low. I sat there on the ledge, trying to keep warm in spite of warm clothes, the log, and the heater constantly running. Grief is cold and sends needles into your spine. I played Keith Greeninger and any soothing folk or classical music I could find. The music and the flames put me in a trance, my eyelids heavy and swollen from crying. But looking at the fire and listening to music made me feel that my pain was safe.

Somebody put a note on the door to give us a little privacy, but I still remember answering the door every few hours to sign for flowers. I never saw so many flowers in my life. The pastor from Greg's church came over and brought communion. I accepted any kind of ritual or blessing.

Somebody handed me a yellow lined notepad as a reminder to begin planning funeral arrangements. It had to be done. A bunch of my musical girlfriends came by and sat on my bed, planning the music for the service. It all came together. When people ask me how I managed to come home and deal with the jobs of honoring and burying, I hardly remember. My eyebrows go up and I concentrate and focus. It is a phone number I must recall. I was on automatic pilot. I learned you have to count on others who love you, the real friends, the jewels, just know what to do. Suddenly the services are over and the sun rises the next day. My mind drifts to the game we played as kids. One person falls backwards without looking and the others catch her right before she hits the ground. It's a trust fall.

An old friend Jon Bailiff called me the night before the service and asked me if he could bring a painting he created of my mom. He had met her only once, but he was a close friend with my cousin David and he knew her well through stories. I sensed something sacred when he went on to tell me that he saw the article in the local paper and that my mother told him to paint her. He stayed up all night painting, so it would be ready for the service. When I looked at it, I nearly fell over. It was her spirit, but it was a transformation of her. She had this yellow aura about her, and she looked so pleased. People couldn't stop staring when they walked into the service and saw it, a huge monumental tribute.

"Jean Permison"
by local artist Jon Bailiff

Mom's Eulogy

Shattered but still whole, shattered but still whole... A kind friend wrote these words down for me the other day. Our family has been surrounded by love, support, food, prayers and the one phrase we all say when a tragedy hits the ones we care about: "Is there anything I can do?" I suppose we are all children now, sort of waiting in the dark. Shock and fountains of tears roll down my face like ugly make-up. I don't know if it hurts more to be alert and try to make sense of this all, or simply to imagine what life will be like without these five people I love so much.

Today, I want to honor my Mother's life. Simply put, I was as proud of her as she was of me. We could talk about practically everything. As busy as she was with all of her clubs, hobbies, art and music – she never interrupted me when I was talking. When we made time for one another, which was usually bi-weekly, we had our quality time. We spoke on the phone at least every few days, and lived a few miles away from each other. Usually I called her while I'd be taking a warm bath, and each time she would worry that I'd electrocute myself. She thought I drove too fast, sometimes wore my skirts too short, pushed food on Greg too much... but, otherwise, my Mother just let me be myself. She exposed me to different cultures, and she helped me to appreciate the art in everything around me. Her newest interest was Tai Chi and she had started various new art projects. My Mother walked faster than most tall people. She had oodles of energy, and she sparked everyone she came into contact with. She raised two happy children who, in turn, had happy children.

My beautiful Mother told me when I was small that great minds discuss ideas, average minds discuss events, and shallow minds discuss people. She didn't speak badly of anyone, and she fell in love with the Montevalle people.

She and Charlie were incredible to be around. I teased her when they first met at a party of Charlie's daughters. He was watching her try to drive out of a dirt parking area. He was laughing from a distance, and she was blushing like a school girl. Charlie moved into my old room a few weeks later as a roommate, and somehow, over the course of the next twelve years, they became companions. Charlie and my Mother loved one another deeply and teased each other constantly.

Greg and I have always said that we want to be just like them.

I need to be there for my daughter who will miss her Grandma each waking day, as I will miss my Mother. More than anything, they loved to cook together. I make a promise to take the torch she has passed on to me, as her only living child now.

I am shattered...but still whole. She is on my left shoulder, allowing me time to grieve, but gently encouraging me to carry on our family culture of loving, of creating family and extended gatherings, and appreciating the beauty of simplicity. She often said, "Never go to bed angry," and I will pass this on as well. Life can be snuffed out in a moment, as we all today can witness. The little petty stuff doesn't matter. My Mother, Jean Permison was and is my hero, and I know she was for many other people too. I pray that if there are angels, they have taken her home and that somehow she can feel all the love we held and hold for my amazing Mother.

It rained all day on February 9, 2001, the day of the service. I didn't want to look in the mirror, and actually I don't think I did. I concentrated on writing my mother's eulogy, standing, and walking. I kept thinking I would fall down in front of all of these people.

There was a rainbow when we pulled into the parking place in front of the church. It had rained all day, stopping just before the service was set to begin.. It felt like a gift.

As I stood up to walk to the podium, a fantastic light filled the church, coming out from the stained glass windows.

I felt great comic relief when I mentioned how nervous my mom would be when I talked to her from my bath. I used to call it my office. She always thought I would get electrocuted. I actually felt her laughter as I told that to her loved ones. I brought her clarinet for people to see. There was great love and silence and many people sharing stories informally, both after the service in the parking lot where all real talking happens, and then at Montevalle (her senior community) where we had the reception. It was beautiful to hear and watch these seniors talk about how giving and fun she was. They couldn't get past my mom or Charlie not returning. We were all there, stuck at that exact sentiment for a very long time. Somehow it breaks my heart even more when the very old and the very young must endure bad news.

Bob, Ileana and Emily October 1999

Bob, Ileana and Emily's Service

The next day was Bob, Ileana, and Emily's service. To say I was numb wouldn't be completely accurate, because I was riddled with emotion, but there is such an exhaustion and anti-climactic, reflective aura, which follows any meaningful memorial service. It seemed unfair that I would have to attend, speak, and somehow get through another public gathering. The Fire Department did a phenomenal job working out the details and the convergence of the fire engines.

A limousine came and picked us up, en route to my father's house in San Mateo, about an hour and 10 minutes away from Santa Cruz.

My father, Arthur wore my brother's firefighter hat. It was pretty touching. He looked smaller than when I saw him last. He was sighing and shaking his head. It was too surreal to look at him in the eyes. He had an imaginary shield around him anyway. Lisa, my dear friend Loel from Seattle, and my mother-in-law Naida rode with us. My stepson, Ben looked very handsome and was unusually quiet. Greg looked pale and far away, and Carina was pretty but obviously distressed. I don't really remember checking in with her, there were just too many people around and things to do. She looked grown up, Carina, but in a premature way. The concern and pain on her face didn't match

SALUTE FOR A COMRADE

JOHN GREEN — Staff

Assembled firefighters salute as family members of South San Francisco firefighter Bob Ost arrive at St. Robert's Church in San Bruno Friday for a memorial service. Ost, his wife and infant daughter died in the crash of Alaska Airlines Flight 261 off the California coast.

Mourners gather to honor firefighter

By Laura Linden
STAFF WRITER

SAN BRUNO — Family, friends and dozens of uniformed firefighters from around the Bay Area gathered Friday to mourn the deaths of South San Francisco fire inspector Bob Ost, his wife, Ileana, and their daughter, Emily.

The Osts, along with Bob Ost's mother and companion, died aboard Alaska Airlines Fight 261 on Jan. 31 when it plunged into the Pacific Ocean off the California coast.

They were remembered as a loving family whose lives ended at their happiest.

"We all had the experience of knowing them — it was a wonderful experience for all of us," said Chris Debro, who worked with Ileana at Alaska Airlines.

Uniformed firefighters from departments on The Peninsula and across the Bay came aboard red trucks to honor Ost, who had been with the South San Francisco department since 1985. Ileana Ost's relatives came from her native Mexico City.

Those who spoke at the service, at St. Robert's Catholic Church in San Bruno struggled to comprehend why tragedy struck at a time when things were going so well for the Osts.

Bob, 39, and Ileana, 30, had

been married for four years and were as happy as ever — especially with the addition of Emily, born four months ago. They were growing closer to relatives who where sharing in the joy of a new child.

The energetic Bob Ost was sinking his teeth into remodeling their San Bruno home and was recently promoted to the respected post of fire inspector.

"I feel like I could still call you," said Bob's sister, Janice Ost-Ford. "I will never make sense of this tragedy."

Ileana worked for the airline that flew the plane on which she died. She loved her job as a station manager for Alaska and her co-workers loved her.

"She had that rare combination of beauty, strength, wisdom and serenity," said co-worker Chris Debro.

Ileana was a synchronized swimmer in Mexico City, but she was also the brainy one in the family, said her sister. Berenice Kolber. Her fluency in Spanish, English and French drew her to working for an airline.

She was upbeat and lovingly tolerated Bob Ost's daredevil pursuits — rock climbing, hang gliding and parasailing.

But she was, joked Debro, "against Bob taking Emily, hang gliding."

South San Francisco Fire

JOHN GREEN — Staff

Dozens of firetrucks make up a procession on El Camino Real in San Bruno to honor firefighter Bob Ost.

They were remembered as a loving family whose lives ended at their happiest.

Chief Russ Lee remembered Bob Ost as someone who couldn't stop learning and trying new things. "He had that lust — he loved to seek out new challenges."

But he learned to temper that drive when it came to his family.

When Bob Ost became tethered to a 40-hour work week upon being promoted to fire inspector, it was tough, because he realized he would have to choose some pastimes over others, Lee said.

But then Ost realized it wasn't such a sacrifice.

"He said, 'I know the most important thing is spending time with my family,' " Lee recalled.

If there was any solace to be had, the mourners agreed, it is that the family is together. "None of them could live without the other," said Kolber.

The service closed with the mournful sound of bagpipes rising into a gray sky.

44

her carefree young 13-year-old body. She looked like something bad had happened. You can say this about any age, but I truly believe that teenagers wear their hearts on their faces more than others. As we got closer to the church, traffic was stopped and there was a whole entourage of fire engines. I saw my niece Ashley and my nephew Axel, wow... it was really hard. We were all raw.

I stepped out of the fancy car and faced no less than 500 firefighters in their Class A Uniforms. They saluted us. I have never in my life been saluted.

I looked at the packed cathedral. I saw candles burning softly and noticed the religious art around the church. The truly difficult part was recognizing people I knew, and seeing shock and pain blending together on their faces. The hardest moments of the day included reading the tribute to my brother, hearing a eulogy delivered by Emily's cousin on Ileana's side, a first grader, and hearing the last call, where the dispatcher from the department indicates an emergency call. A voice came over the loud speaker and said Bob's name, and it took a toll on everyone. Then the bagpipes came and Amazing Grace was played. Bob's service, this tribute to his young family, I will say it was the most difficult thing I had ever experienced. This is what I wrote:

My dear brother, I am still in shock and disbelief that we are separated by different worlds right now. I have never in my life felt as close to you as I had for the past year or so, seeing and talking to you very often face to face, and somehow I have to realize that I will never see you on this Earth as I know it again.

Yesterday we had a service for Mom, and it was really heart-warming for me to see a packed church of people from different backgrounds and ages coming in her honor. I expect the same for you today, as we all prepare to salute you, and looking around the room, and feeling everyone's pain as your little sister always could, I will see that we are a very loved family.

I don't know where to begin. They brought me home from the hospital when you were three years old, and we had the typical brother and sister kind of relationship. I wanted to be like you, and follow you, and I drove you crazy. We agreed on some stuff though, like tearing off the sides of white bread and rolling it into a ball and watching "Leave it to Beaver". We agreed that it was great fun to wreck the house when Mom and Dad went out for the evening, and then pretend we were asleep when they came home. Or we would kick each other's butts and threaten to tell on each other and then make up when we would hear the garage door open, knowing their Volkswagen had just pulled in. We grew up both surrounded by different friends, but we reunited around the music of Neil Young and when Mom and Dad divorced and we lived in different houses. You picked me up and threw me in freezer shelves, and when I was a cool smoker in high school we used to blow smoke in your face to get you mad. At one point I drove alone to Yosemite, to sort of find myself after I was 18. You gave me concise directions, and I of course got lost, but after awhile I landed there and I just remember a lot of rain and solitude, the first time I was ever really alone. To tell you the truth, you loved Yosemite so much, that I wanted to know your world. I remember how proud you and I both were when our daughters were born, and the joy that Mom and Dad had when we would visit them. The song Cinnamon Girl comes to mind, as we would dance around your house with our daughters in cowgirl boots. Axel came along soon after, and you had the greatest nicknames for him like "Lumpy". You very soon after joined my world of being a single parent. You didn't feel sorry for yourself, even after you announced the news at a family get-together, you were "Just the facts Ma'am" kind of Bob. You focused, like you always could do as a kid, and you became an Electrician, a well known Tandem flyer, a more accomplished Mountain climber, and of course a veteran firefighter. You and I got together a lot more at this time, as Carina, Axel, and Ashley loved one another and they loved visiting Santa Cruz. Axel was becoming more like you with the love of practical jokes, and Ashley can just start laughing and

46

Bob & Ileana getting married (Carina watches)

put me over the edge.

I hold dear a memory of the five of us going camping for a few days, before you and I had a significant other. We talked all the way there, driving all night with our kids sleeping in the back seat. It was one of those times that one could feel the crossroads of their life. We were tired and empty in our souls, but gave to our kids 100%, I guess it's the Ost trait.

Seems at the same time, God found Greg for me and Ileana for you. Everyone who knows you talks and still talks about your transformation. Ileana's love for you was and is incredible. She changed your life, and you never looked tired again. Her sisters and Mom became our family. I remember at your private wedding at the beach, that Mom and Guadalupe just smiled at one another, not being able to speak each other's languages. It was universal, their babies had found live, and they were happy. You and Greg were brothers, and Ileana was my sister. Her beauty and kindness should be bottled and sold all over this world.

The 9 months that she carried Emily was the most exciting time in all of our lives. Dad was turning eighty and would say, even when politics were bad, that it was worth sticking around for the arrival of Emily.

You and Dad grew closer and closer, and it was his ritual to see you all each Sunday Emily was the queen, and the image I hold in my mind so clearly is you fixing your house with Emily in a snugly on your chest, Ileana cooking for you and kissing you on the cheek and telling you that lunch was almost ready.

My sweet brother, I am so amazing proud of you and I still think that you are going to call me, as you were doing on a regular basis to tell Greg and I what new sound your Emily could make.

I have lost 5 people I love so dearly, and I will never be able to make sense of this tragedy. Bob, Ileana, and Emily, I shall honor you all and light a candle for you daily. I shall watch over poor Dad, as I will watch over Ashley and Axel.

Poor Dad, nobody should have to out-live their son. I am shattered, but still whole. I need to carry the torch which was passed to me, and I will try to never let any of you down. I miss you all terrible, and I shall close by saying that at least you are not one but three, and you returned to the sea. God be with you, and also with us as we mourn.

Kim, Bob and Dylan left after the service, Loel flew home, and the flowers began to die in our house. It was time to get used to things being very different. I needed to sit by the fire and play the music, which helped my tears flow, but I needed to begin the tasks ahead of me as well. I suppose this was the time I learned to take care of business, and then to take care of myself, and to treat these jobs like two hands being washed at the same sink.

I took a month off from my job. I felt embarrassed by this somehow, as I just wanted to pull my own weight and not call attention to myself. I saw my Principal Mary Akin at my Mom's service, and it took me aback. Her face stands out to me, as she looked very moved sitting in the middle of the church. She cared enough to come, and I recall that she looked so business-like in her nice suit. Still, she had the softest shoulders as she hugged me. Mary put together a huge basket filled with cards from my staff. Many staff members had their students make me cards, so this basket of cards was tremendous. Some of my favorites were hand drawn dolphins and the kids telling me in broken English and poor spelling that they loved me and were sorry the airplane fell on my mommy.

I began making phone calls, lots of them. I found that even customer service people from Macy's knew about the fatal crash and genuinely seemed to care. Most of them would offer a "God Bless You" or "You are in my prayers" type of comment before putting me on hold or passing me on to their supervisor. It was actually quite nice. It made me feel that they were sharing a minute of also being vulnerable, that this plane could have carried their loved ones. There was a lot of local coverage on the news, and I suppose the crash was still relatively "warm" and fresh in their minds.

I learned that no matter how nice people seemed, it behooved me to get their names immediately and to write it down with the date we had a conversation. Nothing is worse than having an official tell you something pertaining to business and then getting a bill, which isn't supposed to come. It's quite ugly when you are feeling like a victim and then your deceased love one gets an unfair bill, and you have to start all over again with the explanation of the death and your relationship to the person. God forbid if you are ever in this position of being administrator to an estate, GET people's names and write dates. It may sound trivial, but I have felt heartsick over somebody excusing a late phone bill and then receiving late service charges. Choose your own fights, because that will come too, but save your energy, that is my advice.

Nothing felt right or would feel right, but somehow staying in the house and passing the day in familiar surroundings felt the best. I went to a few initial counseling sessions, but I was a zombie, and if something was said to me, no words penetrated. That is how it was, you just try to put one foot in front of the other one, and you go through the motions. Some days are horrible, and some are just hard, and none would be easy in the first year.

I couldn't stop staring outside. If I am expecting a friend to drop by, I seem to have the urge to look for them outside, seeking signs of their arrival, such as the sound of a car pulling up, the yellowish color of their headlights, a car door closing, footsteps, something…

Upon coming home after the crash, I looked over my shoulder all of the time, I looked at the sky, I stared outside. I was waiting, it was so still and quiet outside, that it gave me hope that I was somehow in their world, that I would be allowed in if only for a moment. My breathing was shallow, as I also felt dead.

I kept waking up each day, and slowly gained my appetite back. I needed a haircut, my nails grew, and I got my menstrual cycle. I was alive, and I needed to be strong, as crushed as I felt. My good friend Pilar's words kept haunting me, as they still do: "Shattered But Still Whole". I repeated this to myself whenever needed, whenever my own weakness sets in and I felt defeated by the thunder around me. I took refugee in the words. I have heard that God never gives you more than you can handle, and I pondered this too. But God didn't do this, he or she or it doesn't make plane wrecks or bombs or evil doings, man does. This stuff can sure keep you up at night.

I had began the special education program to earn a Master's through San Jose State University two days before the crash, and somehow the impending work and the nagging sense of work completion set in. I wasn't involved physically in the crash, after all, so I didn't feel excused. I believe these were a few Saturdays a month for the semester, and I had missed one or two already. The winding road through Highway 17 had always cleared my mind, and I looked forward to getting away from the ringing telephones. I didn't like how every phone call somehow needed my attention, and the attention to detail, which screamed for my tired eyes and delirious mind, it felt suffocating to me. I only liked the night, because the noise stopped. I would wipe the counters in the kitchen, make a list of agencies I needed to call the next day, fold laundry, sit on the couch and stare out of the window. Again, it felt that if I were patient enough, shooting stars would appear, I would hear my brother tell me something, they might call somehow, some message from out there would show it's mercy. I felt like a kid from daycare waiting for my parents after all the other kids got picked up. I wanted to panic, but I would just look outside and wait for the sound of their arrival. They never ever came, and I still secretly wait.

Happier Days – Carina, Jean, Charlie, Janis, Greg and Ben.

The Crash That Made Me Crumble

When the ball dropped into the year 2000 I distinctly remember telling my mother what a great year this would be. After all why wouldn't it, I was getting straight A's in school and everything was going perfect. However like the saying goes "what comes up must come down." In my case, that saying referred to my life, which was getting ready to take a big fall. After only 31 days into the new millennium I reached the worst point in my life. It was then that I lost my grandmother and my only uncle among many other loved ones in a horrible fatal crash.

My grandma Jean Permison was one of my favorite people in the world. I saw her on a regular basis, probably at least twice a month if not more. She was the most active 70 year old ever, she taught the exercise class at Montevalle (where she resided). She also participated in Tai Chi and was also extraordinarily artistic. Most seniors I know complain about their aches and pains, not my grandma she was in perfect health. Most grandmothers make steak and potatoes, not my grandma she was making won ton soup, spaghetti, sushi, and tamales. She had probably cooked any type of ethnic food possible. I know most of my friends hate seeing their grandparents, but it was never like that for me. I looked forward to seeing her all the time, and I loved dinners at her house because they were filled with warmth and laughter.

My grandma and I had a very special connected bond; we used to always cook together, sew, play ping-pong, and paint ceramics. She has made a huge impact on my life because she helped raise me. She was and is the closest person to me next to my mom. When I spent the night at her house our favorite thing to do was to wake up and talk in bed for hours. She use to say she wanted to live until she was a hundred and see all my grandchildren, with her health that could have easily happened. I loved talking to her, she never judged me and was always sincerely interested in my opinions on issues. She supported whatever I wanted to do in my life, which always changed daily. When I was younger I wanted to be a psychologist so she would make up fake problems about people and then have me solve them. Then when I was older I wanted to work with the police and draw criminals based on a witness description. She made up descriptions of people for example; tall, white, male, brown hair, green eyes, I would then draw a sketch of the person. When I wanted to be a chef we would make up a menu and then cook whatever my mom ordered. That's just a couple of examples of how she always stood by me.

The last time I saw her was her birthday. We took her out to dinner and bought her a bread machine. She was so excited, all she talked about was us making bread together. I remember when my Uncle Bob called and invited my grandma and her companion Charlie for a weekend in Puerto Vallarta, she was so happy. I kissed her goodbye and told her to have fun and take lots of pictures!

I remember when my mom came into my room and told me a plane had crashed coming back from Mexico. I had a friend over at my house that day and I said "oh how sad" very nonchalantly. My mom then reminded me that my grandma Jean was returning home that night and it was an Alaskan Airlines plane that crashed. We both knew that my Uncle Bob's wife Ileana worked for that airlines and that's the only airline they ever took. I told my mom "no way, stuff like this never happens to people like us." Well my mom called the airlines anyway and they told her that they couldn't give out any names yet. She called everyone to see if anyone knew what time they were supposed to arrive.

By that time I was getting nervous, with my eyes glued to the television set, waiting for the airline to call back. I just sat there frozen watching the helicopters circle the Pacific Ocean looking for people on the six o'clock news. My throat felt like it had a bowling ball inside of it. I could hardly swallow. All of sudden the phone rang and everyone paused as my mom answered it; she let out a huge wail and repeated if they were sure. It was at that moment that I felt my entire body go numb. I then remember running to my mom and balling my eyes out, even that word doesn't express what I was feeling at the moment. In my mind there was hope that everything would be fine, I thought they would pull them out of the ocean and they would be saved. Unfortunately things don't always go the way we want them to. I knew and lost five people on that plane, all of which I love dearly, My grandma, my uncle, my grandma's companion (who was like a grandfather) my aunt Ileana, and my 4 month old cousin Emily who I only met three times.

I felt cheated out of my family, I never had anyone close to me die, and then in a second I lost five of my favorite people in a horrible and tragic way. There isn't a day that goes by that I don't miss them. All of the holidays and birthdays aren't the same without them. I was never able to make bread with my grandma or sit in bed and talk to her again. I hated the fact of not being able to call up my grandma or having our famous family gatherings at her house. The thing that kills me is that none of this had to happen. It could have easily been avoided. Corporate greed, people not wanting to pay a little extra money on fixing a jackscrew caused it. If people just did their job correctly I could still have my family here. The only way I could cope with all this was just thinking of it as though my family was on a "long term vacation."

By Carina Ost

Bob mountain climbing 1980

Bob

Bob was the chess champion in high school,
The shortest but strongest mountain climber ever.
Bob was born with wild blonde hair and sea-borne blue
    eyes, a tamed but mischievous sailor type kindred spirit.
Bob was born in 1960 in New York City to two
    Bohemian- type peace loving people.
Bob was a very respected, hilarious, worldly, sometimes
    reserved, passionate young man of 39 years.

Bob fell in love with mountains in his 17th year.
I blew cigarette smoke in his face and thought this would
    be a short-lived crush, like the girl from the ice cream
    parlor down the street.
He saved his money for climbing gear and kept returning to
    these quiet titans and I could not understand the need.
Bob marched to the beat of a drummer who didn't come
    to my room.

Bob and I played funny jokes on each other and usually couldn't finish a sentence while recalling childhood and
teenage years because we couldn't catch our breath while
laughing. Though our parents divorced when we were 14
and 17, there were many funny and happy things that took
place before. Our own children wanted to hear the infa-

mous pranks over and over again like a hose in a water balloon soaked neighborhood that only children can truly appreciate.

Bob didn't speak of his deepest feelings but you could guess how he felt by watching his face. He had the most handsome blonde/red whiskers sprouting from his face like a fall leaf, looking for the first day of school to welcome children. His mustache was ample and devilish making a dashing first impression, and centering his small-framed face quite cleverly.

Bob loved The Three Stooges more than anything. He watched the re-runs over and over again when we were small, and as an adult he had their picture framed. He wore their tie, roaring avidly at the slapstick humor, usually spitting and showing off his dental work and molars with his wide-open mouth.

Bob was frugal and saved coins and stamps as a young boy. He was very conservative when it came to safety and new climbing and flying equipment. He hated shopping and new clothes but loved new tents and any kind of climbing or flying gear. He saved his firefighting days off to be in Mother Nature's arms, kissing each horizon hello and goodbye like a little boy waving on a carousel.

Bob adored his children and talked of them incessantly. They were marvelous creatures to him, not just his extension. While Emily is with Bob in the other world, heaven, or a big puffy cloud somewhere, I sneak looks at Ashley and Axel, when I can. The shyness, the humor, the intensity carried through the bloodline like a proud Native American dancing in a traditional ceremony.

Bob, Ashley, Greg and Axel 1996

Bob & Emily

Jean & Janis singing together for Charlie's last birthday.
August 13, 1999

Jean

Little Jeannie, I would call her, as I had for years. Her nickname came to me from an old Elton John song about someone with "So much love". Every time I think of her, we are arm in arm, our eyes and noses touching, and I am calling her Little Jeannie. We were exactly the same height, 5 feet, 1/4 inch and we both round that off to 5'1". We have earned the extra 3/4 inch, it's not always easy being small in such a big world.

My mother, Little Jeannie, was the most adorable, toughest, yet most gentle human being in this whole world. I can't do anything but smile when I think of her, so everyday I smile, at least just a little. My friends have always adored her. She had her own style of dressing and talking. She had a knack for making others feel important. Her words were always sincere, or else you wouldn't hear them.

Friends ask me what it was like to grow up with Little Jeannie. I tell them she was a late bloomer. She was the most fun in her fifties and beyond that. I think that's when she found herself. After she and my father broke up, she took out her clarinet again. She joined Green Earth Singles, she took creative writing classes. She loved healthy food and healthy living.

Once, after high school, some friends of mine invited her to try "funny cigarettes". She had heard about it quite a bit, and used to play clarinet in an all girl rumba band in Harlem. She had smelled pot, but really had no interest in it. I admit it, we really wanted her to try it; she made us all laugh without even trying. Okay, the truth is, it just didn't work. She laughed at the time she was supposed to inhale, and after a few attempts on this one occasion, I realized she would stay pure and naturally high all of her life. I would tease her about this experience, as she insisted she just liked being in control of her mind.

My mother had oodles of energy and would sometimes trip over things and into people because she was always doing, going, moving. Her hands were red, a fiery red burning color. Her hair was a rich medium brown, and she had great natural waves. When she went gray, she simply did nothing, and the outcome was a striking salt and pepper mixture. Her eyes were a friendly hazel, and she looked the best in purple, which she wore a lot. She spent a lot of money and time on her teeth. She had inherited poor teeth from her family, but nevertheless won awards for the cleanest teeth and gums from her dentist. My mother spent a good twenty minutes a day flossing and using the water pick, and polishing each tooth as if it was a gem.

My mother would go crazy when she heard live music. Her feet would begin to tap to the rhythm; she *couldn't* sit still. Over the last few years of her life, her clarinet playing got better and better. She played in a few coffee houses, and I am proud to say she played at my wedding reception. She hit the notes to "Hava Negilah" like nobody's business.

In addition to her musical endeavors, she made incredible batik hangings and clothes. She had more orders than she could fill. Making art and music and being happy were her passions. Jeannie also loved doing Tai Chi. She exercised daily. She had an occasional half glass of wine. Then her nose would get red and she would burst into a smile and say, "Boy, my arms are getting tired" in the most playful Brooklyn, New York accent ever heard. My mother never really finished her wine – she was affected so easily and quickly. I think she was so damn happy anyway that anything extra was like whipped cream on a very sweet pie.

Men typically liked Little Jeannie more than she liked them. I had a job with Toyota as a customer care hostess right after high school. By then my mom was single, and I was working with a widowed car salesman named Bill. He took us both to Reno one weekend and really wanted to start something with her. I remember how she blushed when he paid too much attention, it probably was good for her ego, but she wasn't into the superficial. She was reading self help books, cooking new recipes, really enjoying coming into her own.

My mother never really would be one to sit home and wait for the phone to ring. She was re-defining herself at this time. Finding a new companion wasn't even on her "back burner," I don't think. She had one boyfriend named Ralph Garcia, They dated for a number of years. He had green cat eyes and dark olive skin and he took her to Hawaii, New York, and treated her well. He was getting transferred to Maryland and asked her to go with him. She said she couldn't leave her kids (Bob was twenty-two or twenty-three, I was nineteen or twenty).

I think when you miss someone so incredibly much, they sort of move into your insides. As I write this in a quiet café, I wonder what she would want people to know about her. She smiles in my heart when I tell people what she would do in a situation. When I praised her, she would remind me that I was so far ahead of where she was at my age.

I have always felt proud of may mother. People didn't walk over her, they respected her and the fine line she drew in the sand about everything. Once a houseguest simply stayed too long. They had agreed on a date he would hit the highway, and the day came and passed, he was comfortable, as everyone was in her cozy places. She walked up to him, got very close to his face, and stated how she felt, that she needed her place back, and that the day had come. That was it, no bargaining, wavering, no apologies. It was so clear and beautiful.

Sometimes when life has gotten me tossing and turning

at night, nervous with the anticipation of a confrontation, I soothe myself with Little Jeannie's wisdom. God I learned so much from this lady. She repeated sayings at times, but they were the good ones, and I never really minded. "What is the worst that could happen?" That was her favorite, and it actually works if you ask yourself at any moment of uncertainty. Usually, the consequences are not that bad, that is what I learned.

Little Jeannie also NEVER tried to make anyone feel guilty. If she had trouble sleeping, it was because she had difficulty making a business decision or a decision between pieces of furniture or tile colors. I lose sleep because of not wanting to hurt someone, or anticipating how somebody will react. This is how we were different. I wish I could be more like her in that way. She could say "too bad" and let the chips fall where they would. I agonize over giving people several chances before I want to give up.

I think my mother wanted people to walk with their heads held high, not worrying, but slowly moving towards their personal goals. She would want me to remember that. She wished I didn't wear my heart on my sleeve, but I was the sensitive, late, bed wetter who wrote poetry in first grade about visiting people in convalescent hospitals.

Little Jeannie was the perfect Grandmother. After I divorced my husband, Carina and I lived with her for a short time. I know it must have been hard to have crayons and stuffed animals on a couch that used to be clean, but I know she was concerned about me financially and morally. She had a roommate from India, and was conscientious about not disturbing him as we were not in the picture when he moved in. All three of us girls slept in her room mostly in her bed. Carina loved her grandmother very much, and called her "Working Mama" where as I was just "Mama". I didn't work at the time because Carina was so young.

My mother never complained, but at some point I could tell she needed her own room back. We never fought, but I wanted to honor her, and allow her to sleep alone again, the way I knew she slept the best. When her new love, Charlie moved in, and I was in graduate school a few miles away, she seemed completely content again. I would egg her on, years later, "Come on Mom, you didn't need a baby in your room again, especially when you had to work over the hill every day...". She would just smile, and nudge me to save some of my tip money in case I needed it for an emergency. Being practical, and not giving her attention to somebody when they were trying to guilt themselves were two more of her gifts.

My mother, my little Jeannie, is strangely within my reach in an unreachable way. I miss her though, in ways that I imagine lovers and spouses miss each other when one departs before the other. I miss how her skin felt when we all slept together, the three generations. I loved putting my cold feet over her warm thighs. "Warm me up, Mama", I would say, and she always did. Most of our best talks were in bed on weekend mornings, when she didn't have to wake up at 5:00 a.m. We talked about everything, and then she'd make healthy pancakes. Neither of us were dating at the time, and we both felt like we were at crossroads in our lives.

As Carina got older, and up until the crash, she'd spend the night fairly often with "Working Mama." Like mine, her most meaningful memories were also of laying in bed on weekend mornings and talking about everything.

I am rambling on about the serious side of Little Jeannie. That was only her "day job," as it were. The other side was very silly and fun. She made funny tee-shirts with suggestive sayings, she liked to laugh, she liked amateur plays and fancied diamonds in the rough. She didn't like jokes played on her, but she was a good sport, anyway. I am laughing a little but still feeling bad about the night I stood above the shower, feet on the toilet seat, holding a huge pot of cold water. It sounds so sick now, but we were having this really silly night remembering old times and then she went to do her half hour tooth care routine, followed by her shower. It was a work night for her, and I tried talking her into staying up late with me. Carina was already asleep, and I guess I missed adult interaction. So I was standing on the toilet seat just waiting for the right moment, as she was in the shower. I looked down on her, but she was lathering her hair with shampoo, oblivious to my presence there. I slowly dumped the water on her and she shrieked. I couldn't stop laughing. She didn't play jokes like that on others, but she never got too upset either.

I knew how much I loved my mom as early as I could remember. It is such a sharp pain that I never told her goodbye, that I couldn't give her one last kiss and hug goodbye. This stuff becomes very vital when tragedy robs you of it. I have trouble imagining how she must have felt the last minutes on the plane. I told her my whole life that I couldn't live without her. When I was little, she would tell me that I told her that dying meant you fall down, and that I would never let her fall. This haunts me so much. Did I know something back then? How many times have all of us, the families of the crash victims, imagined the long plunge into the ocean?

For many months, the Coast Guard and the rescue parties in Point Hueneme couldn't find any trace of my Mother's remains. It bewildered me so much, yet there was almost something noble about that; I almost appreciated the mystery. I imagined that she had turned into a dolphin or maybe a mermaid. One evening at dinner, a uniformed policeman came to the door to deliver the news. Her hand and a piece of her foot still wearing a white tennis shoe had been found. I liked the dolphin fantasy so much better, and I super-impose that image when my mind wanders down dangerously graphic roads.

In a strange way, I can relate to my mother more as a child I've lost than as my parent. I wanted to protect her forever, she was my innocent, magical little flower. I have the most trouble looking into the eyes of the mothers I've met who have lost children on the flight. I imagine them having the same kind of protective and unconditional love for their kids as I did for my mom. Knowing it was in the same category made it unbearable. My Mother sat on my lap, that is just how we were together. She was so damn fun just to take to concerts, to taco bars, the hairdresser, wherever. There is nobody who can even come close to filling the void. I feel her, I have her pictures all over the house, and the hole is still in my throat choking me.

More than anything, I didn't have to explain myself to my mother. She just knew me. Nobody will ever love me in the way she did. How can one say goodbye to that? I need her. I thanked her for everything, told her how much I loved her all of the time, so it's not like we had unfinished business, but the sheer reality that we are in different worlds just kills me, and I can't get past that.

I used to talk myself down every morning for the first year or so. I reminded myself very matter-of-factly that she was gone. I wanted to call her, I wanted to drive to her house. I imagined that maybe she had swum to safety and found a fisherman to rescue her and dry her off, and then I could drive out and pick her up.

I recall my first birthday without Little Jeannie, in April. I bought a hot tub because I knew she always wanted one. I filled it up with water and sat outside. I did this almost every night for the first year until Cody was born. I'd make a cup of tea, and look for her in the stars. I'd feel the closest to her at these times. My eyes would cross as I looked for "signs" outside until my eyes would burn. At some point I realized that it's the *feeling* of loved ones we are blessed with. But we just aren't able to see them exactly as we knew them. Still I looked and looked and waited and hoped. My doctor knew that taking hot tubs were helpful to me in healing ways, so as long as I didn't make it too warm, I was allowed this luxury. For me it was an escape and offered me sanity. I would finish washing dishes with my big swollen belly, and as the flood of my emotions would take over, I would quickly walk outside, get in the warm water, look up at the sky, and exhale. I would hear a cricket, or a slight noise, and I would get a thrill, maybe my mom was coming for a visit!

At that moment your heart expands to such dimensions

that you can get a little lovesick and you don't think straight. Still, I stared into the night sky, even on rainy nights, with the slightest chance of a possibility that she'd show her face in a branch or in a star.

I can only say that I loved her more than anything in this world. I pray she stays with me, from the dawn to the darkest of the nights, guiding me and continuing to teach me. If you see a timeless, short, gray haired lady playing the clarinet with a twinkle in her eye, and she has a New York accent and she has her head and heart on a good path, tell her "Hello, Little Jeannie."

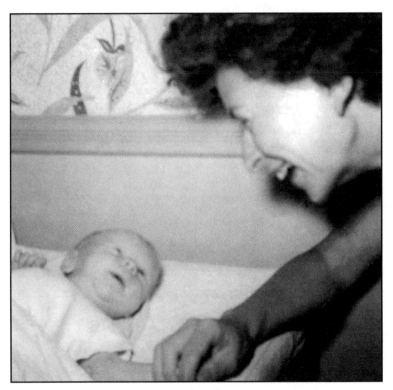

Jean and Bob 1960

Jeannie
by
Janis Ost Ford
January 14, 2000

I wrote and played
this little song to
my mother on her
birthday.

Born in Brooklyn
under the Capricorn sign
People learned quickly
    she had a strong mind ⌒

A champion at punch ball
    and clarinet blowing
She wasn't too orthodox
    cause her artist was showing ⌒

Was a Greenwich Village hippy
    in the usual time
Hung sheets like curtains
    Got giggly and weak arms from wine ⌒

Life spun it's tangled web
    took this lady to the west
She raised a family
    oh she was the best ⌒

She bought a gift store
    called it the Gift Horse
Meditated and made won ton soup
    oh gentle, so gentle was her force ⌒

Well things got foggy
    a divorce was long due
Everything was changing
    her teenagers too
(She was reborn to herself, at age 52) ⌐

She charmed her way into H.P.
    boy did those engineers talk
they never saw a lady move so quickly
    in her skirt and Birkenstalks ⌐

Years passed on –
    she got the Golden Handshake
Now she takes her time in the morning
    and even makes pancakes ⌐

Now she's the Queen of Montevalle
    and loves her tai chi
the sexiest senior there ever was
    Jeannie's so free ⌐

A dozen years later
    there's still Jean and Charlie
Which one drives the other more crazy –
    and who, but who gets put over the knee? ⌐

She's careful how she spends,
    fanatically healthy how she eats
Jeannie, Jeannie, Jeannie makes our lives
    so sweet and complete ⌐

There's Jeannie, Jeannie, Jeannie
    coming around the bend
Besides the mother of me,
    she's my best friend.

Charlie & Jean

Charlie

He was perhaps the biggest man I had ever set eyes on. Six foot tall, sailor, engineer, lumberjack shirt wearing wonderful man with a deep voice. His eyes told you he cared about whatever you were talking about. His stomach said he liked good food.

Magnificent blue eyes, so filled with watery emotion, hiding behind glasses because the intensity would knock people over.

Mighty man with the white mustache and beard. I had never been hugged by anyone with more love in an embrace. I felt comfortable with him the second I saw him, wanting him to be partners with my mom.

It wouldn't matter what kind of partner, as this man looked as if he could take care of a galaxy, and he could, and he did.

When formality flew out the window, Charlie could make you laugh so easily, and he kept a handkerchief in his pocket to wipe the laughing liquid from his eyes.

I noticed him watching my mother. It began when she and I were invited to his daughter's home for a Christmas party. There was a softness in his face, he seemed amused by my mother, he broke into a shy smile. He was like Santa Claus watching a little girl he was fond of. They avoided each other's eyes, so much that the gaze to disconnect was actually two bow and arrows shooting at the same target.

She couldn't park into the dirt road, there were too many cars crowding her as we both struggle with understanding space. And Charlie was everything of space. He was born with sharpened pencil, an exactness, perhaps a compass inside of his ears. He smiled, stretched out his long arm, and attempted to guide her. Her hand was slipping off of the steering wheel, she drove in, out, reversed, came forward. I laughed, he looked puzzled but amused, she blushed like a warm glass of wine sitting in a window sill. This was the beginning of the start of it.

Weeks later I called him. A funny Santa Cruz friend told me to "Always replace myself" so I coolly offered the room in her house to him as I was moving away to campus. A week or two later, he moved in his large jar of mayonnaise next to her whole grain bread and alfalfa sprouts and the two people more than a foot apart in measurement stood firmly, that he would be a tenant and she would be the landlord and this would be a trial. They lived as best companions until death did call.

They were, hands down, the most opposite couple, not ever getting why one would do things so oddly. Through time, I saw that he kept her helium balloons from carrying her off to the moon, and she showed him that great big, serious men could still be happy and young little boys. That is what I think at least one lesson was.

When Carina was in kindergarten there was a small mouse in my house. I was hysterical, not being able to go about my day for fear of seeing it, but being afraid to harm it. Charlie came over at 10:00 that rainy December night and took over. He gave me a bear hug, told me I was like my mother, and got rid of this terrifying rodent. At that moment, I knew I would never be the same without him in my life, and I am not.

Charlie waxed my car and helped me with math. I noticed how he cleaned. I would go out and buy the same dish soap and my kitchen could never touch what Charlie could do so effortlessly. He whistled when he worked and he was always working, helping somebody, or listening. He called me "Dear" and "Angel" and regularly asked me about anything going on in my life. Charlie was the most nurturing blanket I ever put on.

Charlie and my mother lived in two houses together. Their magical bond lasted the dozen years they knew one another, since meeting on that dirt road. They were adored in their senior mobile home community. Another retired couple wondered aloud why they didn't consider getting married, and Charlie just laughed and said, "Why ruin a beautiful friendship?" At his 70th birthday party, I played a song on my guitar I wrote for him, he had a tear in his eye. At the end of the party, I gave him a watch and he said the years with my mom were the happiest days of his life.

When my grief took me to the bargaining table, I wished I could have at least ONE of them, but then I realized they needed to hold hands and surrender together, like Bob, Ileana, and Emily. I would give my arms to have just one more warm hug from Charlie.

Janis & Charlie

Emily

Her picture smiles down at me everyday like a gentle rain.
Her little pumpkin face, expressive eyebrows, perfect little
   lips, her mouth which never sprouted teeth, breaking
   into a big helpless smile, her sweet round little four
   month old body…
Emily was a perfect and proud flower, she could not have
   been better.
Her father used the word WONDERFUL to describe his
   little baby girl, and it fits.

These words do not come easy. Emily disappeared as
   quickly as she came into the world.
Little baby girls are supposed to nap with their bottoms
   up in the air, catch ladybugs, draw hearts and sit on
   their mommy and daddy's laps reading Sesame Street.
   Emily never got to do that, in fact she never blew her
   first candle out. Her Grandpa always said she was
   going to be an astronaut. Is she now smiling at us
   from the cosmos?

What can I do but miss the times we never had?
What can I feel when I see her picture but heartsick and sad?
What can I do but love my own baby, wishing she were
   still here?

Tell Emily's story to anybody who wants to hear?
A beautiful child from two races with the happiest smile
to see
Had only 4 months to spread her love, then went away to
where it began,
Where she dances on waves and whispers to the sand.
Emily, sweet Emily, I will cherish holding her little hand
in mine
Only a few years ago, but feeling like the time lapse of
infinity –
And one day I shall see her again, riding the dolphins and
singing of the trinity.
Until then, I light a candle each day for her, but I cannot
cry every day
As I was called to be the mother to Cody, and he wants to
play,
I will never ever forget her sweet memory, her time here
Like a shooting star, so far, but in the same way, very near.
I will love her forever, Emily Ost – the angel baby…

Emily & Ileana 1999

78

Ileana

Sweet, sweet dark eyed Ileana
Hovering over my brother with pure love and devotion
Thick Spanish accent, delightfully chopping away at big
    English words
She enchanted all of us with her well-mannered ways and
    her excitement for each season.
Little by little her shyness dissolved, a new essence filled
    our drinking glasses.
Whether she pushed a broom, tried a new recipe or re-
    arranged the furniture-
Ileana did it with grace and a selfless flavor.

Nothing was more awesome than when she showed off
    her big, growing belly
While Bob tugged at her sable locks and said, "We'll call
    him Elvis"
She laughed and threw her head back, beaming.
She never looked quite as beautiful as the day she held
    Emily in a blanket, telling me how happy she was to
    be a mom.
She inspired me always, as we were new wives a year apart
Laughingly I'd tell Greg that I could never be as sweet
    and subservient as her,
But secretly, I wished I wasn't as feisty and maybe

narcissistic

Deep down, she probably liked herself more than I like
    myself,

Why then, did she get a permanent red light and I am still
    on the freeway?

Had there been more time for us, she would have shown
    me how to love someone more than myself without
    losing myself.

Ileana's time here was so pitifully short.

I miss her big smile and the sound her shoes made as she
    pranced down the hall holding her new baby in one
    hand and serving hot lunch for the company.

Doing it all, and still having clean floors and wearing nice
    shoes with sensible heels.

With my lips tightly closed and my head in the big open
    sky, I attempt to conjure up each memory we had
    together,

In pools, at restaurants, in parks, during Christmas,
    Thanksgiving, playing bingo, baby showers, and most-
    ly in kitchens, where women seem to connect in pow-
    erful ways.

I miss the connection, I miss the most wonderful sister-in-
    law, and I miss the gentle spirit, the dynamic woman
    who truly loved my brother until the end.

Bob & Ileana

Cleaning Out Mom's House

Upon returning from Point Hueneme, I found myself in the back of a rental car driven by Karolee. We past my Mother's exit, and the weird noises came out again. I think somebody may have taken my hand. This was the exit I'd taken for years and years, it just took me by surprise to see it now, as if it were a teasing neon light advertising a ghost town. It was very windy and cold outside. I knew entering the house the next day would be impossible but necessary. I felt like a dad with a weak stomach, forced to take a dead mouse caught in a trap outside to the garbage. It was just a necessary job. Hating it, being terrified, not wanting to look and face the music, all of these excuses wouldn't cut the mustard of a final death and the brave entrance into a house which would change my life forever.

It was cold in Mother's house. I walked slowly, carefully, peeking out of my snotty and wet piece of Kleenex. Going into each room, closing and opening and opening and closing doors as if I were both the intruder and the detective catching the intruder.

Wanting to keep everything, as it was, wanting to respect each cold pencil, each plant, each spoon, even the miniscule dust ball on the answering machine.

Nothing is more chilling than touching the clothes of the recently deceased. But at that moment, anything she wore was a relic I could smell and clench and cry into, and so I tortured myself by standing in her closet and putting every one of my senses to work, I groped every single article I could find...

Finally diving onto her bed and burying my head in her soft purple sheets, where I shook and whimpered, too tired to go into the night, admitting there was nothing left inside.

Cleaning Out My Brother's House

My brother's house looked like a shrine. Somebody had put a huge wooden rosary over the front door. Old flowers and new flowers, teddy bears, lit candles, notes and cards. The South San Francisco Fire Department left a huge spray of flowers on a stand. It was breath taking, an honor. My brother had begun his remodel, and like so many aspects of his life, he was living in the middle of his pilgrimages. There was so much to do all of the time, nothing was ever quite done.

The drive from Santa Cruz to San Bruno is about an hour and fifteen minutes. The first time I had gone to Bob's house after the crash is a bit of a blur. There were quite a few people there, including Ileana's mother from Mexico. Everybody was crying, looking around. Emily's toys were neatly put in her room, the dishes were cleaned, everything just seemed normal, like they would be coming through the door at any time. I remember there was talk about where Bob's will would be. I wanted to be helpful, but a strange and self-righteous feeling from within didn't want to disrupt anything. His house, their house, should be a quiet museum to simply walk through and bow heads. It was a futile, childish thought. When tragic accidents occur, there needs to be movers and shakers, those who don't take notice to all of the flowers outside, but the wills and needed keys inside. I am not and was not that kind of person, not in my big brother's house.

It was freezing. I kept burping a very foul smell. No matter how often I brushed my teeth, this awful taste and smell kept surfacing.

I spent days trying to make sense of his office. Maybe it worked for him, but I could find no rhyme or reason for the way in which Bob organized his files.

Ileana was incredibly neat and organized, probably more than anyone else I knew. Nobody in my immediate family inherited that type A gift; we weren't slobs, but there were always piles in our houses. There was always a sense of the process of clearing and cleaning out, but never immaculate housecleaning.

Pictures of Bob's kids, Ashley and Axel, were in every file and folder it seemed. Bob's flying stuff (para-gliding) electrical jobs, firefighting evaluations, Ashley's dental bills, and jokes were stuffed into a single file.

Everything was slow motion. It was time-less in this quiet, dead, cold house.

I recall the sound of the heater and my strange, strange crying patterns. Stopping, starting, wailing, hitting walls, weeping quietly, and then starting all over again. A lot of friends of Bob's came by, and the remarkable South San Francisco Fire Department helped out a great deal, but I was left alone in my brother's office. When Greg would come in and check on me, I pretended to be efficient, but it was a farce. I was Bob's little sister after all, and I needed to remain a bit dependent and inept in the setting of his house. It was hard to just look for a will and locate pertinent bills without having emotion and being clumsy.

A copy of Bob's will was located, and then I remembered him asking me some months before if I would take care of his business should anything ever happen. It made me feel so good. Greg was the only guy in my life who Bob ever really liked (Firefighter brotherhood?) and since I had gotten together with Greg, my relationship with Bob blossomed and got better and better.

And so, little by little, truck load by truckload, I gathered the bills, which had to be paid, and I took them with me. I made copies of the will where I was officially named as the "Administrator" of the estate, and I made dozens of copies of the death certificate. I contacted my friend I used to teach with and remembered that her husband practiced probate law. I asked him to help out in this mess, and I suppose I did a few duties each day from an endless list.

Months and months later, I sold the house, and contacted his banks, putting everything in one account, but these are all jobs and expectations that any dummy could do. The real job, the dirty job in the trenches, was entering the house knowing that he would never set foot in his house again. The food in the cupboards would not be eaten, they would never look at their photo albums again, and Emily would never play with her baby toys or be rocked in her chair. Ileana's clothes were neatly put away and hung, and these clothes would never again be worn by her. This stuff, these heart-wrenching truths were the hardest. Desperately, my brain went through a process of attempting to bargain, to see a way out of this mess. As a teacher, and a mother, there are always options in my daily life. When things get tough, my girlfriend Jeanette and I sit down with a cup of coffee and we brainstorm ideas to change or better the bad things bothering us. But plane crashes are different. The sudden, terrifying needle prick reality of sheer horror is deafening, immobilizing, and relentless. There was no way out of this, nothing to un-do, no letter to write to try to change a situation. It was a horrible screeching sound, glass and blood tumbling through mid air, and then silence. My job would be to wash my face, take a deep breath, and take care of business. Clean, organize, bury, delegate, honor, and remember, in that order. I detested being the little sister in control. Oh how I needed my mom. Where was she?

Somewhere in the heavens cuddling her partner, her son, her daughter in law, her Grand daughter?

I felt abandoned, it finally hit me. I heard others talk about this feeling and I could finally relate.

85

My poor father could barely walk into the house. He looked so disheveled, so old and broken. Bob was good about checking his car, fixing his appliances, doing those typically male oriented jobs that my sweet but mechanically challenged father could not do.

I felt so sorry for my father in these times of going to Bob's house, but inside I felt hatred and self pity that I was alone to do the hard stuff. It was like burying a horse with my bare hands in a rainstorm. It was ugly and gross and hard, and I had to do it.

My father wouldn't recall this I am sure, but I promised myself to conjure up everything in the past years since the crash. A few weeks after the crash he was pacing outside the un-painted, half stucco house, and finally came in. Bob, Ileana and Emily's beautiful faces were framed in the hallway. My dad saw this, walked out, and claimed he was hungry. He wanted to have someone drive to Jack in the Box and bring back lunch. I granted his wish, and cried in the car by myself waiting in the drive-thru line to place my order. People die in plane crashes and there are still happy voices greeting you from fast food machine chains trying to entice you to super-size your order. It was too much for me.

I brought the food back for him, and watched him eat his hamburger with his little hat on his head. He looked like a four year old to me, and I hated this reality of having to take on a big role of the parent in this scenario.

I watched him eat his burger, click his tongue, swallow too fast, and all of the things that drove me crazy about his eating habits when I was a teenager. Bob and I always laughed about this stuff, and now I would watch him alone.

I felt so damn sorry for him, ketchup and mustard on his gray whiskers, his eyes so teary but he could offer nothing but a bite of his burger. I cried and cried and hated, knowing this was but the beginning. The house was so very cold, so very, very cold. It was too much for me.

Taking Me Home

This was the first dream I remember after the crash. It will haunt me in a delightful way until I take my last breath. It was realistic, calming, and the most visually beautiful thing I think I have ever seen in my life.

I am in a hospital or clinic type of place. Someone asks me if I want to see my brother. I don't, I am so afraid and I don't want to see how bad he would look after a crash of this magnitude.

Nobody is around. I am holding my finger in my mouth, terrified. I am standing by the door. I also feel drawn. Either somebody tells me it isn't too bad, or the mystery pulls me to stand by the door where the body is. I see a gurney. I walk closer to it. There is a sheet and a young blonde boy in it. I look closer. He is sleeping, he is about thirteen years old or so. He sits up, and he smiles. His eyes hold the most magnificent blue color I have ever seen. He is looking around the room, he doesn't see me, or we just don't talk. I see lights dancing around him, the room is lit up and he is slowly turning his head, he is a teenager with porcelain skin and these amazing eyes, just smiling. Somebody or something says so clearly, "The saints are here to take you home." Bob says, "I KNOW" and then the dream ends.

This was the best dream I ever had. Bob was not the

least bit religious, but he looked so peaceful in this dream with the most beautiful expression on his face. I super impose this dream when the nightmares take over.

Dreams

Freud said we know our dreams. Some say dreams are just our sub-conscious, and like anything else, which is experienced so differently, there are no right or wrong answers. I know that I was given some very unusual dreams the first year especially.

I believe in some small way, we are working things out in our dreams, and just like we throw up when something is wrecking havoc on our systems; we dream about things and people we have yet to work things out with.

My main re-occurring dream was dealing with Bob's death. My brother saved people's lives as a profession, and I bet my sweet life he used the last minutes of his own life trying to help someone with their seat belt, or having heart problems, or he was calming people down. I know, or at the very least, I have the hunch he didn't have time to deal with his own mortality, or if he did, it was very quick. As his only sibling, someone trying to put scrambled pieces of the puzzle together, he may not have known he was dying (did any of them? Probably not. I know Bob assisted others, I just know that) but regardless, I worry he didn't know this would be the end, and that he had less time to process than the other passengers. My dreams, you guessed it, all seemed to have the common thread of me telling him what happened. I believe this dream haunted me twenty – thirty times.

An Early Dream

I am driving into a small parking place in front of the mini-mart 7-11. I am walking in, and there I find Bob walking by the candy section. He is cool and sort of yawning, asking me what is new. I start crying and shaking and there is stuff in my mouth preventing me from speaking. I sound garbled, not able to speak, he looks at me as when we were fighting teenagers, like I am the dumbest person he had ever seen. I want to tell him that he is not real, he is not flesh and bone, he is dead, but there are wires and a thick glue or gum-like kind of material in my mouth and I can't formulate a sentence.

More Dreams

Bob comes over my house and only has a short time before he has to be somewhere. I GRAB HIS ARM, I AM CRYING AND HUGGING HIS UPPER BODY. He gives me a hug, but keeps me at a distance and tells me I am acting weird. I want to bury my head in his chest, like a scared kid hiding in their mom's skirt, not wanting to be seen.

This dream begins this way and has different surroundings, but this was the theme so times. Sometimes I see Bob's face in a crowd in many dreams, and the similar feeling in the dream surfaces, I want to grab onto him and hold on, but I am speechless and in tears.

A Later Dream

I see Bob on my old deck in La Selva Beach. I have this strong discipline not to cry. Bob hates when I see him and cry. My voice, as I hear it, is muffled and weak, but it doesn't cry. "Bob, you are not here. You are dead. Nobody told you?" I ask. His eyes are blue as always, but they are not looking at me, they are sort of crescent moon shaped, and he seems robotic. I tell him over and over that he is dead. He has no response, he just stares ahead, and I start crying. I put my head on his shoulder and hold him, as I look at his expression, which is like a neutral mannequin.

A Kid Dream

Bob and I are kids playing in our backyard in San Rafael, where we grew up. We are showing each other snails in our pails. He is on his bike and I am on my tricycle following him. He goes on a street with thorny bushes, and he is gone. I can't find him. I wake up saying "Bobby, where are you? Bobby where are you?"

A Breakthrough

I see Bob walking around by himself. He seems to be at an open-air market of some kind. There are a lot of clothes and items for sale around. I take a deep breath and tell him that something bad happened, that he took my Mom and Charlie away on a plane and that it crashed into the ocean and that he was dead, in fact they are all dead. I tell him that we are looking into what happened, but that Ashley and Axel are okay and that it is all okay. He tells me he is not dead. I tell him that if it didn't happen, it will happen. I feel somehow relieved that I can get the words out. I think we hug in this dream.

Seeing my Mom

There is a dirt road I am driving on. I see an old gray haired man running toward me with open arms. I think he is a poet I knew from San Francisco. I see my mom. She looks very young and cheerful. She is wearing denim over-alls and a scarf of some sort. She is touching my hair, rubbing my shoulders. She is standing with two men. Neither one is Charlie. She introduces me as her daughter. She tells them I am beautiful, I feel self-conscious; I tell her she is the one who looks so great. She is hovering right next to me, I feel so happy to be near her. One of the men has longish gray hair and is making jokes. He then takes a huge jug of apple juice and pours it into his mouth. The whole bottle is upside down, he is taking it all in. My mom is clapping and egging him on to finish.

We are still outside but my mom disappears and there are rows and rows of lawn chairs. The night is dark; there are a lot of stars in the sky. Blue figures are spinning in space; they seem to resemble TV's, or some high tech kind of appliance. I started to scream, I do not know why. They were spinning; these devices, and they had numbers on them. I seemed to be giving a talk at this outdoor place. I was sobbing and then giving some data about what time the flight took off, who was on the plane, etc. A lady with a split in her front teeth stood up in her chair, and said that she was a Doctor and was with a patient when she heard of the plane crash. One by one different people stood up and said where they were then they heard the bad news.

Rain, Horses, Healing, and Jessica

It's raining almost every day.

The answering machine is overwhelming, too many messages.

I drive Carina to school, come home, and make lists.

I sit by the fireplace and stare, inert, at the burning log. I watch the February showers. I have a counseling session with Jan in a few hours. I want help getting the screeching noises out of my imagination. I feel helpless. Where are their bodies? It is not real until I see proof.

I feel watched by everyone. I am barely holding on, but adrenaline and good work ethics save me. I must go to my list, box things up at Mom's, call her insurance company, and cancel her plans. On the weekend I will go to Bob's house, sort, pack, weep, and finally collapse against his wall.

Jessica is soothing to be around. She is my guitar teacher, now becoming a solid support. She leaves such kind messages. I like hearing, "You don't need to call me back." She is home with her son Eli, four years old. She invites me to walk with them, looking at flowers and plants.

Today she invites me to his horse-riding lesson. I almost decline, but something stops me. Jessica has received training as a counselor. She listens so well. I figure she'll help me name my strange and distraught feelings.

Something extraordinary happens out here, on this property in Santa Cruz on this February day.

Jessica is talking to Jody, Eli's riding teacher, the care-giver for the horses. I have the chance to be alone.

Eli and Jessica have Marfan Syndrome, a very rare connective tissue disorder. They have certain restrictions with physical exercise. I have never heard of Marfan Syndrome before meeting them. Jessica has explained to me that Abe Lincoln also had it.

Jessica is the wisest person I know. She is tall like Abe was. And honest. She checks out library books often. I think they may be related.

Anyway, Eli is doing well with his lesson. I watch him wave as he rides around the track on a big brown horse.

Jessica walks up to me and hands me a horse brush. With a quiet sense of knowing, she says softly "Canela is very old. She would probably love to be brushed". Then she walks away. This ancient cinnamon colored animal seems nervous when I first approach her in the stable.

Later on, however, she puts her face close to my hand and she moves in very closely. I begin brushing her mane. Her eyelashes are magnificent.

I lose track of time. I get so much into the act of brushing and tuning in that I forget who I am and what I am doing. All that I know is that I can't stop crying. Canela and I have a very intense stare down. I feel as if she knows everything that has happened, and somehow I connect to her life. I am still brushing her mane when Jessica and Jody walk up to me, asking if I have any history with horses. I can't think of anything out of the ordinary.

All of the sudden, I remember. My brother and I went to Horsemanship camp when we were kids. We were there with our old family friends, The Pepper Boys, David and Ben. Our parents had been friends forever. What stands out the most for me from that time is taking care of the horses and learning to ride.

My brother and I loved practical jokes. He read "Mad" magazines and loved a good laugh. He snuck in "Ex-lax"(a laxative in the form of chewing gum) into his duffel bag. He heard it worked well. He told me he wanted to give it to

94

Ben as a prank. I had forgotten about it until the last day of camp when we had a horse show for the parents. Over the loud speaker, everyone heard the announcer calling the name "Ben Pepper" over and over again.

Thinking back I suppose Bob felt a little guilty, as poor Ben was pooping his brains out, stranded on the toilet. He never made the show. Over the years, Bob and I would reminisce about this and fall over with laughter.

I get a little taste in my mouth of what is to come. Childhood memories are all there, locked within each of us. It has only been a few weeks since my only sibling was taken from me, ripped out of his own skin. I will not laugh with him again. The rain has not ceased; Canela walks slowly with her soft mane. Jessica rubs my back for a moment. She seems pleased that I have had a release. We go back to her house. She plays her guitar and sings so sweetly for me.

Jessica is a healer, a wise soul.

There is something so familiar about her.

Her soulful eyes don't blink as she asks me questions about the feelings of losing a sibling.

I am so sad my mother didn't get the chance to meet her, as we were new friends. She had become my guitar teacher, a free teacher for any educator in Santa Cruz who wanted to play music with children. My mother was so pleased that I was making the time to learn something I wanted to know so intimately. She couldn't believe Jessica was getting me to sing in front of others, even!

The last time I played guitar was for my mother on her birthday. Now, I don't know if I can pick it up again. I look at Jessica, gaining strength. We sit in her living room, saying nothing for a while. It is so comfortable. I never knew I could count on something so solid as a new friend who understands me.

I remain sandwiched between strong and wonderful friends. Those who laughed with me in high school and those who are just now looking in my compartments. There is softness with my suffering.

Rising from the fall

Santa Cruz woman preserves the memory of friends and family who died in the Alaska Airlines crash

By JANIS OST FORD

SITTING IN FRONT of the fireplace, watching the big raindrops hit the front window, and then gently fall, I hold the phone and catch myself not blinking for awhile as I am put on hold once again. I am either waiting for the car insurance lady or somebody who represents the company who is to locate their body parts, and make positive identifications. All of the hundreds of phone calls mesh into one now. Occasionally there is pretty music between the phone calls, or I will put some significant music myself as I go down the list of people I need to call. There is still that fresh smell of flowers in my house, but the petals have fallen off of many. My eyes dart to the over-flowing basket of sympathy cards. I think I have heard from everybody by now. Somebody comes back on the phone, I hear the CD changer make that sound of something ending and a new piece of music starting. I will occasionally look at my watch so that I am not late picking up my daughter from school. Some noises and subtle things make me aware of time and space, but mostly I catch myself rising and falling. "Yes, my name is Janis. I lost my mother in the Alaska Airlines crash last month. That is right, Jean Permison, she is now deceased. Even the customer service people don't know what to say, and I can hear them fumbling between saying what is in their hearts, and what they are probably accustomed to saying. I have never seen so many raw and honest feelings in my whole life. I have never been hugged more and held more,

> I can't think of them in pieces on the ocean floor, I think of the other "peace" because that is where my mind and heart feel the most comfort.

attendant from Alaska Airlines who volunteered years ago to be there with the families if a plane were to crash, never really thinking that she would be called to do this. I liked showing her family pictures and just talking to her about everything. I remember having to describe my mother's toenails and what kind of ears she had, and telling them about Bob's big knuckles. I remember feeling so proud of them as I gave my blood to be used for DNA. In a funny kind of way, I felt patriotic. Now I am back home in Santa Cruz. I have two houses to deal with. Thousands of photographs, memories, a huge network of support and candles, and ringing telephones. Some people tell me that they have contacted a family member or friend that they had not talked with for several years after this tragic plane crash. There have been miracles out of this ugly mess. There have been drops of water in my driest of days.

They have found four out of five of my family members. I miss my mother every second, and yet like all of the veterans of mourning say, "One can really feel their loved ones and so they are never really gone". It is true, and yet it is a lie. It is a rise and a fall, a lit candle and the darkness, a hunger and a full feeling, it is all of that.

Both services for my mom and Charlie, and for my brother, Ileana and baby Emily were incredible. Our family was honored to have a Native American Wiping Away the Tears Ceremony through the San Juan American Indian Council last week. We are grateful.

Mostly when I feel homesick, I think of

Continues first column next page

Continues 2nd column next page

Janis Ost Ford with her mother, Jean Permison.

and felt more alone and more loved in my life.

Occasionally I think about what it was like when I was flown with Greg and Carina to the crash site. I remember the bus rides, the family briefings, some executives crying from Alaska Airlines, walking the halls in the middle of the night, oh yes, the eyes of a beautiful African American chaplain telling me that I have lost so much. I remember having so many tears at that moment that I couldn't see, I just fell, and this chaplain just held me. It was like one of those Trust games you do at a summer camp when you are a kid, you fall backward and trust that your support behind you can hold you up. I was always good at that game, and I guess I still am. I remember my mother-in-law watching me so sweetly during a big buffet breakfast. I guess I was just staring at a plate a food. She lost her husband and her mother some years ago, she knows when the food won't go down. I think of Aunt Ruthie, how much I wanted her to be there, and after not seeing her for 13 years, they flew her in. I wanted to hear that New York accent and just be with someone who knew me as a baby, someone who loved my family and could remember stuff with me. I could feel her crying en route, and my wonderful cousins from New York and Chicago and Walnut Creek would be on their way. Jeanette, Lisa, and Tori and Joanie were there as well, and soon I had a whole wall of people I loved and could fall on. I remember finding Jeanette's room in the middle of the night, and just laying down with her and not being able

our dinner get-togethers, our laughing and the fact that we all loved each other so much. I had just given my mother a massage for her birthday and told her how beautiful she was. We took her out to dinner at Adolph's, and the staff there sang her "Happy Birthday" and gave her vanilla ice cream, her favorite. I told her when I was a little girl that she would never die, because I would never let her fall. My mind races to every child memory I ever had. It was always sweet between us. She was always there for me, and we could talk about everything. I tell everyone to have reconciliation between their families and to honor each member. Tell people when you have goofed, tell them in a good way when you have felt hurt. Do not bury the pain. My brother Bob and I were never closer than we were when he boarded that plane to take my mother on a special get-away for her birthday with Charlie. I cry when I look at our photos from Christmas Eve, but I heal from this cry. It is how I rise from the fall. There is one photograph of my mom feeding baby Emily. They are still together, they have to be. People want to know how my father is holding up. Nobody should out-live their children. He told me when he was here the other day that he wished he could believe in something the way I do. I can't think of them in pieces on the ocean floor, I think of the other "peace" because that is where my mind and heart feel the most comfort. They would want me to remember and cherish, but certainly not to stop living and loving. Every one of them chose life. God or Spirit did not do

Continues 2nd column previous page   *Continues next page*

Mourners erected a shrine to Flight 261's passengers and crew on the beach at Port Hueneme.

of that look of determination and fire in my mom's eyes, and I decided to keep being enrolled at San Jose State. Even when I am weary, if my daughter needs to visit her grandma's house in Scotts Valley and smell the spices, it is my duty as her mother to do that. When I look at my husband in his uniform, I shall always see my brother. I shall try to find the beauty in all things as my mother did, and never go to bed angry as she would say. When I see a big smiling man with the warmest blue eyes telling stories, I shall think of Charlie. When I see proud new mothers, I will think of Ileana, and I will smile when I see bilingual children because that is what Emily would be like.

So much has been taken from me, but so much has been given to me and will remain with me. I want to thank every person who has touched our lives during this incredibly difficult time. Thank you for your ears, your heart, your food, flowers, and prayers.

The Welcoming Of Lawyers

I opened every Hallmark card ever made. I heard from people as far back as high school, names I hadn't thought of in twenty years. There was a nice conviction of being cared about, that this plane crash so close to our backyard had profoundly affected a lot of people. Although the act of opening each and every card may have been monotonous, I was truly touched receiving each and every one. In my opinion, sending cards with any kind of sentiment is a wonderful thing. It didn't matter how many there were, I read each one and have re-visited each card several times over the years. By all means, send a card to someone who has lost a loved one. Do it sooner than later. I liked it the most when folks would write something other than their name on the card. In this day and age, getting a card and perhaps an e-mail or two were the best ways to know people wanted to reach out to me. I needed the phone to do so much business with, so perhaps my situation was not ordinary, but the phone was an appliance I was asked to hold while staying polite. I hated the ringing telephone. Looking back, the playing of Keith Greeninger's music and the fireplace constantly going were my comforters, they represented my dire need to retreat within the core of my quiet, sad, reflective soul.

I believe there are forty-five days of grace time where lawyers are not to approach any family after a plane crash.

One day in March I had just gotten back from work. Even though I was glad to be home, the different world of work kept surfacing in the front of my mind. I would think about my students, their testing results, their placements, their progress, new reading and writing techniques I could try on them. My wheels would spin for hours. It helped me to focus on things other than the crash and my new responsibilities. I enjoyed filling out forms and zeroing in on my students. I came home after a typical long day and systematically opened a dozen or so cards. I noticed quite a few large manila envelopes, looking very professional. I didn't recognize the name on the front. Out of sheer curiosity, I began to open these packets. More and more of these packets arrived in the following days. They all told me how sure they were that this was indeed a very difficult time, this is why they were here to help me. Some talked about their track records whipping the airline industry, others listed the amazing schools they went to, positive things other people said about them, etc.

It was very awkward and falsely flattering if that makes sense. It was as if someone with a history of never being noticed became gorgeous overnight, and was asked out by the whole town the next day.

Our recycling can was grossly over filled the next few weeks. To report that I had received 15 packages from different wrongful death attorneys would be accurate. It's not that I wasn't ready to begin a case; it was the way in which I was solicited which bugged me. I must admit that these firms and individual attorneys were only doing their jobs, and better getting a packet in the mail than a phone call. Still, I hated getting these packets; and yet can't think of any alternative way to find clients, or for families to find representation. Just one of those things you must go through after a plane crash, unless of course you do nothing.

My probate attorney was preparing legal documents on my behalf for my mother, brother, and niece's cases, and an attorney working with Nurenberg, Plevin, Heller, and McCarthy Co., L.PA called him. They have two offices, one in Cleveland and one in New York City. Apparently, a gentleman by the name of Jamie Lebovitz was hoping to fly out here from Cleveland, Ohio to meet us. He sounded persistent as all heck.

It was decided that he would meet Jamie Lebovitz for lunch, and they would come over to our house right afterwards.

I felt particularly fragile and irritable on this day. When I know somebody is trying to sell me something, I catch myself folding my arms and looking at my watch nervously. For one thing, I am a sucker and like to try new things, so I try to at least look intimidating, or like a hard sell. It seemed so different waiting for Jamie to visit our home. I was incredibly sensitive to his goods, rather I needed what he was selling, and it was so personal and confidential that I wanted to hide. I remembered looking at his packet a little bit early on, and was aware that he was representing a lot of Flight #261 families. I felt teary as I quickly tried to clean off the kitchen table and vacuum. There are so many damn pieces of paper after horrible things happen.

There was a knock on the front door. Jamie had a firm, yet very warm handshake. He looked at Greg and I directly in the eyes and began his visit by earnestly giving us his condolences. What struck me right away was the serious look on his face and the sincerity, which hung on his face and words. He wasn't overly friendly, yet he certainly wasn't impersonal. He let us know that he would do everything in his power to bring the faulty parties to justice, that we had enough on our hands. He showed us books made by his assistant, where victims of previous crashes were honored. It suddenly dawned on me that other planes had crashed; other family members were left behind, just like me. I took my time to study pictures and read stories. I tried to fight back tears. I was talking about my job at school, answering Jamie when I noticed him watching my face closely. I remember trying to convince myself that I wasn't going to cry until he was gone. I had gotten through his "interview" with us and thought my voice was rather clear. Jamie's look haunted me, it was one of those rare non-verbal interactions we have few times in our lives. I will never know if I looked intense enough to get a concerned look back, or if somebody with strong perceptions knew that I was holding back. At any rate, we all agreed that Jamie would represent us. Jamie took his cell phone out of his briefcase and explained that he would go outside to call his wife and kids at home, giving us a chance to discuss the beginning of our working relationship. I recall him commenting that he was sure we all agreed this was a good match, as he felt certain he'd end up representing us. I had never witnessed a more confident man in my life. It wasn't so much an ego talking as it was authentic experience, crystal clear confidence.

A few months later, Jamie's assistant Tamara flew out to meet us, another completely efficient hard worker. The water must be good in Cleveland, Ohio. Tamara is a bright woman, married to a policeman, mother of two young boys. I thought she was a lot more reserved and conservative when I first met her. It took a little while for her to let her hair down, but that's okay. I don't know how she does her job, and Lord knows she does it well. She travels all over, documenting the lives of those killed in plane crashes, and helping Jamie with various tasks preparing for trial.

I learned that it's the airlines and their insurance carrier's motive to minimize a person's life; it's the family's job to tell the world what these awesome passengers were really like.

Tamara asked leading questions, writing down everything like a thorough reporter. She asked what my brother was like growing up, how did he get on in high school, what kind of dad was he? Was my mother in good health, were we close? How did my family celebrate holidays, where was I when I heard about the crash?

I found my responses dull, my voice monotone. I do not know if this is how they were received, but as I gave the information asked of me, I had this huge perception of vagueness and answering questions with short responses. I know my body was in shock, and I had learned to de-sen-sitize a bit. Combine this with being tired and being bombarded with tasks of legal issues and making decisions on people's properties, this was perhaps why I didn't sound animated. I wanted to do my family justice, I wanted to gush over them, elaborate on the brilliances of my mom and Bob, and yet-the reality of them being dead was as surreal as the person in front of me asking probing questions. It was like a job interview I was aware I would not get as I continued to answer the questions. I know I didn't sound polished or bright. I rubbed my eyebrows, yawned, trying to remember the year my parents divorced. Any memory I had was with the four of us, and when a memory came to life, I wanted to stay with the images on the screen. This went on, until I heard my own voice, realizing I didn't answer how my brother's grades were in high school because the moment my ears heard the question, I was zap back in the late 70's of high school. I was recalling a day he gave me a ride to high school and I was thinking about the parking lot of high school and what my brother's dashboard looked like. I was in slow motion, and the world wanted me to be quicker, sharper. Just answer the facts ma'am. I didn't sound smart, and this bothered me. I wanted to tell Tamara she should have known me before all of this, as I was fairly quick and funny. I am not funny anymore. When your family dies suddenly, with no warning, a lot of humor goes out the window.

Alaskan Airlines invited me to give them receipts from my counseling sessions. I thought they wanted to see me successfully go through the stages of grief, I thought they wanted to see me healed. They accepted some of the cost, not all of it. They decided how many sessions it would take. They allowed 10, and then Dr. Relovich screamed at them on the phone, reminding them of how many losses I was dealing with. They maxed out my visits at 20. A magical number of 20, a box of Kleenex, and I should say "God Bless you, Alaskan Airlines, what a big fat heart you have, right?

My friend Dan, the one who was at my house when I

first got the news of the crash took me out on the deck to talk once. This came at a time when I was baffled at how attorneys and lawsuits work. "It's like this", he began, "A hand is worth more than a finger, a foot is worth more than a single toe, it's all math, and it's all carefully calculated." I hated math in school, and I still don't get how anything in the world can't be looked at in different ways. I looked closely at Dan's face as he was explaining this to me. Our neighbors was having their house remodeled; there were a lot of hammering and electric saws going. I noticed how much Dan talked with his hands. He has a huge appetite and a big, full belly. Since the crash, I need an anchor to look at when I am taking a lot of information in. I listened to every word he said, but was over stimulated with the saws going, the nails being hammered in, and his stomach sticking out so proudly. He wanted to see that all of this was a game that I was now in. He told me if I trusted my lawyer, I must sit back and be patient, allowing him do the dirty work. I must understand that it's all about how much money attorneys can make, and that these suits take a long time. Dan loved my mother and Charlie, seeing them often. He had birthday dinner with my mom and all of us right before they left for Mexico. "Would you fight these greedy corporations Dan?" I ask. More hammering is heard, the birds are chirping, I'm trying to really key into Dan's response in spite of the outside noises and my fascination with Dan's self indulgent body. "Of course", he chimes in. "You want your experience to make a difference. But once you hire someone, forget about it. They'll keep you informed, go about your life". It seemed easy enough in words, but not realistic.

I have forgiven anybody who has done me any wrong in my life, but not the airlines or the manufacturer of the part responsible for bringing the plane down. My anger is fused with disgust and shame for them. I must admit that I think about it all of the time. In high school I believed in the principles of karma, and in many ways I still do. I want to talk to the guilty parties head on. I don't know quite what

I'd say, but I want to look into their eyeballs. I want them to see the pain they have caused me, my father, our friends and relatives, and the other 85 families as well. It is early to speculate, but it seems as if the plane was brought down due to a lack of grease on the jackscrew. The chief mechanic, John Liotine, was on Dateline News speaking out about the pressures he had from his employer (Alaskan Airlines) to basically be quick and careless with the maintenance procedures on the aircrafts. There was a whole segment on how he was concerned and made a call to the FAA and was still pushed to go against his better judgment and sign off unsafe planes. His work order was subsequently crossed out. This is absolutely the sickest thing I had ever heard of. How criminal, to ignore an accident ready to happen.

At this time, mid-March 2000, I was welcomed into the world of lawyers. I was tired, and having nightmares of the plane doing corkscrew turns and then ripping through the ocean. I was in shock, but optimistic that the bad guys would go to jail, and Alaskan Airlines would go belly up. Maybe I still believed in the Easter bunny, too.

Making A U-Turn

One morning in May I awoke, startled, to the sound of the annoying beeping of my alarm clock. I quickly showered, realizing I had hit the snooze button several times and would be late to work if I didn't hustle. I tried to make a mental preview of the day, but as I lathered my hair with shampoo, an almost paralyzing feeling ran up and down my arms and lodged into my throat. It felt as if my mother and Charlie were so close, they were inside of me. If I allowed myself, I could have easily closed my eyes and landed back into sleep. I realized that I had been dreaming about them, and this connection had been cut short by having to get out of bed too quickly. I recalled taking a class in Dream Analysis once, and the advice given was to go back to bed and finish listening to the dream. (I didn't think my principal would like this idea very much.) I remembered that it was beneficial to be near water to help trigger the dream, even if that meant washing dishes. The key was to be still and quiet and to give time to the dream to re-play. I felt discouraged. This was one of the first strong dreams I had of my mother, and I wanted to respect her by paying attention. On the flip side, I was enjoying my work at school because it gave me a vacation from the responsibilities of carrying death on my shoulders. I needed to be at work, and I was *required* to be on time. I liked my job so much; I liked being one of the first teachers in the parking lot.

I figured if the dream was that important, I could dissect it on the drive. I hurried through my shower, made some coffee, grabbed my briefcase, kissed Carina goodbye and ran out the door. As I approached the on-ramp of the freeway, there was a mist in the air from being overcast. A soft rain came down. Entranced, I watched the windshield wipers glide robotically across the glass. I took a sip of coffee and felt my heart beating very quickly. As I approached a red light, I thought of the symbolic images in last night's dream. My mother and Charlie were aboard a bus. A terrible accident had occurred – the bus had hit a big rock or boulder and my mother had fallen out. Charlie was still riding in the bus, reading the paper. There were broken windows and people were stuck in their seatbelts. Charlie didn't seem to know that my mother was gone. They were planning a dinner party and had taken the bus to go grocery shopping.

Now the scene changed and Charlie was standing at the bus stop, apparently looking for my mom. It was raining and he had his newspaper over his head. He looked calm at first, but then he checked his watch and began frantically looking to his right and left. He appeared angry. I realized that poor Charlie had no idea my mom had fallen out of the bus and that she would not be meeting him. I knew I was the one who had to call and tell him.

By this point in my dream, I knew she was dead. I dreaded telling him. I started to call their number as I saw Charlie pick up the telephone in this rainy phone booth. He looked upset and angry, and I couldn't formulate my words correctly, which caused him to shout "WHAT?" I felt myself whimpering as I tried again to tell him about my mom. My voice came out sounding weak and garbled.

The light turned green, somebody behind me honked. It scared the heck out of me. I started to cry. I wiped my eyes. The driver behind me, unbeknownst to him or her, let me know I was not ready to be on the road. In fact, I wasn't ready to be out of bed. I never ever had an experience like this, where being in the world scared the crap out of me. It wasn't so much the startling sound of the inpatient horn that penetrated me, as it was the pain of the dream. The love between Charlie and my mother, the realistic job I had to do – to tell him that his companion was gone, vanished. I had to be the one to formally separate the pair.

I looked around at my surroundings. I was a mile or so from school. Students were walking in their school uniforms, people were filling up their gas tanks in this part business, part residential section of Watsonville, California on this May morning, and I was drenched with tears and fright. I am not a big crier. This morning tears flowed out of me like a siphoned hose. I felt embarrassed; I felt that I was separate from my body. My body was far ahead of the strong mind I pretended to operate. I looked at my watch. I had five minutes to get to school. My eyes were totally blurred. I passed my friend/teacher's aide house on the way to school everyday. I literally felt like an unsafe driver so I pulled in front of her house. I buried my head in my hand, hoping I could pull it together before she came outside. She usually walked to school because it was so close. Her garden was tidy yet colorful, like her. Isabel was born in Mexico and is absolutely awesome with our special students. She became suddenly widowed a few years ago. She understands sudden loss and I knew she would be a safe person. The interesting piece was that I thought I was doing fine. This dream came out of nowhere, like they usually do. It floored me; it spooked me, and this morning it took over. How could I teach, having innocent kids look at my red face? My eyes were stinging. I got out of the car and knocked on Isabel's door. I didn't know why, or what my plan was, I just did it. She opened the door, and quickly took my hand, pulling me inside to safety. She brushed my hair back as I tried to hide my face. Her softness, but strong facial features were omni present like my mother's constant concern, and it made me weak in the knees to come to terms with my vulnerability. Isabel held me, kissed my head. I felt sincerity, her Catholic presence, a connection, and a reassurance that I made a good decision, making a surprise visit. I couldn't talk, I just bawled. I tried to spit out that I had a bad dream. The words came out choppy and high-pitched. Isabel called the office and told them I wouldn't be in today. I got back into my car, and made a U-turn. I wasn't crying anymore. My face felt sullen and defeated. My dream tortured me enough. I decided I couldn't live without them as I continued home. I pulled into the parking lot of Oakwood Cemetery and just sat. I had a little make-up bag in my purse and thought I would freshen up a little. My eyes were slits, my face looked like a blotchy and tired soap opera actress.

My next move took me by surprise. I drove across the parking lot and went to a florist, buying a flowering plant. I then went straight to Dominican Hospital. The Pastor from Grace Methodist Church had just had her baby the day before. I felt a strong urge to visit her in the maternity ward. I wanted to drop the plant off and see if I could look at babies in the nursery. I didn't want to impose a visit on Rebecca or Hank, but I had this overwhelming need to be seeing a new life from afar. I was self conscious about the way I looked, but it took the back seat to my stubborn nature of listening to my instincts. I walked right into the maternity ward and recognized a former customer of mine when I waitressed at Hobee's Restaurant years back. She was a minister and used to come in all of the time and journal and drink tea. Her name was Barbara. She had an angelic look on her face as she played the harp in the waiting room. It was too lovely to interrupt her and re-introduce myself. Sometimes I think there is a beauty in remembering someone in a kind way without breaking the silence with meaningless introductions and words. Maybe when we spot people we know out in public, we should do a quick inventory of the situation and decide to say hello, or simply recall with a smile. Or maybe I am just shy. The receptionist asked me whom I was here to see. I told her about Rebecca being my Pastor but I didn't want to impose. I was quickly ushered into her room where as I felt like a pesky intruder.

I saw baby Kristen's head peeing out of a blanket. I dropped off the plant and tried to smile. I could still hear Barbara playing the most soothing music in the waiting room. It suddenly wasn't important that I congratulate Rebecca or ask her questions about her birth. She looked tired, as I looked a different kind of tired. I quickly dropped off my offering, smiled at baby Kristen, and left.

Hearing the music, delivering a plant and catching a glimpse of a newborn was the most poetically sound and just antidote to the drive I made to work this morning. The drive that ended in a U-turn. The more I tried to find meaning, the clearer the symbolism of life and death interchanging at U-turns seemed to be.

Going Back To Work

One day during the timeless month of February I was released from work, I visited the school I was teaching at. My co-teachers handled me beautifully; they just greeted me with open arms. It felt as if I had been gone a long time. The custodian waved to me, as I pulled into the parking lot. Many kids on the playground ran up to me. I felt a little over exposed, missing the safety net of my living room cocoon; but at the same time enjoying the thought of being needed and missed. The kids asked me over and over again when I was returning. The first of March was my broken record response. Many of the kids told me they had seen me on the news, and they felt badly about the crash. I didn't know how to respond. Once a student would see me, I recognized teacher friends trying to make eye contact, and I felt conflicted. I felt on a very primal level that it was awkward for everyone, and I vowed to answer all questions, greeting everyone who might say hello or offer condolences to me. I felt watched , as if I were an experiment. The whole experience I lived through and continued to partake daily in felt surreal. I tried to keep my head up. I thought of the eulogies I gave at the services, and just being on my school campus required the same discipline and a not turning back kind of attitude. These people cared about me, and the kids were affected.

I had to stay focused and be present, this was all I really knew. Stephanie, a lovely third grader with Downs Syndrome took my hand and kissed it. Her job was to take the roll to the office each day. We held hands. She only said two and three word sentences, it felt very comforting to swing hands and walk across the playground together. When we reached the office, I told her she could walk back alone as I knocked on my Principal's door. Mary, my principal, gave me a big hug and quickly ushered me in. She told me that a sub had been helping out in the Resource Room, and I could take all of the time I needed. I told her I still felt as if I only needed a month, and wanted to come back soon. I left feeling eager to return to routine and hard work. The warmth and compassion felt so good that it actually filled me, I felt that I could be productive. I missed having a sharp mind. Walking past the classrooms and hearing singing and kids reading aloud and laughing reminded me that there was control and order in a school setting. I didn't want to stand out and be felt sorry for. The busy routine and endless tasks of the school suddenly delighted me, I wanted to be a part of it. A sense of shyness circled around my head , but I felt very alert and capable, wanting to return. The mood in my actual classroom was different in contrast. My co-teachers seemed to sense that behind my smile and intent to return to normalcy, I was hurting and not sleeping much. They saw through the make-up. As determined as they hopefully viewed me, I sensed they had a hunch of how low I had been crouching in my attic. This is what makes special education teachers a commodity- at our very best, we can see the whole picture.

The Kindergarten class had made me Valentine hearts with special messages. Meade, a local writer and advocate for special education, was placed to help out in our busy program. He ran IEP's, and helped teach our larger groups of students. I could not have returned to a more peaceful and accepting environment.

I left feeling very lucky. Driving home, I thought of words to say as I would try to come up with the best translation from English into Spanish. Again, I just wanted my old mind back. It was like being drunk while convincing myself that I had nothing to drink. It bothered me to realize how grief had taken me hostage. The stress or the almost month away of hearing constant Spanish was taking a toll. I couldn't think of how to say "They died in a plane crash." I knew "Ellos se murieron," I knew "avion" for plane, but it stopped there. I found contentment with "Tengo mucho dolor en mi corozon." I have pain in my heart. I wanted it to come out fluidly. I wanted to practice Spanish and forget I knew English because my emotions were so overwhelming I didn't want to accurately name what I was feeling. It seemed like a nice escape to go back to work. At the end of the month, my regular paycheck went automatically through my bank. I hadn't really even thought about it, but found myself pleasantly shocked that I missed a month of teaching and somehow got payed. I meant to thank someone for this, but didn't. For all the bad luck I felt I had tapped into, acts of kindness and compassion were hand delivered to my heart daily.

My first day back on the job was a movie in slow motion. I was answering questions all day long, the children's faces close to mine, bells ringing as new groups of kids came and went. Questions ranging from how come my father didn't go on the trip, to the multi-repeated ones of who the loved ones were in my family. One girl in fourth grade named Aimee asked me if my family actually died in the airplane or in the ocean. It truly was a fabulous question. Night after night I would unconsciously torture myself with images of how I thought the crash transpired, but Aimee's question put everything into perspective. There was so much innocence in that question, and yet such a direct scientific yearning of needing to know what happened first. I offered , "They were probably very banged up while in the plane because everything would have fallen all over the place, but they would have died when the plane hit the water at such a fast speed."

My job is set up by taking small groups of students at a time. The last hour of the day I do paperwork and test children. I found great comfort in being physically close with my students, reading with them, sitting closely with them as we would decipher worksheets and maps together. I felt super sensitive to their voices, their smells, and their needs. It was almost sad for me when the bell would ring and they would gather their belongings and head back to their homeroom classrooms or to recess. I wanted to establish an immediate momentum with them. It felt like it was the last week before school was out, I wanted to be sure they were at peak performance and retaining everything. One student named Robert left his map in his homeroom classroom, and I took his carelessness personally and seriously. I wanted him to be prepared, careful, and ready for battle as it were. I felt an intensity to help prepare Robert for the big real world. Did this new spin on my life make me a better or worse teacher? I have no idea, really, but I felt authentic as I never had before. I took my job more seriously than ever.

I had my lunch in the staff room. I felt incredibly aware of everything going on around me. The crunching of Mr. Smead's carrots were churning and splitting in my eardrums. The beeping of the microwave was magnified, the compassion in teacher's voices discussing concerns of different students made me feel a part of something important. Towards the end of the afternoon, after I taught my last group, I put on classical music and began working on student's goal pages and reports. I read everything quickly and thoroughly, and the whole picture, the core of each student, seemed to present an immediate and dire need for attention.

Everything was so serious and time was of the essence. Holding a ballpoint pen and creating a healthy balance between mainstream classes and special attention in designated areas for my students became the only area of my concentration. I came to love paperwork. I could lose my whole being inside of it. My handwriting seemed to improve, my thinking felt very clear. I promised teachers on campus that I would make observations of targeted students whom may need some extra help, and my drive to school was spent thinking about these students and how I could arrive five minutes earlier each day. I told jokes and brainteasers to students I didn't know during morning recess and helped tie shoes, mediate fights between anxious second graders. I would bring containers of fruit and offer it to students who arrived too late for cafeteria breakfast. I took student's pictures and hung them all over the classroom and brought a fountain into our class to create a calm feeling. I felt an absence of grief when I was at work. I thought that darkness and death couldn't find me if I was busy doing good things and being an effective teacher. Mary, my Principal would watch me encourage a group of kids to throw away papers on the ground before school and wipe down the slide with paper towels. I gave the kids gold slips, which were then saved and pizzas were raffled off to the winner. She would smile and wave at me and I was on top of the world. I loved my job and more than that, I felt close to God or to a higher power that a new renewal in life was manifesting inside of me.

There was only one problem, the weekends would come. My mother's house needed to be packed up. I had to deal with the current situation of coming to grips of my mother's remains not being found. I had to look after my brother's house in San Bruno and begin the task of boxing his possessions and furniture. When faced with the lack of control and the bleakness of these tasks, I missed learning new words in Spanish and being a special friend to my kids at school. I needed the closeness to the Lord I experienced when I listened to them read aloud. I wanted Monday to come around so that I could feel useful and productive. I continued my classes at San Jose State and saw a direct correlation between my being a good student and a stable position at my elementary site. I wanted to do well so that I could serve, hence, I got lost in my work

One of my extracurricular responsibilities at my job was to be part of the Sunshine Committee. Typically this entailed giving birthday cards to teachers and staff members, recognize deaths in the families, retirements, planning end of the year parties, making sure that plants/gifts or farewell small gifts were in place when teachers moved on. I found that I got to know the whole staff rather quickly when I took on part of this job. I volunteered to collect money from each staff member and be the bookkeeper. The more people thanked me and appreciated flowers we would send off as a staff, the harder I worked and wanted to please.

Once in awhile a person I didn't know very well would throw me off guard and tell me how terrible they felt for my loss. I tried to put this out of my head when I was at school. Through time, I wasn't at all the center of attention, nor did I feel watched. I was able to blend in, and Monday through Friday I was able to heal myself through my service of giving to children. It was a nice deal. It literally saved me, I believe.

Carousel Of Pain

I run all over to get away from myself, and I always come
    back to the center, to the middle, to my core.
Keep my mind busy, please give me work.
I will do anything but enter my mother and brother's
    houses; they are not there anymore. They will never
    come home.
I have their keys in my purse. I have their blood in my
    body.
I feel them, but can't see them.
I will never hear their voices or hold the small of their
    backs again.
I close my eyes and hear our dinner parties. Laughter, the
    most comfortable laughter I have ever heard.
It is silent now.
I walk like a widow. I can't smile. I have so many deci-
    sions to make.
Realtors and bankers hold Kleenex for me.
I cry at the bank. I cry when I sign Janis Ost Ford,
    Administrator of the Estate.
I sign this everywhere.
This came out of the blue.
Who really has their life in order?
Who imagines they will be tied to a seatbelt as they spin
    out of control thousands of feet above the sea?
Who anticipates a one-way trip with a round trip ticket?

My mind and body are so tired.

I want a baby.

I want anything new and life affirming.

I think I will never make love again, dance again.

I go to sweats, I am under the ground, sweating and calling on Great Spirit to hold my family in the stars.

I meet Leonard Crowdog. We do a ceremony. He looks at me with these deep-set old sad eyes, he tells me they went straight to the stars. Chief Sonne says they are smiling down on me.

Still I sit alone, holding my insides.

I am a little girl, I want to hold a blanket with something living and breathing inside of it.

There is nothing rooting me, I am air rising, my sadness fills a room like smoke.

I buy a hot tub on my birthday because Mom isn't here anymore. Nobody holds me the way she did.She loved the warm water on her thighs, as I do. She knew I needed to stay warm as I looked for her outside. Nothing makes sense in the day. It is loud and bustling. But the nights are long and revealing. She will come closer to me at night, as the moon does.

I sit out alone, night after night.

I want her to show her face.

My tears form and fall,they say it is cleansing.

All I know is it comes out effortlessly.

They call me to come back into the house.

I have been in this warm water too long

I need my ghost family and my own family needs me.

I am either in a trance or I am swallowed by my work.

My father comes for a visit, I try not to cry in front of him, it usually doesn't work.

He can't bear to see their pictures all over the house.How do we erase our past? Everything is triggered. Everything is raw.

We are both so wounded, we collide into one another.

He is blind and I am mute.

I do dishes because it is a quiet task. It is easier than sitting

and feeling.
Sitting and feeling make me feel as if I am waiting.
And they do not come home.
Their footsteps have stopped.
Their souls are in the water, softly and dramatically being
    pulled by the moon, in and out, around and around.
It is such a sad carousel.

Funeral Homes and Fertility

I recall sitting very nervously in the waiting room at Oakwood Funeral Home and Cemetery. The man in charge was most respectful, and like most local people, had read the paper and knew about the crash. He showed us catalogues with different family markers. I was sighing a lot and feeling very antsy. It was hard to "land" and talk about burial business. I was asked to write out my family member's names and birth dates on a special form, one letter per each box. The gentleman, John, explained that it was important to get the ball rolling and have this company begin the tile work. He left the room several times so that Greg and I could discuss matters. My fingers took a long time to complete the forms. It was so terminal, so damn difficult to admit their departure from the world. What was the difference how big the letters were and if their ages or birth dates would be listed? I looked at Greg looking out of the window. It was raining. It was very peaceful in this still room, with caskets and respect for the dead or eternal sleepers, but I couldn't complete my task. Something was very wrong. My insides were still churning, I was still burping an acidic taste. I was losing weight, I didn't feel right. I wanted to explain my inertia to Greg, but the words couldn't come. It was close to my birthday and I was feeling very nostalgic.

"Greg," I began slowly..." I think we should have a baby." The room, already quiet, went incredibly silent.

There was such a sense of finality sitting in a funeral home. It was confusing without their bodies. The only control I felt I had was petitioning to go off of the pill. Although I experienced occasional maternal pangs over the years, this moment pushed the idea to the front of my head, and it overtook me. An immediate surge of a deep longing to bare a child took hostage of my body.

I finished the form and grabbed Greg's hand. I put my left wedding finger next to his ring and squeezed his hand tightly. "Let's just do it" I said. My impulse to create new life was the swing which rocked my grief. The mere possibility of making this emptiness go away anchored and propelled me. My mind was at peace when I imaged rocking an infant in a warm blanket.

I recalled my last ten or so conversations with my brother. They always ended with him asking me to consider having another baby. His acceptance of my life with Greg, and his new happier energy was contagious.

I looked at the sky for a long time that night. There was not a doubt in my mind that we would attempt to bring a child into this troubled world It was a glimmer of hope. I suddenly felt that I could go on, that everything really was going to be okay. I actually began to see stars in the dark nights instead of tail lights from jets.

A New Baby

My special time to think and reflect is on my way to work and on my drive home. I play music in my classroom and as soon as I buckle myself in the car, I am looking for the best songs on various radio stations. The silence is hard. I stare at the clouds and I am afraid of getting lost in them without the distraction of singing. There are so many airplanes going by. They haunt me, but I stare at them just the same.

I turned thirty seven years old. My mother had me at the same age. I brought up the idea of a baby to Greg, but I am afraid he thinks this is stemming from shock, and that perhaps I am not really wanting the ramifications of following through. I was the one who wanted a kitty when we adopted our cat Jiff. I adored him as a kitten, and after a few months, the thrill wore off a little and I wasn't terribly excited with how nonchalant cats can be. Greg grew up with cats, and certainly understood them more than I did. Needless to say, Greg really is the one who has taken care of Jiff these past eight years. But a baby is different, I feel ready...

I think of my father aging rapidly, especially with this recent loss in his life, and the open sky terrifies me when I consider his mortality. My last conversations with brother Bob play back in my pounding head.

"Have a baby, oh, go ahead, just have a baby." It still

haunts me now. I want to challenge God, the God who may have been responsible for looking away when these innocent victims took their last breath. No, I don't really believe this, but I want to be a fertile reminder to my higher power that I will carry on. I will not be broken. Like dear Pilar says, "I am shattered but still whole." I have a surge of anger and vitality. I am feeling so young and orphaned, yet old and sick of being messed with. I think of Carina as a little girl and I want to touch her warm red cheeks again. I try to conjure up the memory of being pregnant. I think of my poor father and how he talks to all of the new mothers at the mall everyday where he gets his coffee. How does he cope to see little baby girls now? Does he say anything to them? What if I were to hand him a little Grandchild in a year or so? What if I were to hand myself a baby to love? Would this bring joy to Greg, to Carina and Ben? I think of the milestones, the car seats and high chairs and diaper bags, and I seem to return to an image of a sleeping baby who looks a little like my mom, a little like Bob, a little like Emily. What would they say about this idea, this vision? I have always been spontaneous, but this desire to create from the ashes of death and destruction is now overtaking me. I will not renew my birth control pills. I have heard a woman is not very fertile after being on the pill for as many years as I have been taking them, but it's ok – I can wait. I am usually too exhausted from work and nightly tears to make love anyway.

I miss everyone so much. Just the thought of my mother's sweet face and voice and Bob's practical jokes makes me cry. I weep for the loss of them, I cry for the unfairness of their lives cut short. The clearer my mind seems to be, the possibility of having a baby appears to be the most clever decision I have ever made.

I will slowly wipe my tears away, and ask the universe to grant me only wish in this life- to be given a healthy baby.

Keith Greeninger

One of my first and strongest memories of my mother stems from when she took me to see a live performance of the play "Hair" in the early 1970's. I wasn't mature enough to be embarrassed by the nude scene, but wasn't quite sure what I thought or felt. I was rather in an in between stage of development where I looked at my mother as an anchor to see how to react to people taking their clothes off during the final scene. My mother was in tears. I watched her closely. Driving home in her Volkswagen, she told me that music and words moved her very deeply. Years later, I not only got "what she was saying," this very phenomenon also trickled into my bloodstream.

One day in 1999. I was driving home from my Kindergarten job in Boulder Creek as I heard an amazing song on the radio about a Native American woman by the name of Jenny. The images were giving me goose bumps, and I didn't know why. I just liked what I heard. I could see and hear and feel and smell Jenny. The song talked about her "grave yard cough" and her "beating the steering wheel like a drum." I pulled into my garage and stayed in the car in case the radio station disc jockey announced whose song this was. After a good fifteen minutes or so, the name Keith Greeninger came over the sound waves. I wrote it down. Money was tight as always, and I barely bought any new music, but this song stopped me and provoked me in a very profound way. A few days later, I heard another song by him on KPIG this same local station, only this time they mentioned Keith was doing a concert right in my town at my favorite club, the Kuumbwa. I went out and bought his CD, obsessing over it. He lived locally I found out, and my guitar teacher and close friend Jessica told me he was doing carpentry work for her. Jessica's husband makes guitars and they were friends with Keith. We were laughing about how good artists make guitar-playing sound so easy. I was struggling with chords and playing simple songs, but even more moving to me than Keith's guitar style was his ability to touch my soul with his lyrics and strong voice. I took my friend Jeanette to see him live in concert and then became even a bigger fan. It was sweet to see his wife and children attending his concerts as well. During intermission his son, about four years old was telling the crowd in the patio that he was Keith's boy.

I played Keith's music over and over again. My friend Sara Poyadue was very sick at the time, and the title song on the CD "Wind River Crossing" gave me chills. It helped me make peace with the fact that Sara would not be here for too much longer. It talked about "Underneath the turquoise sky, a raven smiles to find, that everything is dying, everything in time."

I listened to this CD when I cooked, cleaned, made lesson plans, stared at the sky, ate lunch in my classroom, etc. There was something haunting about it, I knew this music intimately, and it knew me.

When I returned home from the crash site, Karolee took my hand and walked me into my living room. She asked me what I thought I needed. There was nobody I wanted to talk to. There was nothing I wanted to do. I was still cold to the bone. I sat by the fireplace and put on Keith's Wind River Crossing CD. Karolee and I sat next to each other and wept silently. Greg opened the mail and took care of business.

It was time to plan memorial services for my mother and brother. A couple friends were over helping me to create some ideas for the services. The Fire Department was really helping with my brother's, but my Mom's was staring me in the face. The phone rang and Greg answered it. "It's for you, it's Keith Greeninger." I felt a little nervous. He could have told me it was Neil Young and I would have had the same reaction.

A very nice man was on the line. He told me he was a good friend of Jessica Turner, who he knew was also a good friend of mine. She thought he might be able to sing at the up-coming service. He regretted to tell me that he was doing a show out of town; but that I had his condolences and he would stay in touch. It was perhaps the nicest gesture a stranger ever bestowed upon me. It touched me on so many levels. Somebody with that much talent would call someone they didn't know and tell them they wished they were able to sing at their mother's memorial service. It touched me that Jessica cared enough to even attempt connecting me with someone I held with so much regard. The older I was getting, I could see that I was moving away from energy dominated by male/female unconscious intention. I was motivated by Keith's friendliness and humanity on a level so much more mature and lasting than in younger days of crushes and projection. I hope I am conveying this accurately. I appreciate the difference.

One night during dinner a policeman came to the door. He had a letter in his hand that stated some of my mother's remains were found. I was struck with mixed emotions. I had this fantasy my mother had turned into a mermaid or a dolphin; I was disappointed that she apparently was still a mortal. I was equally relieved that I would have a piece of her, some fraction of evidence of her beautiful and innocent body.

The remains of the victims of flight # 261 were cremated and placed in burial urns. Alaskan Airlines had a policy of having one of their employees deliver the urns, or they would send it through UPS. I was uncomfortable with both options. UPS was way too impersonal. Having an employee of Alaskan Airlines deliver it to my door seemed like a forced and potentially confrontational relationship in some way. I asked special permission to have Karolee Samac, my family care friend, bring the ashes to me.

It was a warm late morning in May. Karolee drove up in a rental car. We looked at one another for a moment and teared up. We embraced, her six-foot frame and my five-foot frame. We said nothing for a minute or two. I walked her outside to her car, and she carefully placed a brown box in my arms. The mere thought of my mother's energy being stifled in this plain, silent box bothered me. I didn't know what to do with the box or where to put it.

Karolee, as always, was respectful and ever present.

We sat outside on the deck for a while as the sun grew warmer. We made plans to get outside and spend a few hours together before she needed to get back to the airport.

Jessica called earlier offering to spend some time with me. She had been a constant in my life, always seeming to know what to do and how close to get. The experience we shared in the horse stable with Canela was spectacular and eerie at the same time. I have learned to trust the timing of people like Jessica in my life. Jessica and her four-year-old son Eli came over. I introduced the two tallest friends I had to one another, and went into a shy and delicate mode. I wanted to open the box of ashes, but I didn't. I wanted to talk to Karolee about her life and the airlines and how she was managing, but I didn't want to start anything. I wanted to talk to Jessica about our guitar class and basically catch up, but I felt shut down. I wanted to play with Eli as I easily and regularly do with other young kids, but I felt stuck. I was grateful to have two women over who genuinely cared about me, and yet the heightened awareness of my suffering caused me to feel that I was taking too much room in the apartment of compassion. I wanted to get away from it, in the way I could escape at work. I would have been perfectly happy running some bath water and sneaking off into the tub. Karolee told Jessica how much she enjoyed the Keith's Wind River Crossing CD I had sent her, and like me, she wanted to turn all of her friends on to this special music.

Jessica called Keith and arranged that we all meet at his parents' house. We talked a little bit in the car, Karolee and I. Jessica was following behind us in her car. We were going to meet Susan, Keith's wife, planning to buy some of Keith's CD's from her. Karolee didn't want to talk much about herself but she spoke of her girls so enthusiastically. I gathered that Karolee's marriage wasn't a bed of roses. I wanted to be a good listener, as she had been for me, but I could tell her relationship was a private and delicate subject. We walked into the fitness center where Keith's wife, Susan gave massages. She was warm, genuine, and very beautiful in an earthy and natural way. She gave me a big hug, and thanked me for being a big fan of her husband. I was so relieved there was no weirdness or misconstrued jealousy or mistrust. Susan is petite and actually holds you when she hugs you. I felt right away that this was a woman with whom I wished to be a friend.

We said goodbye and headed out to Keith's parent's house, where Keith was expecting us. He had just returned from a gig in Oregon. His parents have a nice atrium style house overlooking the golf course. Jessica got out of her car and hugged Keith, who was holding his little girl of four months. The silhouette or shadow of Keith and his little baby caused me to stop in my tracks. Keith, whom I had only seen from several feet away at concerts, was now right in front of me. He was the same stature as my brother; medium height, strong, rugged looking. He was holding his four-month-old daughter, and all I could do was fight back the tears. I wanted it to be Bob and Emily. I wanted to meet a musician I admired so much when I was happy go-lucky as usual. Whatever was slowly walloping up inside of me was now moved and pushing outward. The artist in him would make it hard to pretend to be anything but the broken woman I was. I was scared to death as I got out of the car. I grabbed my insides and stuck close to Jessica.

Jessica and I had held a family Seder together the month before with her family and mine. I felt such a familiar bond with her. I trusted that this meeting was supposed to take place, but I felt incredibly raw and exposed.

Keith says hello with these warm blue eyes and gives me a hug. I immediately feel emotional and start to feel myself crying. I can not say the typical "Nice to meet you" or "I am enjoying your music". No words come; I look down at the ground. I feel like a little child who has spilled or broken something sacred and yet I am forgiven. Keith does something quite profound. He hands me his daughter Tenaya and walks into the house. Jessica smiles and follows him. Karolee is out of sight.

Holding Tenaya is holding Emily. I feel I am saying goodbye. Tenaya is so much lighter than Emily, but something is the same. I feel love for her, and know that it is okay to just hold on tight and let myself grieve. Tenaya is sound asleep so she is fine with me holding her as I am. Time allows us a pleasant meeting with nobody around. In this moment, I sense a rippling, pounding, aching in my heart, which tells me, I need to be a mother again. Keith returns and tells me that it is an African legend that holding someone else's baby and having the will to create life makes women lucky and fertile.

Soon I meet Keith's mom and dad, and like Keith, they allow me to take my time and rescue me from the necessity for small talk and formalities. I don't remember if I told Keith I was contemplating having a second child, or if he just intuits. It doesn't really matter. The honesty, the compassion, and the blessings of the day are my salvation.

A short time later, we all drive to the beach. Keith brings his guitar. As the day grows later, Keith looks out into the ocean and proceeds to play some original folk and Neil Young songs. I look out as far as I can, and try to make peace with my brother being gone.

As profound as it was to receive my mother's ashes today, what I feel more than anything is a reminder that Keith knows my soul somehow, and it is my time to weep and remember, and let go. Karolee asks him to play a few of her favorites, but I am in a trance. The Neil Young songs transform me at all his concerts I saw with my brother. Now I drift back in time and watch my brother and I as we grow up together. I am almost hallucinating, as if I am watching a movie about my loss and myself. The end of the movie is Bob dancing across the sky and each chord Keith plays on the guitar is like a kind, old friend putting blankets on me and telling me I can be a little girl and rest. The music assures me that everything is going to be okay. For a few uncounted minutes, I believe that no worry or nightmares burden my spirit. There are no phone calls or decisions to make. I am rocked on the water, I feel God or Spirit in a way I never have before.

The sky grows dark as we all say goodbye. Keith tells me he will put me on the guest list at his upcoming show.

Karolee and I pick up some Chinese food to go and head back to my house. I walk past the urn, not sure when or how I will open it up. Karolee has to catch a plane in the next hour, so she wolfs down some noodles as we attempt to absorb the entirety of this spiritual meeting which has just taken place.

No music has ever touched my life in the way that Keith Greeninger's musical healing has. When I decided to write a book, in the sincerest hope of befriending others in grief, I knew that a sample of Keith would need to be inside of every book. One of the nicest things he did for me was simply play his guitar and sing, and not ask me to talk. He played while I bawled or processed or simply was given the strength to walk down that lonely corridor of acceptance alone. If I have learned anything, it is that death is a process and we come to terms with it at different times in various ways.

Keith told me that he remembered my mother going to one of his concerts. It was a small mountain bar in Ben Lomond, right outside of Santa Cruz. He was impressed with her feistiness and love for the music. She played clarinet professionally, and just about went out of her mind when Dayan, a member of Keith's band *Water* began to play clarinet. People offered her their seat, as it was a tiny place, and she declined, dancing and clapping her hands. God, I miss her and our shared love for music with meaning. I thank the stars above for Keith, and the incredible opportunity I have to become his friend and thank him. I pride myself on the dozens and dozens of people I have introduced to his music. I have given him some of my brother's clothes, and we have become closer friends with the passing of time.

KEITH GREENINGER

PORTRAITS BY SHMUEL THALER

STORIES BY WALLACE BAINE

Keith Greeninger spent many a day as a kid on the beaches near Rio del Mar noodling around with a guitar. That may explain why his music feels so free and spacious.

The singer/songwriter is known for his rich, naturalistic sound — folk melodies of relaxed, slow-flow beauty.

Keith was part of the once-popular folk trio City Folk with fellow singers Kimball Hurd and Roger Feuer. He's also played extensively with the group Water, led by guitarist Dayan Kai.

But he's most known for his solo work, best exemplified in his 1997 album "Wind River Crossing" and his most recent work, a collaboration with Water called "Back to You," both showcasing his rich, textured singing voice.

Though he's a Santa Cruz homeboy, Keith has lived in Vermont, Colorado, Alaska and Central America. He helped established a folk festival in British Columbia that combined the talents of famous North American acts with Native musicians and dancers.

Those themes of wanderlust are central ingredients to his music, which is laced with metaphorical and literal references to nature.

Now he lives in the Happy Valley area of Santa Cruz with his wife Susan and two kids, working on material for a new album.

"You really can't hide who you are in your music," he said. "You can mask it, but in the end, it's discovered."

Dear Janis:

Thank you for the very nice letter you sent dated June 17. I wanted to let you know that the Embassy Suites hotel in SSF dedicated their fire control room to Bob. He had done the inspections on the facility; the manager of the hotel said they wanted to dedicate the facility to Bob because he was so nice and helpful to them.

Enclosed are some pictures from the ceremony on June 26. As you can see they have erected a sign outside the hotel and the door to the facility is marked "The Bob Ost Fire Command Center."

I admire your strength; I think about Bob a lot and miss him very much. He is a very special person.

You & your family are in my prayers.

Take care

Jackie Kious
S.S.F. Fire Department

Janis & Mom 1999

Mother's Day 2000

The sun is shining through my bedroom window. I hear my mother saying, "Good morning sunshine!"

I know today is Mother's Day. My therapist told me to take good care of myself today. I didn't really have any plans, only to be with Carina. She wanted to get off out town for the day. Once again, I did not know what I needed. All that I needed was gone, dead, silent, intangible. I have spent so many evenings in the hot tub, staring at the stars and at the different shapes and phases of the moon. Greg is going to Sacramento with his mother and two sisters. I feel like a downer, I do not want to be around people. I think of all of the places I would take my mother to today. I think of last year, sitting at my kitchen table with pregnant Ileana and her mother and sister. I think of every Mother's day I can remember. Homemade dinners, brunches, restaurants, plays, picnics, the years fade in and out but the characters stay the same. They were always special and sacred, and now they will never be the same. I want my kids to have fun memories of Mother's day, so there will always be an element of having to remember "Show Time". That is, no matter what, the camera is rolling, and the show must go on no matter how ready or prepared I feel. Even when I am starving for nurturance, I must feed. In the act of giving, I will feel my mother softly nodding at me and encouraging me that I am strong enough to stand on my wobbly legs without her.

Carina is eager to leave. Greg is feeling awkward about leaving me on a day he knows will prove to be very hurtful. I feel worse when people are expecting me to be weak and they are right. I want to hide. Carina and I head out Southbound on the freeway. We drive to Carmel for a nice breakfast. We bought bathing suits for the hot tub and just messed around all day, eating and driving and silently experiencing the loss of our key player, the amazing Grandmother/Mother.

I try not to stare at all of the mothers and daughters out and about. Seeing happy gray haired women with lots of energy and wearing tennis shoes causes me to swallow hard and keep my head down. It is still unbelievable that my mother with all of her passion and vitality has become an urn of ashes. I feel abandoned,cold, and alone. I think of the song "Somewhere Over The Rainbow" and I weep with shaking emotion. Wherever she is, she knows I can barely stand it without the continuation of our incredible bond. I want to see her one last time, I want one last kiss goodbye. I know she is free, but it doesn't come close to easing the pain.

June 2000

I took a pregnancy test at home.
This was my first smile since the crash.
I have landed. I am pregnant.
It happened, it's here, it is a blessing.
I asked for it in my prayers, in my sweats, in front of so
    many candles.
I am a few weeks pregnant. There is a baby inside of me.
    A seed of hope.
New prospects fill my head.
I struck a little gold after months of suffocating anger,
    disbelief and shock.
It happened so fast, it almost seems unbelievable.
I dare you God, let me believe in you again.
I call my father as I hold the plastic applicator.
Greg is beaming, Carina is laughing, and even my father
    sounds lighter.
This baby will not be Emily.
This baby comes from all of them; he or she comes from
    the wreckage of the plane.
This baby came from everyone's tears.
I almost detect happiness in my own eyes.
I stare into the mirror.
No, you can't tell yet, a baby sleeps silently and secretly
    from within my walls.
I will hold this baby up all over town.

Nobody will feel sad and sorry for me again.
I am redefining my fate.
Please let him be like my mother, please let her be like my
    brother.
Will all five blow a whisper of hope onto this brand new
    flicker of light?

December 2000

I can feel my little boy kicking and swimming around.

I am so excited he is a boy. I will call him Cody Robert.

I just had a baby shower; there is so much love for this little unborn child.

Nancy, my doctor, gives me his sonogram picture at every visit; she knows I need this reassurance, he is healthy and fine. Just not ready to come out yet. I hate waiting. I rub my swollen belly, counting the weeks and looking at pictures of everyone.

It is too painful and raw to imagine my mother not exposing him to cooking, Bob not being able to have water fights with him, Ileana not teaching him Spanish, Charlie not showing him how to be mechanical, baby Emily not playing with him.

I imagine instead, they are all inside of me, guiding me with love. They wash away my tears with the promise of their coming. Did Cody begin where they ended?

Time unravels, but barely makes noticeable steps. I weigh more, my stomach is ballooned out, but this life and death stuff echoes to me like a lost seagull. I don't know what it is saying, really. I know I have to keep on loving and giving thanks, as orphaned as I feel.

Christmas and Hanukkah

Christmas and Hanukkah have just passed, thank God. Wrapping paper and empty boxes have made it into the trash bag, and it's quickly approaching the New Year. My belly is still huge and swollen and his heartbeat and occasional hiccups can still be counted on to bring me a smile. It reminds me of Mona Lisa, or perhaps a rhinoceros smile, in that it is nothing it used to be, it is not full or childlike these days, but it is a start, and I can still feel a little excited. My 34 and a half-week fetus is my flickering candle, my search light on the big dark ocean, my hope, and my whisper in the fog.

My dear friends know what this holiday season would feel like. Their hugs have encompassed me, they hold on a little longer. My relationship to my Mother was no secret to anyone. We were publicly and privately very entwined; the same sized women, with many of the same quirks. We could talk about virtually everything together, and we laughed and cried at the same stuff. The kind of friends who say the same thing at the same time and rarely take notice to it.

This morning I awoke early, with a dream still hanging on my sleeve. It is a typical dream. It is the landscape and the set stage for the place where my Mother would sit. This morning I was ordering salads and a bagel for us in a downtown café. I sat down with some packages, I guess we were shopping, and my Mother was using the restroom. I divided the food, and was looking over my shoulder to catch her coming out of the restroom. I recall now how many times in my younger days that I enjoyed scaring her. I liked jumping out of places and surprising her. She laughed and screamed when I was seven and when I was twenty-seven. Either my own consciousness or the long wait in this café caused me to wake up. The same reality bites me in the cheek everyday now, my mother will never again eat a salad with me, or allow me to jump out of nowhere and say "Boo" again.

My daughter Carina dreamed that a plane crashed on our small court the other day.

I received a call recently that a small portion of my Mother was identified through my DNA, these are the kinds of adult stuff that ruins my dreams and my flowing memories of childhood. It is the most sobering and awful feeling to have, these interruptions of the crash.

What do I do? How do I cope? I wear my Mother's clothes, I try to keep in touch with all of the people who loved her to keep the memories alive, I ask myself what my Mother would do in certain situations, I decided to have a baby two months after this tragic plane crash. I can honestly feel my five beloved family members encouraging me on, like sages above me, reminding me to look at the pretty pinks and purples in the sky when I lay in my bed wondering why these happy lives had to be ended so quickly after returning from an innocent vacation. Remembering my last conversations with my brother, as he would pester me to have another baby after so many years because he was so thrilled with his four month old Emily.

The tears do not surface every single day as they used to, but the broken glass in the throat, the incredible void, the anger towards the airlines and the careless makers of the plane all stir in my blood, same blood which also feeds my unborn child.

I am somehow standing between two worlds, hurting and healing, holding on and letting go, pushing out and pulling in.

Family member clings to memories, sees hope in the birth of a new life

Bill Lovejoy/Sentinel

Janis Ost Ford shows a memorial plaque to her brother, a firefighter who died in the Jan. 31, 2000, crash of Alaska Airlines Flight 261.

By DAN WHITE
SENTINEL STAFF WRITER   SANTA CRUZ

D eath and life are neighbors in Janis Ost Ford's dreams. They are neighbors in her waking hours too.

As she drives along Soquel Avenue, she can't help but see that Dominican Hospital, where she gave birth to a son last week, is next to Oakwood Cemetery.

That's where her mother, brother, sister-in-law and baby niece were buried after the crash of Alaska Airlines Flight 261.

The graveyard holds only the remains the salvagers could recover. They continue to find more.

A year ago Wednesday, Flight 261 dropped into the sea about 40 miles northwest of Los Angeles, killing all 88 people aboard.

Life and death intersect in Ford's stories. One afternoon, fresh from watching her then-unborn son's heartbeat on a hospital monitor, she came home to a letter asking if she wanted her mother's socks. They were badly damaged, the letter said, but did she want them?

Crash: A year of lost time in aftermath Flight 261 tragedy

'A loss of time'

On a recent afternoon, Ost, 37, rested in her Santa Cruz home and spoke about the past year. She was wearing her late brother's South San Francisco Fire Department shirt, which is much too big for her. The bilingual special-education teacher at Watsonville's H.A. Hyde School began her maternity leave earlier this month.

One hand held a cup of orange juice. The other rested on the bulge in her belly. Ford kept a neutral expression whether the subject was birth or death.

The birth of her son is one of the few things that has cut through the week-to-week reminders of the crash.

Once the salvage people in Houston sent a big package to her via UPS. From the outside, it looked like some sort of gift. But inside the envelope was a binder, weighing 15 pounds, with photos of the unclaimed goods from the plane.

Luggage. Purses. Jewelry. Underwear.

Ford has done everything she can to keep her forward momentum. She's filed a wrongful death suit against Alaska Airlines. So have 46 others.

Federal investigations, and the lawsuits, have focused on airplane-maintenance problems and the failure of a 2½-foot-long jackscrew, which helps control up-and-down movement in the tail of the twin-engine MD-83.

Ford's lawyer, Jamie Lebovitz, said he's seeking compensatory and punitive damages "well into the millions" for 17 families including the Fords. The Ford case was filed last summer at the Federal District Court in San Francisco.

Lebovitz said the negligence is indisputable.

"The cockpit voice recording reveals the flight crew was struggling to maintain control of the airplane, and had they heeded the warning signs ... apparent to them well over an hour

before the plane crashed, there is reason to believe the airplane could have been brought down safely."

The lawsuit gives Ford some feeling of recourse.

And, of course, she has her son, born 6 pounds, 8 ounces.

But none of these things, even the child, can erase what Ford describes as a "loss of time."

"Sometimes you go outside and look at the stars, and you wonder where people go," Ford said. "You hear them all laughing." Ford flew to Ventura County this weekend to meet with survivors near the crash site. She expects 800 relatives and friends of victims. She's taking her young son with her.

The baby is supposed to be the antithesis of the crash. But in some ways he's linked to it. Ford wouldn't have had a second child if the crash hadn't happened. Her late brother urged her to have another baby.

"He kept saying, 'Go for it,'" she said. "We needed some joy. There's going to be a lot of love for this baby."

The baby was born last Sunday. Janis Ost Ford named him Cody, because that's what her brother would have named his daughter, Emily, if she'd been a boy. His middle name is Robert.

Pieces of memory

The crash happened at the tail end of a life celebration.

Ford's mom was turning 73. She and the others were returning from a trip to Puerto Vallarta.

Janis Ost Ford knows they were carrying cameras. She wishes the film survived the crash. It would have been nice to see what they ate "and how much fun they had."

The plane was flying from Mexico to San Francisco International Airport. It only made it to about Anacapa

Island. It fell off the radar screen at 4:21 p.m.

Other pilots saw it happen.

Aviation experts say this is one of those accidents when the victims had plenty of time to be afraid before the plane hit the water.

The crash is "not an unusual case," said Ford's lawyer, Lebovitz. "Except in the sense that there was an extended period of time when the passengers and the crew of Flight 261 underwent some extreme forces.

"G forces, aerodynamic forces, as this aircraft was out of control and ultimately flying upside down. ... I tell you there is no question, no question, these people were physically injured before (the plane hit the water.) One pilot reported that the plane was cartwheeling."

Lebovitz offers detail after detail of how he thinks Alaska Airlines could have prevented the crash. But wondering about malfunctioning parts doesn't comfort Ford, who remembers the moment a family friend called and "sounded very strange on the phone.

"She said, 'I don't want to worry you, but when is your mom and Charlie coming back? Have you turned on the news? A plane crashed returning from Mexico.'"

Frantic calls to the airline. Last-minute travel arrangements to Southern California, by plane.

Ford's memories come in jagged pieces: feeling removed from mind and body; needing medication to sleep; the plane flight to L.A.; the airline employee who sat up all night with her.

Welcome Cody

Kim, my sweet angel friend for more than 20 years flew out for Cody's birth. She is also a neo-natal nurse.

Phil Caylor gave me a wonderful acupuncture session with the hopes of opening me up. I didn't want another C-section. I wanted this baby out, and desperately needed to be with the other Flight # 261 families on the anniversary. These were my two priorities.

Carina also attended the birth. With Keith Greeninger's music on in the background, I pushed like hell, and at 5:13 pm on January 21, Cody took his first breath.

Jeanette, Laynee Bluebird and Janis
January 2001

Welcome little Cody,
Your mother and father dreamt of your arrival for a long
    lifetime.
Your mother and father needed laughter in this very quiet
    house.
Welcome little Cody,
You are tiny and powerful.
So helpless but wise
So full of stardust, mercury, and molecules of a bright star I
    can't see.
You came to heal and remind broken backs that there will
    be dancing again.
You came to whisper into tired ears that new words would
    sound delightful.
You came from beautiful ancestry
You are such a part of them

But you are Cody Robert
Your own person
You are slowly opening your eyes
I could stare at your unopened spaces and newness for
years without moving.
I am in awe of your perfect-ness.
May your stay be long, sweet Cody
My only son
My galloping seahorse
Racing slowly in swirls of greens and blues and purple hues
Speaking without talking
Breaking all rules of gravity and science
You take my breath away
You give me the will to love again
To accept the death so close to me without taking me
You were sent or thrown down from heaven's prettiest
mountaintop
And my promise is to love you forever and keep you safe
and warm
And if I love you too much you will forgive me because
you know your mother can't help herself when her
young gypsy soul is wide open.
When her heart is pierced with fiery love for her angel
child.

Cody & Janis

Cody

January 21, 2001

I just read an absolutely wonderful grief book called "The Anguish Of Loss" by Julie Fritsch.

There were only a dozen or so pages in it. It was so profound, and shall I just say the author filled me the way I needed to be filled. The book was short prose/poetry corresponding with exquisite pictures of clay pieces the artist / writer made after the loss of her infant son. Julie's clay sculptures were bent over, pleading and bleeding, so common to those of us who grieve regularly. I looked up her phone number in the local directory here in Santa Cruz as I learned she also lives here. I knew myself better, I wouldn't call, but knowing she was somewhere in my community made me feel less alone.

Thank God people share their personal stories publicly or we wouldn't know that others cry in the night.

I recall a few times during my pregnancy with Cody that I would imagine something bad happening to him in utero or during birth. During this tumultuous nine-month time, I talked myself down a lot. That is at least how I described it to my therapist. When my head goes crazy with thoughts, I sort of try to explain things to myself, kind of like a coach telling their client they only have two more miles to run or twenty more pounds to lift. I did so much praying that Cody would emerge before the 1st anniversary. I tried to visualize holding his new body to my chest, as we would travel to the crash site together.

My husband, my teenager, my step-son, my father, and my friends were all my pillars and my anchors, but nothing snapped me out of my spaced out time warp like the birth of Cody. I thank my lucky stars that he came out with a healthy beating heart, a yearning for recognition to be his own person.

Nursing

Sometimes I think I like nothing better than simply holding Cody in my arms. Nursing him, touching his soft golden hair. I don't need anything at the store, there is nobody I want to call in these moments. I listen to folk music and look out of the window. There is a soft rain trickling down. The sound of the heater is quite comforting. All is calm, as I watch Cody nurse and touch his left ear with his curious, dimpled hand. There is nothing comparable to nursing a baby. I feel very sad for mothers who tried and couldn't nurse effectively, or for those who chose a bottle for whatever reason. I am not one who typically feels pretty, but I am the closest to feeling pretty when I nurse. Why? Because I am doing what I am supposed to do. There is no ego, no commercialism, no heating or cooling involved. The milk mother nature supplies to me is warm and right. I space out and stare, and occasionally I glance at Cody who shares my expression. It's as if we are in another world, another time. We might be seeing things not visible or hearing the colors of the sunshine streaming through a window. Maybe we are quietly contemplating the maker of the rain. We are two pretzels embracing, two beings completely in love, needing one another and saying nothing. The mother giving, the baby taking, a timeless bond, instincts never learned but simply known forever, frozen in time.

Families to unite on crash anniversary

San Mateo resident Arthur ...st lost his son, ...laughter-in-law, ...ndaughter and -wife on Alaska ...ines Flight 261, which crashed ...n. 31, 2000, off coast near Los Angeles.

JOHN GREEN — Staff

By Josh Richman
STAFF WRITER

Five-year-old Calvin Gemmell still talks about his grandmother's husband, the kind, guitar-playing man named Dean who used to spend about two days a week with him while his parents were at work.

Sometimes he and his grandmother, Susan da Silva of Benicia, listen to tapes Dean Forshee made of his conversations with Calvin. Those tapes, and the good memories, are all that remain.

Calvin, his parents and his grandmother will be among hundreds of friends and relatives who will gather in Southern California on Wednesday, one year

■ Crash investigation continues as lawsuits pile up
NEWS-6

after Alaska Airlines Flight 261 plunged into the Pacific off the Ventura County coast with 88 people aboard.

Some will go to share their grief and remembrances with the only other people who truly know their pain. Some will go not for the communal experience, but on an individual pilgrimage to honor those they loved.

Others won't go at all. For some the memories are still too painful, or it's a part of their life they've chosen to leave behind. Some question Alaska Airlines' motives in paying the families'

Please see **Crash,** NEWS-5

Crash: Oakland probe started before crash

Continued from NEWS-1

way.

Since the plane crashed on its way from Puerto Vallarta, Mexico to San Francisco International Airport last Jan. 31, most of the public focus has been on the crash's legal and regulatory aftermath.

A federal grand jury investigation of the airline's Oakland maintenance facility began well before the crash and still continues; the National Transportation Safety Board held a three-day public hearing last month to gather information for a report coming sometime this year; and a batch of civil lawsuits are pending against the airline.

But Wednesday, relatives say, will be a day to refocus upon the human toll. Several memorials are planned in Ventura County; it's possible that a flotilla of private boats will ferry families out to the crash site near Anacapa Island.

da Silva and Forshee, 47, had been married five years; he

was a professional musician who gave guitar lessons and played in several bands.

"We've had other memorials for Dean, but my grandson, who is five, didn't get to participate in all the previous activities," da Silva said. "We're taking him to Southern California because I think it's a good opportunity to help get closure for him."

da Silva has another reason to go: she has gotten to know the families of several other people who had been on the plane, "especially the family of the man who was sitting next to my husband."

"It's clear to me that the guy sitting next to him, whose name was Bob Hovey, seems like a wonderful guy. My husband was a very outgoing guy, and I'm sure they must've talked. They went through this terrible thing together, so I want to be with Bob's family on the anniversary."

Hovey, 50, of Emeryville, was the Bay Area manager for ice cream purveyor Gelati Celesti.

His brother, Chuck Hovey of Murphys, Calif., said going to the memorial will cap a very difficult year for his family.

"My wife and I, my whole family, had decided not to go down, but at the last minute we decided to go," he said. "We're just wanting to be with other families ... it's a time to be there and support each other."

He's not sure about taking a boat out to the crash site, however: "We're just going to play it by ear. It's pretty gut-wrenching and I'm not sure how much I want to get back into it."

Phil Salyer of Sebastopol lost his wife Ellen, 51. He hasn't come to know the other victims' families, he said, but he feels a primal need to be near the crash site on this anniversary.

"She's buried in Sebastopol ... I go visit her grave on a regular basis," he said. "I guess I'm going just to be there, to experience it, just to honor her and remember what happened to her."

First Anniversary

Cody is tiny.

My heart is full.

I am so thirsty and tired, but glad to be on my way to Southern California. I look at Lisa sitting next to me, on the plane, God I am so lucky to have her in my life.

Greg is so protective of Cody, only 9 days old.

We arrive in Los Angeles. I am used to people making room for me with my big ol' stomach. It is different now, people get so near, they want to see Cody up close. I am so proud of him, yet there is no barrier between my baby and the world. I wish there were a gate I could occasionally close.

A van picks us up at the airport. It is a cold and long ride to the hotel. I nurse Cody somehow as he sits in his car seat. I feel like the strange lady at the circus who can get her body into the most pretzel-like form. I am a sleep-deprived contortionist. I am filled to the brim with a milk supply, and it hurts unless he is nursing every few hours. It is a quiet ride to the hotel. I think of Lisa's daughter Jessica. I feel somewhat guilty about taking her mother away, again, one year later. In a rational moment, I know that Lisa is a great Godmother, she is here because she wants to support us. Mostly Lisa is next to me because she loves to help. I still feel badly. Jessica was teary and worried. Would I feel different, as a 6th grader, knowing the odds were in my favor of not having another plane crash, but still terrified

Families gather to mourn victims of ill-fated flight

By PAUL CHAVEZ
THE ASSOCIATED PRESS

LOS ANGELES — A year has passed since Alaska Airlines Flight 261 suddenly spiraled out of control and smashed into the Pacific Ocean, but pain and anger remain for families of the 88 people aboard who were killed.

The victims of the Jan. 31 disaster in the waters off Point Mugu will be remembered in memorial events Tuesday and Wednesday that are expected to draw nearly 800 relatives and friends.

Fourteen members of the Ost family will travel from across the country to attend services paid for by Seattle-based Alaska Airlines and to view wreckage of the plane stored at the Navy base at Port Hueneme, northwest of Los Angles.

They'll remember Robert Ost, his wife, Ileana, and their 4-month-old daughter, Emily, who died in the crash along with Ost's mother, Jean Permison, and her companion, Charles Russell. The five were returning from Puerto Vallarta, Mexico, to celebrate Permison's 73rd birthday when the crash occurred.

"The first month was really difficult," said Fred Ost, 48, of Skokie, Ill., who is a cousin of Robert Ost. "Trying to work at my job was difficult, I was getting choked up frequently. ... It took time and slowly I'm getting over it and life goes on."

Robert Ost, a 15-year veteran of the South San Francisco Fire Department, and his family will be remembered privately by his 81-year-old father, Arthur Ost, of San Mateo, who won't attend the memorial events.

"I will not go and be a pawn of Alaska Airlines," Arthur Ost said. "I know they're doing it purely for public relations."

Arthur Ost said he'll talk by phone to his daughter, Janis, who will attend the ceremonies, and grieve in private when the anniversary arrives.

"I'll just think about it and mourn the death of my son and hope that someday we'll punish Alaska Airlines or their insurance companies," he said "My own personal wish is that the CEO of Alaska Airlines, John Kelly, would personally pay for it by going to prison. It was under his watch that these vile things were done to save money by putting up these airplanes. That's my wish."

The twin-engine MD-83 was bound for San Francisco and Seattle when it fell out of the sky eight miles off Ventura County, near Anacapa Island.

A ranger on the island and pilots of other planes saw the jet go down. Boats set out from the mainland and their crews searched in rough seas as darkness fell, but there were no survivors. Eventually, wreckage would be pulled up from the ocean floor.

The anniversary comes as the National Transportation Safety Board continues its investigation. The agency held fact-findings hearings in December and is expected to release a final report with a probable cause for the accident in the next few months, NTSB spokesman Terry Williams said.

The crash has spawned many lawsuits family members against Alaska Airlines; plane manufacturer McDonnell Douglas and its new owner, Boeing Co.; and companies that played a role in manufacturing and maintaining the jet's jackscrew, a key part of the MD-83's horizontal stabilizer that is suspected of causing the crash.

A federal grand jury in San Francisco also has been investigating the airline's maintenance operations at its Oakland facility since 1998.

The grand jury and NTSB investigators have been examining maintenance records of the downed aircraft's jackscrew mechanism, which controls the angle of the horizontal stabilizer on the aircraft's tail. The jackscrew's threads were found to be stripped.

The NTSB also is reviewing the types of grease used on the jackscrew assembly to determine if two lubricants are incompatible if mixed and whether the grease used on the aircraft cause corrosion.

Alaska officials have denied any wrongdoing and maintain that repeated tests showed the wear was insufficient to require replacement of the jackscrew assembly.

The crash occurred after the pilots reported an apparent jam in the mechanism, which lifts or lowers the plane's nose in flight. Pilot Ted Thompson and co-pilot William Tansky wrestled with the problem for more than 30 minutes before the aircraft suddenly plunged, upside-down, from 17,900 feet.

---

that I might not see my mom again? I am so sleepy and certainly don't want to guilt myself that Lisa chose to be a true friend and leave her family for a few days. I guilt myself anyway, I am good at it. Does the airlines have any idea how many families they unintentionally but actually screwed up, the direct effect of the plane crash?

We pull up in front of the hotel. Soon we unload our suitcases and all of Cody's baby paraphernalia. There are a lot of families embracing that long, sad way, and it becomes very apparent that there will be a lot of emotion in the next few days. I see the Red Cross people, I feel drawn to them. There is compassion on their faces, I want to thank them. I have a fantasy of having one of them put Cody and I on their lap so we can just weep and nap. That is all that I want to do, a sweet surrender. My adrenaline and hormones are kicking in; I guess I forgot what hard work having a baby truly is. I have not slowed down in this surreal year.

There are booths set up in the hotel lobby, boat tours, hanger tours where families can view the actual wreckage of the plane. To my right there are lines to pick up the newly made memorial books with 88 bios, one page on each passenger. I want to get to my room and lie down. The incision the Doctor made when Cody emerged is hurting, my feet ache and there is such a collective, sobering sensation painted with sadness in the air. I lay down, falling asleep immediately with Cody. I smell his newborn smell, breathing it in as if it were an undiscovered drug. I lose track of time for a while. I see my Aunt Ruthie and my cousin Fred. I clutch onto their clothes and pull them in close. Hugging them is a direct connection to Mom and Bob. I don't want to let go. I like the hug that is tight and safe and allows you to hide. I don't like ending the hug, as you have to look at faces and tell the truth. I know I should be so absolutely engrossed with the miracle of Cody's birth, but being here in L.A. brings the truth and reality of this visit back. I feel my face twitching as I try to hold back the tears.

Either the first night or the second night we are all in a huge room decorated with lights. There are candles on the tables, and a museum like room to visit with memorabilia on each airplane victim. There is a lot of crying, a lot of hugging. Ileana's beautiful sisters and her mom are there. They look just like her at this time.

The press is around. The sky is dark and lonesome looking.

I am eating breakfast, Cody is in a serape. I see a widowed mom, a Flight 261 family member, and her little boy who looks like a kindergartner. I want to talk to her, but the oatmeal is not going down very well and I am anxious to get out of this lobby cafeteria. The waitresses are all so nice to me, I consider reminding them as to why I traveled here with my infant. Maybe it's better to say nothing, as it keeps everything simple. I remain silent, leaving the hotel restaurant.

On the eve of day before the first anniversary there was the most breathtaking musical remembrance for the victims. I believe it was the Philharmonic Orchestra playing, while each victim's face was super-imposed on a large screen with the background of clouds. It was in alphabetical order, so we'd know when our family member's turn came. This tore everyone up. We all left speechless, it was so powerful.

Woman wipes tears while sitting on bow of a boat that ferried family and friends of air crash victims to site of the crash off Point Mugu.

Marking 88 Lives One Year Later

■ **Flight 261:** Victims are remembered in tributes at spot where Alaska Airlines plane went down last Jan. 31 off Point Mugu, and at a cemetery in Westlake Village.

By STEVE CHAWKINS
TIMES STAFF WRITER

Twelve months after Alaska Airlines Flight 261 plunged into the sea off Point Mugu, victims' friends and family members paid tribute Tuesday, ferrying to the spot where the plane went down and attending a burial service at a Westlake Village cemetery.

For many relatives, these events have been the most public expression yet of the grief that penetrated their lives a year ago today. More than 850 people have come to Ventura County for the two-day observance, which was organized by a group of family members and paid for by the airline.

"We've had so many tributes, private memorials, and amazing moments with friends," said Paige Stockley, a Seattle cellist whose parents, Margaret and Tom Stockley, died in the crash. "But this is something so huge, and most of the families want to be here. I can't explain it—it's like homing pigeons."

Eighty-three passengers and five crew members died in the crash last Jan. 31. There were no survivors.

Last summer, Stockley, whose father was a wine columnist for the Seattle Times, helped kick off the planning for this week's observances. At the dock where her parents moored their houseboat, Stockley and relatives of about 50 other crash victims sketched out plans not just for these ceremonies but also for a permanent memorial that will one day be situated near the Port Hueneme pier.

On Tuesday, Stockley and several other families toured the par-

158

The next evening we all had a buffet dinner together, which ended with a speech from the coordinator of this anniversary memorial. It was so nice to have Karolee there, the family care contact person, yet we both kept our conversations simple. When I first saw Karolee, I felt a bit nervous, uneasy. Her energy is nice and clean, I very much like being around her, but I feel slightly conscious of both of us not really able to be close. It is almost as if she and I are different colored people, heavily involved, and our parents are prejudiced. It feels as if we have to hide our relationship, as innocent and mutually supportive as it is. Karolee mentioned to me sometime later that the family care team was intended to be short-term care, and she was asked to refrain from having a relationship with me. Again, I experience that bizarre feeling of getting the role in a freak show. Due

CARLOS CHAVEZ / Los Angeles Times

Relatives and friends of Flight 261 victims watch as 88 birds are released—one for each person lost—at Westlake Village cemetery.

STEVE OSMAN / Los Angeles Times

Harbor Patrol station in Port Hueneme served as gathering point Tuesday for family and friends of Flight 261 crash victims.

tially reconstructed wreckage of Flight 261 in a hangar at Point Mugu. "It was pretty shocking," she said. "The airplane was in a million pieces. A lot of Kleenex were going around."

Stockley said a National Transportation Safety Board investigator told family members at the hangar that the agency was committed to

pinpointing the cause of the jetliner's abrupt 18,000-foot plunge on its trip from Puerto Vallarta to San Francisco and then to Seattle.

A lawsuit against the airline and the plane's manufacturer on behalf of 55 families incorporates claims of negligence. The first hearings related to the suit are set for March.

Please see ALASKA, B5

to horrific circumstances, I stand out in a crowd, people will either go out of their way to protect me, defend me, and will always know what is best for me.. Ay-yi yi. I suppose the impending lawsuits, and any confidentiality from Alaskan Airlines to Karolee's ears could be tricky. We will forever be aware of the heaviness in our hearts, so we remain quiet. I suppose our eyes and hearts have their own conversation, in which there is huge depth and connection.

An active family member stood up after a dinner and reminded us to remember what brought us here; it was a very poignant silence.

The actual memorial was on the beach, as close to the crash site as we could get. Cody was fast asleep on Greg's chest. I felt tremendous love for Greg. I felt sorry in the sense that he was caught up in all of this. Do I hear more guilt coming from my direction?

The day finally came, January 31, 2001. I dreaded this day, and yet when the sun came up, nothing major happened, I was still there, I lived through the first year! It was time to get ready to board the busses to the site. People in this area were incredibly respectful, they stopped traffic so that the caravan of busses could make their way and keep together. Police on motorcycles led us, it reminded me of Bob's service, so patriotic to the fallen.

There were hundreds of chairs all set up in this pavilion. There were dozens of bouquets of flowers. After music and

MEL MELCON / Los Angeles Times
Buses carrying family and friends of air crash victims leave Valley Oaks Cemetery in Westlake Village after a private service Tuesday.

ALASKA: Victims of Crash Remembered

Continued from B1

In boats piloted by local volunteers, about 60 family members embarked from Oxnard's Channel Islands Harbor on Tuesday morning for a somber cruise to the crash site about eight miles offshore, near Anacapa Island.

Some clutched teddy bears that had been given to them by Red Cross volunteers and Ventura County emergency personnel.

"At first they looked puzzled," Ventura County Fire Department spokeswoman Sandi Wells said. "But I told them it was just something to hold onto, and they understood."

At sea, the boats slowly circled the crash site, where a wreath of roses bobbed in the waves. Some mourners hugged and some prayed alone. Others dangled their legs over the sides of their boats and turned their faces toward the sun before tossing carnations onto the water.

Some of the relatives flew from as far as the Philippines for the observances. A pregnant woman recently had her labor induced so she could attend with her newborn baby.

Earlene Shaw of Olympia, Wash., had been in Ventura County for two weeks, taking long, contemplative walks on the beach. Twelve months ago her husband, Donald, was returning on Flight 261 from Puerto Vallarta, where he was looking at a condominium the couple planned to buy for their retirement.

Glimpsing the crash site makes it "feel like you can get a little bit closer," said Shaw, holding back tears. She was joined for the ceremonies by 21 of her relatives.

In the afternoon, California Highway Patrol officers escorted busloads of mourners to a private service at Pierce Bros. Valley Oaks Cemetery in Westlake Village.

Remains still unidentified— three victims are unaccounted for—were interred there beneath a stone inscribed: "To the spirits of the 88 lost. We celebrate their lives and remember them with love."

Terry Sparks of Seattle, who lost his 20-year-old son, Ryan, wept.

"There's some of all of us in there," he said before the service.

Five clergymen, representing Christianity, Judaism and Hinduism, spoke at the memorial.

After 16-year-old Karla Gilbert, a niece of one of the victims, sang "Amazing Grace," 88 white homing pigeons were released—one for each person lost.

The mourners' day was to end with a dinner and performances by the Southern California Mormon Tabernacle Choir and operatic performer Kimball Wheeler, who sang a piece from Gustav Mahler's "Songs on the Deaths of Children."

"Being a mother myself, it's always a bittersweet experience to sing these songs," she said.

Today, a memorial stone will be dedicated and a private service held on the naval base at Point Mugu, where the initial efforts to search for survivors and retrieve wreckage were coordinated.

In addition, photographs and everyday mementos of the crash victims will be available for public viewing.

The "Circle of Love" display at Oxnard's Performing Arts Center incorporates everyday items that were meaningful to the victims: a guitar, sewing machine, a snowboard ornamented with stickers. A homemade cross that drew mourners at Hueneme Beach for days after the crash stands in a corner

160

A cross, above, on Oxnard's Silver Strand Beach serves as a memorial for Alaska Airlines Flight 261 crash victims. Left, one of the boats carrying family and friends of crash victims moves toward the site of the crash, which occurred a year ago today.

Roses bob over spot where 88 people died in Alaska Airlines crash.

Earlene Shaw of Olympia, Wash., was among mourners who visited crash site near Anacapa Island. She lost her husband, Donald, in tragedy.

A boy holds a teddy bear distributed by Red Cross volunteers and county emergency personnel for family and friends of Flight 261 victims.

with a cowboy hat tied to it.

The display is open from 2:30 to 5:30 p.m. today.

Times staff writers Tina Dirmann,

Tim Hughes, Matt Surman and Margaret Talev along with correspondent Jenifer Ragland contributed to this story.

some inspirational messages, a grief specialist spoke.

The most piercing moment for me was when they read each name at 4:22 while each family member let a butterfly free. There were 88 butterflies to signify each victim. The one I set free for my mom hung on for a moment and then flew in a gorgeous angle. The one released for Ileana landed on Cody and stayed for a moment. I felt her. I felt everybody on that plane. Ileana's mom was praying in Spanish and weeping for her baby, it was on one of those moments to sting, yet cherish forever. No words can do this event justice. I walked Cody to the water. The ocean was very peaceful. Many family members took their shoes off, putting their feet in, basically taking the moment to be fully present. The bus drivers were respectful and didn't rush anyone.

I lay my head on Cody's warm, sleeping body on the ride back to the hotel. My one prayer had been answered, to have this day enveloped with trepidation slowly come to a close. To hold my newborn, with the remainder of my family close by. I wished my dad and Ben could have been here to witness the love in this crash area, but I carried them in my heart as I held Cody as close as I could, hoping I could send all the good spirits I felt their way.

Meeting Claire

June 2001

I don't recall the weather outside or what you were wearing.

I just see your eyes and the soft lines on your face.

My heart pounded a few hours before the Family Group meeting would begin, in anticipation of being introduced to you.

I thought I could avoid your eyes, putting my hand out quickly to shake yours, maybe enough people would be around and we could be interrupted. It seemed like a simple, but cowardly plan.

You heard of me, as I heard of you. The line in the sand was drawn, it was time to look up.

Our losses were momentous, huge, couldn't be blown out of proportion if they were grossly exaggerated. I had to admit to myself only that I would feel more sorry for you than anyone.

As soon as our eyes locked, it was over. We clutched on to one another. I felt your insides shaking, or were they mine?

You asked to hold Cody, and his arms strangely were already out to reach for you. I think he was 5 months old on this Sunday in Seattle, Washington in a donated room at a church where mourning families could unite and pretend to be getting on with their lives.

I had trouble talking at this meeting. We were to vote between various artists who were competing to make a monument for our lost families. I couldn't talk because while you held Cody in a corner of the room during the meeting, I turned around just in time to watch you smell his hair. It killed me Claire, it killed me because I understood, and had your baby survived and mine didn't, I would have done the same thing. I loved you for this, and I hated the enemy, our shared enemy, a million degrees more because you were a new friend to me. I felt your rage as I was next to you in this sleeping bag of sorrow.

We stayed in touch a little through e-mails, but it wasn't and would never be the same as our initial meeting. If I never see you again, I see you everyday sweet woman, strong woman, warrior mother, losing your only two angels in one horrible swoop. They tell me you were at the airport when you heard the news. You were flying home, eager to see the girls the following day after their returned trip from sunny Mexico. My whole body chills when I imagine this. You had a good working relationship with your ex and it was his turn to take the girls. You did nothing wrong, and yet your life got destroyed, your partners, your mothers, David's family, Blake and Coriander's teachers and friends and classmates, and so on and so on and so on.

But you were the one who gave them life, they were nourished by your milk and lived in your home and had their artwork on your refrigerator. It is so damn wicked, so unfair dear Claire.

You are the one left to hear footsteps which do not come.

You are left to hear their singing, while nobody is in your home.

I think of you going into their room, and looking at everything, screaming and falling asleep to the sound of your rage.

I have carefully suggested that you have more children or adopt, and yet I could understand your reasons for not

164

doing this, as easy as I could take my own advice. Claire I think of you constantly. You make me hold on to Cody tightly, aware that something could go wrong with nature or man. He too, could be taken away at any time, with no warning. I saw him put olives on each finger the other day, realizing that I could put my whole life on hold just to watch him slowly eat these olives off.

I have looked at sad art, heard beautifully composed music, felt purple fuzzy sweaters, and smelled imported teas, often I have wanted to send you these things but I don't. I am careful for anything you might feel or not feel as I honor and respect you greatly. I know in my heart that these are just objects, and perhaps if you know that I think of you when I see moving things, that this will be enough. I know that nothing will ever be enough for you because your children were killed. Killed in the same lousy plane that my family was killed in, and we are forever bound and connected with bloody thread

I often wonder how you can stand it.

Promise me, please, that one day, in another time, we will be with our families again and we can hold on until then. Nobody who loves us, whom we love, deserves another loss, so we must hang on, and cherish the pictures and the sweetness that was. God bless you, if there is a God.

It is raining today Claire, and I don't have a smile today. I stare at the raindrops and feel as if my face is also raining, it is gray and dark and everything looks miserable today. Forgive me Claire for having two children and still feeling miserable. I choke when I see the rain and I know I will never see my mom or Charlie or my big brother or Ileana or baby Emily again. I feel like they were my children, and I failed to protect them. When it rains, I am alone, and it's scary as hell without them.

I weep for you Claire. It's scary as hell out here without our families. It's scary as hell out here.

2002

January 31, 2002

Carina and I went to go see the new movie, "I am Sam" on the eve of January 31st. It was, by far, the very best movie choice we could have made. It was like a magnificent ride through the countryside right before a dreaded interview. For the duration of the movie, I was right there with Sean Penn, Michele Pfeiffer, and this delightful new young actress Dakota Fanning, who couldn't have been more than the First Grader she portrayed. It was refreshing just being out in the night air with Carina, not towing around her little brother in his car seat. We rarely have the opportunity to be alone together.

Carina didn't mention much about the impending anniversary, in fact, she said nothing. I watched her face a few times during the movie. She was already grown. I liked how she laughed aloud and didn't care about the volume. I was conscious about not touching her, not dressing like I was trying to look young, not having coffee breath. I resisted asking her any personal questions about high school, chatting about random things, and similar things, which fifteen year olds despise about their clueless mothers. Chewing a lot of gum, and trying to stay a few steps ahead works in my favor. We didn't argue on this night. We first ate sandwiches at a deli, side by side, and then thoroughly loved a movie together.

As I expected, I tossed and turned all night. It amused

me how environments don't seem to change when another year turns over in the calendar. We hold this rage, or this breath holding sigh as we look at our watches, but time stays the same, mountains remain big and vast, oceans keep their busy jobs. As the night turned into day over the misty Santa Cruz sky, things felt just about the same. I made a fire and drank a cup of coffee. Carina open and closed doors grabbed her books and left for school. Greg took the day off in anticipation of being needed or at least available for me. I was certain I had once annoyed him with my vagueness of "How to plan out and spend a dreaded anniversary." In therapy I had learned to simply be prepared for anniversaries and holidays, like taking the day off, thinking of a few things that might ease the pain. Staying in the bath alone all day appealed to me, but Cody might not go for it. A part of me knew what Greg was thinking and not saying. It was like knowing the strange creaks and nuances of a house one has lived in for a long period of time. Greg may have been sensing that this day would end up like a Valentine's Day. I ask for nothing, yet I end up acting somewhat cool because deep inside I am wanting more. It could be compared to reading a Hallmark card rather quickly and setting it on a coffee table without a word. Maybe I withhold a legitimate expression.

He was right, no matter what, this day would upset me, and nobody and nothing could really improve the situation. God Bless most men for wanting to fix us emotionally ready and bleeding females, and damn them for thinking we wouldn't do it for ourselves if we could.

I went to my girlfriend Tori's house for a massage. I kept my eyes closed most of the time, realizing how tight my body felt.

She and I reminisced a lot of my mother. The massage was peaceful and enriching, and yet I still felt anxious. I caught myself imagining a walk into other family group's bedrooms on this momentous day. Immediately I thought of Claire, and an image of a deer ran over with its guts exposed came to my troubled mind. I tried to switch screens, thank you Dr. Relovich, but it didn't work. How could a mother possibly bear getting out of bed on this anniversary? Poor JoVanna, two months after burying her husband, she gets to wake up to this anniversary. I have to stop comparing myself to others, even when I think it's therapeutic in that my shit weighs less. It's all bad. This day will be horrible forever. I wished that we could be together on this dreaded day, the many families feeling similar to me. There is beauty in knowing we are not alone. It almost feels too early to make it on our own. Even though I have never been part of any kind of self-help group, I felt so anxious, I didn't know what to expect. I was walking on an emotional landmine.

I wrote for a little while, I took a bath, but tears didn't surface. My eyes burned and I felt as if I were in a constant state of daydreams. I would stare into a translucent bubble and catch myself not blinking. As I would try to recall whatever fleeting thought I may have had, I was off on another bubble. I thought about work a lot. Often I second-guess my report writing, my ideas for implementing different reading strategies, whatever. Often my teaching feels overly empathetic and lacks a repetitive, no nonsense, and remedial approach. Ah, who really knows? If I delivered the mail every other day, I would probably second-guess the way I open mailboxes, park my mail truck, and waddle with my big butt up people's driveways.

I thought about Port Hueneme. I wondered if it was raining, if people went to the beach and touched the sign about the cursed flight. I wondered how the artist Bud Bottoms was coming along on the dolphin sculpture. I thought about the energy of sadness in that little town, and how many people were and are affected by what happened two years ago. Did Alaskan Airline personnel who knew any of the victims go to work today? I feel for everyone affected, and there are way too many of us. If I don't hold my insides firmly, I will implode.

I wanted to call Karolee, but I figured she was also taking a bath and wishing me peace today. I will think about that woman for the rest of my life. One day, I will volunteer and do something courageous like her.

Carina came home from school and locked eyes with me. I brought the helium machine I had never opened out from the garage, placing it gently on the table. I told her we would commemorate this day in a special way. I slowly blew 5 balloons up, getting a head rush from the loss of oxygen. For my mom, I chose a purple balloon, that was a given. Charlie's was blue, like his eyes. Bob, green, like the meadows he used to fly over, Ileana was a yellow balloon, like the sunflower she was, and Emily was a pink one, a soft baby pink.

Without talking, we put the 5 balloons in my car with Cody's diaper bag. Cody and Greg were sitting on the couch, just kind of waiting and looking out of the window. As we all silently got into my car, I became a little teary; appreciating that the heaviness lodged in my throat earlier today was finally changing to liquid, trickling down into my orifices.

We drove to Seabright Beach without speaking. This is the beach Greg and I always drive to. Whether we are watching the waves, trying to sort out problems, or simply just drink coffee and hold hands, this is where we automatically go. It didn't surprise me that Greg took us there with no previous plan.

Carina offered to stay in the car with Cody as I headed outside with my balloon bouquet. A group of guys stopped talking and laughing as I quietly walked past them. "Are you going to a birthday party?" one of them innocently asked. I felt like Mary Poppins on this cloudy cold day. I wished I could be invisible; I didn't want to be rude or overly friendly and explain why I was taking balloons to my ghost family. The tears began to roll down my cheeks, one landed like a heaping teaspoon of pure salt right into my mouth. I kept on walking alone, briskly, bravely, trance like.

Greg was a few feet behind me; I heard his calm and even footsteps. We hadn't really connected much all day. He put his fireman arms around me and kissed my forehead, very fatherly like. He told me where to stand and release each balloon in order to get the best flight. How did he know I never flew kites as a kid? Damn, I knew I forgot something…

One by one, I silently told each one I loved them, adding a few whispered words as I let go of the string. Bob was the first, and perhaps the most difficult to let go of. I saw him as the Chief, the one who could help the other four find their way. Next I released Charlie, the gentleman, who could follow direction and help the ladies and the baby. Next I released my mom, feeling her pure essence in the deep purple hue of the balloon. Her balloon felt eager to find new territory, although she needed Charlie's compass and sense of space. Ileana was next; the yellow in her balloon was like a big burst of sunshine from a happy kitchen window. Finally, all alone was little Emily, her pink was a soft tulip learning to open up and see the world. Being the last balloon to be released, she soon found the others. She resembled a baby colt running after her mother.

Standing on the cliff, I put my hands over my eyebrows, cupping them so that I could see further. Bob was soaring high and fast, looking for a promised land. Charlie was just behind him, taking off like a stellar soldier. Ileana seemed to be dancing to the west of them, twisting and twirling beautifully. My mom, bless her nomadic soul, was off on her own, rising and falling like a dolphin. She went over a few rooftops, and then reappeared near her son. She then flew with the others, flapping her purple wings like a figure skater teasing the audience. Emily slowly but surely took off with strong force, gliding perfectly between her mother and father.

For one magical uncounted moment, all five were swirling through the sky like synchronized swimmers coming to the finish line.

There were no candles to blow out or people and presents at this party, rather it was a send off. A beautifully sad but poignant going away party for the people I loved the most.

They were five magnificent doves that couldn't be on this soil for too long. They were on a mission, and I was the exotic bird keeper, keeping my eyes on them, being sure they returned home on time to their faraway island I couldn't visit. They needed to be loved enough to be released, so that they could fly free.

Deposition

March 2002

Jamie, Greg and I walk into a high tech building in San Francisco. It is a cool and windy March day. My dad and Carina are watching Cody back in the hotel. I keep thinking of how difficult this day will be for my dad so that I can stop looking so closely at my own insides. I think of a test I took at school recently. Out of the seven named intelligences, knowing myself very well, and having the ability to read others came out first and foremost. I went off the charts. I am overly sensitive; I see the world as everything waiting to be noticed. I can see vulnerability in all species. I wish I was stronger in math and science, but I do amazing introspection and I take fairly accurate emotional snapshots of people.

We check in with a shorthaired receptionist with a strong English accent. The office has modern art and chrome displayed all over. My stomach is tight, overly anxious, throbbing. I tried to get a few bites of oatmeal down this morning. I think I was successful with two. I like the sound my high-heeled shoes make on the tile floor, but I feel as if I am dressed funny. I didn't really know how to dress, I was just told to look conservative. I never really understood that word or the connotation it should stir up.

I ask to use the bathroom. I look around at the company sitting around this long table as I quickly made an exit. Jamie quietly told me who they were, but I can't remember their names. My head and stomach are churning again. I feel like this is an interview for a job I don't want, I am critical of them and also of myself. I tell myself that these airline insurance carriers and attorneys are just regular men who mow their lawn and read to their children on the weekend.

It doesn't help. I feel tears and nausea erupting in my hollow body. I lock the bathroom stall door and put my head in my hands. I ask for my mother and Bob for assistance. I asked that they stand by me from wherever they were. I felt my mother stroking my hair. I thought of a particular tidbit from the psychic Sylvia Brown. She claims that our loved ones on the other side like to touch our hair. I tried to become realistic about my sensation of feeling hands on my hair before or after I recalled this information from Sylvia. At this moment, it really didn't matter what came first. I felt my mother's presence, and God knows I needed it. What hit me harder than anything sitting in this cold bathroom stall was the fact that I felt that I was on the defensive while I remained the bereaved victim of this crash. I was told to answer all of their questions, and that they are allowed to ask me virtually anything they want. This was the first time I was ever introduced to the word "Interrogatories."

I tried to finish my business in the bathroom, but feeling rushed and nervous didn't help flush out my system. Like my tears, my insides were backed up, my mind asking them to be put on hold so that I could have my visit with these corporate monsters. It was time to return to the table. I was shaking like hell. I needed my mommy. I didn't do anything wrong. Is this what innocent people on the stand feel like?

I returned to the meeting room. I was told not to shake my head for the word "no" or nod for the word "yes." I would be taped and thus my voice would have to be consistent throughout the session. I was introduced to the woman taking the transcriptions, and two men in suits rep-

resenting Alaskan Airlines. I nodded when we were introduced. They seemed to avoid eye contact, and it felt the
safest to me to comply with this business like atmosphere.

The questions began. My name, age, occupation and
marital status were asked. Was I married before? When did
I divorce? Did I have children with this man? I found
myself getting politely scolding for nodding and shaking
my head. I guess it is how I naturally answer questions;
with hand and head gestures. There was a little awkward-
ness with explaining my two children from two marriages.
"Have you been married any other times and do you have
any other children?" I told them I had been married once
before and that was it. I felt myself rolling my eyes. I
looked at the attorney's gold wedding ring and figured he
must have come across a former divorcee now married with
a child in his lifetime. I felt incredibly annoyed and we were
only starting.

Questions were popping left and right and in the middle.
I was a tired tennis player, just playing memory retrieval.

Then the harder questions began to sprout and bloom
before my eyes. What was my brother like growing up?
Were we close as adults? What are his children's names? I
felt sarcastic and anger blending together naturally. I asked
for them to confirm if they wanted the name of Bob's dead
daughter Emily, or the living children, Axel and Ashley. I
began to cry. I couldn't help it. I couldn't recall a time ever
being nasty to anyone, never having this feeling erupt
where I wanted someone to feel bad with my ammunition.
What killed me was the way they avoided my eyes. They
seemed oblivious or unconcerned with my growing emotional state. My father used to tell me that the screamer in
any fight was the loser. He said remaining calm was the way
to get the opponent more upset. I wanted to strike these
two men, right across their straight teeth.

Another attorney walks in. We stop the running tape
and make formal introductions. I was asked if I had any
intention of baby Emily ever supporting me financially. I
have never been asked a more ridiculous question. How

could I have anticipated such a premature and obscure pre-monition of a healthy four month old?

I outwardly tell Jamie I do not understand this odd question, thus I can't answer it accurately. We take a break. He calms me down, just a little. He reminds me that there is a blank canvas and my job is to fill it with descriptions/memories of those family members I intimately knew. I try to see myself as the painter or at least the writer. I understand this analogy of the blank canvas but I don't understand how to answer these horribly stupid questions. I don't know where they are going with this. Math has been my worst subject, I feel tricked and confused, and I am damn sure that their question of Emily taking care of me in my old age is a math problem in disguise.

We take another break. I am seeing double by now. They wanted to know about my mother's health. I didn't exaggerate, I just elaborated. I told them of her teaching exercise classes, of doing tai chi daily and eating healthy to a point of being teased. I wanted to drive home. I missed Carina and Cody. I wanted to nurse Cody. I missed my kids at school. I hated the rushing adrenaline in my body. I wanted to feel like myself again. Jamie told me I could show pictures, I guess to help my blank canvas assignment.

As if my audience gave a flying shit of those I desperately loved and missed, I showed them my five angels, explaining where and when each photo was taken.

They thanked me, the transcription lady raced across her keyboard and time ticked on. I knew my father's turn for deposition time was coming up. They asked me if I had anything else to say. I felt my milk supply coming in and a huge lump in my throat loosen. As if a gigantic boulder was gently rocked from the top of a mountain, I became separate from my body, watching something bigger than me break apart and take over. I lost control, and whatever had been inside of me came out, short of vomit and screaming. With any verbal control I had left, I told these attorneys and insurance men about my broken heart, about my not sleeping at night. I told them how much I worried for my daughter, how my life had changed in such a negative way from this accident, which never should have happened. I told them I wanted the guilty parties punished. I told them I was trying to "Get on with my life" and that having a baby was helping, but how concerned I felt for myself. I wasn't quite sure why I brought my brother's shirt along in my briefcase, but I did. Suddenly, without any hesitation, I took this ripped and torn up piece of white cotton out and screamed out, "This is all that I have left of my brother". This shirt was recovered from the bottom of the ocean. He was wearing it. It was horribly disfigured; it looked like it had been in a fire from hell itself. As I got this message out, that this was all I had left, I was sweaty and teary and probably looked disheveled and crazed. And I was. Everything stopped, and for the first time, I saw these men really look at me in the eyes. They looked away as soon as we locked eyes. They had to feel what I felt, if even for a second. Everybody stood up. It was very awkward. Jamie shook their hands, as Greg did. I was wiping my eyes, and saw that their hands were now extended for me to shake. I politely squeaked out that I just couldn't, because of who they worked for. I wanted to go on to explain my answer, but their hands went back to the sides of their suits and they mumbled about understanding or something.

It was over. On the cab ride back to the hotel, my milk began to spill out and stain my blouse. I didn't care. I survived Deposition Hell. It was like having strangers who hated children attend the birth of your baby.

I felt ugly and angry; perhaps it is one of the same. I thought about Jamie's comment about the empty canvas. I thought the finished product would be too explosive and heartbreaking to hang, but I wished I could sneak a look at it when nobody was looking. I then considered if these men would look at me in this way. That maybe in the privacy of a bathroom stall they would re-visit one thing I said and sympathize with my obvious broken heart. Would they secretly hope their bosses or partners of Alaskan Airlines and Boeing Corporation could have spent a little more money on preventing this crash? Or was I just a number, just part of the job, listening to regular people turned hysterical because of their monumental grief?

Mediation

April 2002

We were very blessed to have the opportunity of renting the house next door to our house as it was getting remodeled. It is very rare that things fall into place so easily. Our neighbors told me that they were going to move into their second home near a ski resort hours away. They were renting and found it too financially difficult. I immediately called the landlords, and they came over to meet us. Cody plopped himself down on their laps, it was a pleasant business transaction. I tried to be excited about the prospect of what our house would look like, yet it didn't seem real. My life seemed to be very rote and serious. Work was becoming more intense; children's needs seemed to be increasing. If I wasn't at work, I was folding clothes or emptying the dishwasher. If I wasn't doing that, I was changing a diaper. I tried to look at the blueprints of the house, getting mentally prepared, but it seemed so far away. Summer vacation also seemed months and months away. The present was a holding cell, except for the fact that this sixteen month old in my life was delighting me and giving me reason to get up each day and go through the motions.

Ben decided to stay at his Mother's house more, and although there was a den in the new house, he didn't move his things into this rental. I saw Ben's maturity come, and at the same time, the whiskers on his face were still young. I knew it was hard for Greg to see Ben less and less. Ben was spending time with friends, going to school, and deciding about whether or not to join the Navy. I wanted to reach out to him, but he was independent and not very forthcoming about feelings. He and Carina had little to nothing to do with each other. I felt a little helpless. I wanted so badly to have a normal family life, and realized we all had parallel relationships, but none that were cohesive. I got in touch with a childhood fantasy of wanting to be in the Brady Bunch. I wanted a big, smiling family. I wanted to be a big sister. I wanted to be needed and nurtured. Was everything catching up to me? Was it too much taking care of a baby, taking a college class, having a job, three estates to be an Administrator to, and trying not to worry about my father?

Carina's life was immersed in homework, watching reruns of 90210 and David Letterman. I tried talking to her as she was watching television or doing homework, and I knew I was getting on her nerves. I tried to get involved in my own life, and she complained that I wasn't giving her enough attention. There was no winning. We seemed to be less enmeshed. She felt that I was feeling sorry for myself. I felt devoted to Cody, and found that my joy came from his joys in life. I felt lost without him, consumed with him. As I would nurse Cody at night while listening to lullabies, I felt very young and afraid. I missed my mother and brother so intensely. I needed them. I longed for guidance. I felt God or Spirit a lot while I was entwined with Cody's body, putting him asleep, but I felt empty at the same time. It was like God coming into my room and whispering to me that I was hurting. A reminder that never has gone away.

We had a mediation date set the Easter week I was off from work. As always, it was nice to see Jamie. Again, I was advised to dress conservatively, and again I felt funny and out of place. Jamie introduced me to more insurance carriers of Alaskan Airlines. I felt less hostile, but more sad and destroyed. One local lawyer also representing my baby niece had known my brother and spoke highly of his integrity and great parenting skills. It sent me in that downward spiral. Grief goes down and spins around your body. You cry when people didn't know who your loved ones were because of them missing out, and you cry when they did know them because it makes the person authentic and omni-absent.

I kept on imagining Bob standing above me, with Emily in a little snuggly. He would hate that I was in a room full of lawyers. He never liked the B.S., as he would call it. Usually he represented himself in business and personal matters. The purpose of this meeting was a court appointed session where as we would try to resolve matters and reach an agreeable compensation amount while settling out of the court system. Nothing is black or white. Who can say what a person was or is worth? No matter how I tried to slice it, I was part of a group putting a price tag on a person. This is what I couldn't do, and will never get past this ridiculous attempt. It is impossible, it feels morally wrong, and the gray area is incomprehensible.

I met the mediation Judge and felt his sincerity and scruples were in tact. He reminded me of a distant Jewish relative in New York I had never met. He sat close to me, and gave me real eye contact. I needed that. I needed an anchor. We sat in a nice office in downtown San Francisco. I had trouble sitting still, as the process took all of six hours. Being separated from the other party and maintaining two rooms which the Judge walks in and out of reminded me of buying a car. I wondered if they were going to play good guy, bad guy. During introductions, one of the spokesmen for Alaskan Airlines told me how sorry he felt for my amount of loss. My mouth opened, it wasn't planned, but I told him that I also felt badly for him as they lost a lot of good people too. There was a split second of connection. I thought God might have been in the room. The mood shifted abruptly to the reason we all were together today, and that we would be in two rooms, with only the Judge allowed in both rooms. It seemed like a surreal game show.

I found myself feeling very uncomfortable and almost spaced out, as if I were out of my body. I didn't want to play this game. I wanted to go home.

The Judge asked me what I needed. I began to cry. It was a frustrated, tired, "I feel like I am in another country" kind of cry. I had jet lag without flying.

"I want my family back" I spit out, probably sounding about five years old.

Judge Weinstein calmly kept his eyes focused on me and told me that he couldn't bring them back.

"Okay then… I want these guys to go to jail." I offered.

"Nope, that's most likely not going to happen" he calmly told me.

This led us right smack back to where we began. We would attempt to reach a settlement out of court. This is what I didn't want to do; yet this was the focus of the day's agenda.

The Judge consoled me, and yet encouraged me to hang tough. He saw that I had a lot on my plate, that my losses were big. He became very sweet, almost fatherly or Grandfatherly. As he was talking, I went into a place of half listening and half surrendering. It was like having a big person rescue me from the water. My surroundings were scary; all that I had was this body holding me. He mentioned losing a sister in this horrible ordeal in a hospital. It tore him up, he said. The doctors had made a big mistake, and it devastated his family. "But at a certain time, it is too painful to keep holding onto that anger" I recall him saying. I knew what he meant, but the process, the small amount of compensation offered, and the energy in the room made me certain that the right time had not come.

I was able to say no, push on, and stay firm.

I was exhausted getting in the taxi and going back to the hotel at the end of the day. Greg was very supportive, and felt we were true to our convictions and ourselves. There was a light aroma of victory as I walked out into the cool April air. I said no, shook my head, and walked away with dignity. I felt it was premature to come up with a magic

184

number before the NTSB report came out. I didn't cave; I wasn't a polite little victim girl who happily accepted an offer. I was thirty-nine years old now, and death has taught me to be true to myself. I have a better understanding of mediation in civil law cases now. I will not return to do another. If necessary, I will be contacted on the telephone for a conference. I went home exhausted, it lingered for about two weeks.

Relentless Nights

Relentless Nights,
Why do you torture me so with your open borders and
your timeless generosity?
I yawn, I walk, I type, and I look in at my sleeping family.
I am hopeful that you will offer sleep to me, but you don't.
You are an awful long P.S.
I roll over, offering you a fight, but you win. My head is a
limitless tank of gas and the numbers on the clock roll
on.
In a small way, with great imagination, I am putting it all
together and making sense at night. This is when my
processing plant is at work. I feel smart at night, but it
is a telepathic kind of brilliance, as I speak to nobody.
Spirits dance and I remember what Kindergarten paint
smelled like. I recall the taste of uncooked vanilla cake
mix from the beaters my Mom let me lick.
I am part of the fabric of grievers at night. We are all hating
the night, and yet welcoming the night because of the
clarity of the unknown.
Are we closer to our loved ones?
We don't know, and it is not for us to know.
Are there guards from the other side, blocking and preventing our loved ones from getting too close to us?
What is the veil between the worlds made of, and why can't
we see it?

Music is profound, my memory sizzles. The sound of my
    beating heart fascinates me.
Darkness and silence are the invisible massagers kneading
    my sad back and kissing my tear stained face.
I am simply doing what I need to be doing as I stare at the
    ceiling or out of the window at night.
I am waiting with my questions, and time is the rain
    drenching me, one drop at a time.

May 2002

I know when enough is enough.
My yawns are far from home.
I am always on the freeway it seems.
Diapers are taped on and ripped off, wipes are in constant use.
My phone is ringing; there are people at the door.
My students are getting further and further behind.
I want to please everyone.
"How perfect, you are able to work part time."
They don't know, they don't get it.
I am on overload.
Coffee, gum, healthy food, even Weight Watchers fools me
a little bit - that everything is going okay,
But I know better. Enough is enough.
Flashbacks come back, unannounced and quickly.
They are not from drugs, drugs I do not know.
Post Traumatic Stress Syndrome.
When you have it, you own it, it's yours.
It is foreign to me, but inside of me.
Concentration comes and goes.
When the company goes home and the dishes are clean -
I am sighing.
Please no more falling into the water dreams.
Motherhood feeds me, but takes all that I have.
My husband is good and kind, my kids are healthy, my
friends are authentic and show up -

But I don't smile the way I used to. Death breathes down my back. My mother's and brother's spirits are pleading for me to pick up the ball and run with it, but I am frozen. Frozen in time. I don't know how to ease my own mind. I know they are at peace, but I can't breathe with the residue of their violent parting.

Would hypnosis help? Nothing appeals to me, except the thought of holding them all again, laughing and walking on the same path together.

I get all my work done and wipe off the kitchen table, so that I can think about them.

Hours pass, candles blow out, and I am still waiting for them.

How dare I not embrace my life!

I do, really I do, but when I am alone I wrestle with grief and surrender.

I have to decide between the most penetrating sadness and acceptance.

Everyday I win and lose.

When we are suddenly robbed of our loved one, life hurts so badly.

And enough is enough.

We know we have to get a grip, but everyday it's a battle.

Not to live or die, but to tolerate missing people who gave your life so much meaning that you never feel alone because you are so filled with loving them.

Yet the hole in your heart is so expansive that you constantly feel alone.

Telling Sylvia

I watch my Principal Sylvia Mendez in action. She is a petite, fiery Latina woman who carries herself as if she were very tall. We attend meetings together every Monday. Both Spanish and English roll off of her tongue effortlessly. She knows how to get students talking; she knows how to get parents on the ball. I love how she says, "Let me be real honest" as she leads into why kids need to get a full night sleep in order to be good students. She is telling the parents diplomatically to get it together and help their children get the rest they deserve. She holds everyone accountable. I feel her electricity just sitting next to her.

I consider how I might tell Sylvia that juggling work, mothering a toddler, keeping on top of estate affairs, cooking, cleaning, and all of my daily doings are zapping me. I stand next to her, desperately searching for a neutral opening, and she asks me about one of my students. She is the queen of following through. This woman started out as a teacher's aide, then became a teacher, a Vice Principal and finally a Principal. She runs a tight ship; she is darned good at being proactive, punctual, doing things by the book.

I have to be clear, I want to use my mind, not tap into my own introspection so much. I can't let her down...

Sylvia's car is a permanent fixture in our school parking lot. Her mind seems to be on one thing and one thing only — being an effective leader. Running a school. I blink my eyes and swallow hard as she explains to a parent exactly where this fifth grader needs to be academically, before the end of the year. There is no nonsense about Sylvia. I want her to take me under her wing. She is so different from me, and I like it. Her compliments to me make me feel as if I am walking on air. I work hard, and she leaves me a nice message on a sticky note. I want to work faster and harder and invent something huge and revolutionary!

But something is slowly bringing me to a halt. I am waking up tired. When everyone leaves my resource room, I find I am staring off into space. I don't feel as efficient, it seems as if my student's successes are minimal. Sylvia expects each student to do well. Case closed. My students are making slow, steady progress, not dramatic leaps and bounds.

Also I am afraid babysitting will backfire; I will get a call late at night not to bring Cody. Cody will get sick or Angeles his Friday baby-sitter, will grow tired of re-directing Cody from standing on chairs. On top of these concerns, my house is a major construction site; everything appears to be ripped out, temporary. I am worried, and everything is coming at me quickly. I can't do it all. I chew gum, I light candles, and I pretend to be on top of it. I am a duck gliding along the surface of a pond, but if you look underneath the water, my webbed legs are moving frantically.

I consider going to therapy again, but it's too predictable. So I listen to the quiet of the night when I go outside. I sit in the hot tub, watching the leaves shake in the wind. I am doing too much and won't be good at anything because I am spread too thin. I sigh and think of Sylvia.

She is probably done with her dishes and typing something for school, working on the budget, evaluating a teacher, putting something in order for the next day. I am staring at trees and watching the moon, wondering about my existence and where beautiful souls march on to.

I must talk to Sylvia; I must look at a new way of assessing my life. I watch her, and quietly do my job. I chicken out and write a letter about needing more time at home, finishing my class at San Jose State, spending more time with Cody. It is a letter both to her and to my district. They have been in my arena of support people, even though it is all on a professional basis.

I leave the letter in her mailbox in the staff room, and leave.

The weekend passes, and I am testing my students late Monday afternoon. Sylvia walks into my room and says she wants to talk to me in her office before I go home.

I gulp, and walk sheepishly into her office. She closes the door, and tells me that she will support my decision, and is sorry I am having a hard time. She brings up a concern that knocks me over. I seem as if everything has been okay, at least mostly. She notices I look more tired, but she seems very surprised that I want to take the next school year off. Her concern is a wake up call to me because I see for the first time how tricky grief is, how it manifests in such peculiar ways.

The irony is, for the first two years or so, work was my saving grace. I did my hiding there. I was authentic with the students and staff because I loved them, they accepted me, and I was a hard worker. But my sorrow and grief have been hidden, pushed back, latent.

Sylvia wonders if she upset me in any way. She doesn't know why I couldn't just tell her I needed time. I wanted to jump in her arms and sob at this moment. In all of her professionalism, I see such compassion and obvious self-reflection. I am choked up. This is a moment that will be imprinted in my mind forever. I want so badly to be the old me, who could handle a lot, not doubting myself. Not weak and vulnerable. It hurts me that I couldn't even talk to my Principal. I am disappointed in myself. I feel relieved and protected at the same time. I can never thank Sylvia enough.

It was time to have a need met. A time for my wish to be granted, even though I never wanted it. Maybe it was God holding a mirror in front of my eyes, with the words "I need to stop and slow down" written in captions.

Introspection

I begin writing this on June 7, 2002. It is the last day of school at the elementary school where I work. I have not told many people that I won't be back the following school year. The words won't come out. Only a few teachers I work closely with know. The funny part of it is that I know I am being neurotic. I feel as if I am reading lines from a script, dodging direct questions, talking very superficially. I just can't deal with letting anybody down right now. I KNOW I have to take care of myself. I KNOW writing will be the most healing and productive single thing I could possibly do. I KNOW Cody needs me at home. Yet finding the simplest way to tell teachers and students has been a steep mountain for me to climb. Perhaps I am afraid to have the time I need. What if I were able to concentrate on my feelings, to write every day, to have a stare down with my soul? Then what?

This is the beginning of my adventure. I am the same age as my brother when he was killed. It really is young. Thirty-nine. I sigh. I look at his picture on my desk. Then I go and check the pot of veggies on the stove. The steam burns my finger a little. Like a sunburn at the beginning of each summer, I welcome the sensation. It awakens me just enough.

I listen to the most monotonous voice I have ever heard. The announcer goes on and on about Tiger Woods and some golfing stuff from the T.V. in the next room. I feel annoyed. Maybe I wish I could also just lay down on the couch and watch golf. This is Greg's favorite way to go to sleep. Why does it bother me so much?

Ever since the accident, I have been unable to fully relax. Since the accident, since the accident. Since the accident... how these words haunt me. There was a different me before. I liked myself more then, I really did. Will I ever return to the person I used to be? Mostly, I think I won't.

Recently, I remember my dad telling me I looked nice. It used to be that I enjoyed getting ready for holidays and special events. I used to get dressed, looking forward to going wherever I would be going to. I'd play certain music, depending on the kind of place I would be going. My routine was like a dance almost – a ritual of getting ready, putting on lipstick, opening my mouth really wide and putting on mascara, singing my heart out. Blow-drying my hair, looking at my watch to make sure I still had a few minutes. Anyway, I remember Dad complimenting me, and I remember how I replied "I am damaged goods now." I will revisit that statement for a long time, as I know I meant something by it, but it is very difficult to explain. Maybe writing will help it get clearer.

I contemplate what this book will be like near completion. Who will it be for? For whom do I write? More than anything, I want it to be a book about healing, about honesty, about the strange ways of grief and shock.

I looked for books about loss to read during the first two years after the accident, but it was like feeling very hungry at a supermarket and not finding anything to satisfy my cravings. Maybe I wasn't really even hungry, just hearing a loud knock coming from my belly. I read "When Bad Things Happen to Good People" by Steven Kushner. That book was probably the best of the bunch. I must confess at this point that neither God nor religion have taken an active role in my healing. I take responsibility for this. I wish I could say that my faith has carried me, but that would not be true. I have become more spiritual, but not more religious.

I can see the face of my favorite creative writing teacher, Martin Epstein. I am at New College of California in San Francisco. I am 19 years old. He closes his eyes, rubbing his temples underneath his glasses, saying "Again, again please" as I read my writings aloud in our small class. How thrilling to suddenly be at an alternative college with poets, activists, beautifully colored people and gay men. I felt I had arrived. I could be part of something new and real. My writing was out of control, I couldn't stop myself. I walked all over San Francisco with a journal in my hand.

Here I am, twenty years later, and Martin Epstein is still the good teacher haunting me peacefully, beckoning me to be more specific, if only for myself. I tell people all of the time that I am deeply spiritual, not religious. This is a painting I may never be able to un-veil. I cannot find words to describe the meaning of feeling spiritual in a time of tragedy. But learning to be introspective is the most important thing I learned from these writing classes.

I am still in the middle of the waterbed, I continue to be unraveling, changing courses, waking up very slowly. I am still on this journey of healing, of accepting and dealing, of wanting to be heard while remaining hidden at the same time.

Perhaps if I followed a religion, and could live my life in keeping with quotations and simply follow, things would be easier. I have spent time sitting in churches and temples, looking at candles, and have found my center immediately, because I live there now. I know how I feel all of the time.

This feeling is the same whether I am cooking, exercising, listening to a friend, reading to my young son, writing a check or driving. I am in constant connection to my core which is bubbling over with ripe fruit, falling off of my tree. This is being spiritual, I suppose, knowing who I truly am. Being kind and gentle with myself and others. Seeing the connection and differences between myself and others. Feeling people I love very close to me, even if they are not here. Remembering and savoring love and connection — this is spirituality.

Cody in Red Flannel Pajamas

Last night I couldn't sleep. I wanted to write, but succumbed to inertia. So many thoughts and memories have been in my psyche lately, coming close to feeling like "too much". I wish I could be a simple person without files and tapes running through my head. Perhaps I would even be superficial, not caring about everything and everyone as much as I do. I recall feeling this way back in high school. My Uncle Milty, who was always my favorite poet, would tell me that being overly sensitive was both a blessing and a curse. At any rate, these days I think it absolutely sucks to be a tired person with a full head. Buddhists call it "The Monkey Mind". I must be an ape.

As the night turned into day, I went about routines of motherhood and the task of writing down my truths. Taking the garbage out, I glanced at the moon. She was just a crescent on this windy night, but there was a strength coming out of her. I had a realization that I could take everything I thought about during the light hours and dissect them in my head in the night.

Blowing dry Cody's fine hair after bath time, I thought about what it would be like on the other side to re-connect with loved ones. If bonds are powerful and healthy here, can our loved ones forget about us after they transition? I would think that they remain with us, encouraging, loving, and rooting us on as we remain on our paths. Yet we are rendered helpless at some sort of divine mercy, or at least I am, forever trying to see and hear what I am not permitted to experience.

Therefore I ask if our departed loved ones peer into our worlds in the same way we do theirs? Do they have free reign? I believe they do – that they fly and transform themselves because they are "spirit". I have always felt unable to fit in when my mind spins like this. Others seem to be content with the Here and Now. But I was always in trouble for daydreaming in my classrooms. It is not that I can't take out the garbage or dry my kid's hair, feeling content with the tasks at hand. I am simply anxious to know the bigger picture. I can't help myself.

Cody seems too excited to sleep, and I have trouble keeping a straight face. I never have been one of those parents who implemented or relied on a bedtime, yet I am noticing that going on a baby's schedule doesn't leave me any adult time. Cody says goodnight to each of us half a dozen times. Then in red plaid flannel jammies standing less than two feet tall, he goes racing down the hall to bed, smiling and waving.

I have slowed down from working. I caught my breath. I have entered Cody's world, and I like it. Tears of happiness have formed in my eyes the moment I stare at his little mouth trying to form the words "Good Night". I know this time will not come again. He is so far beyond the most precious thing I have ever put my eyes on. I stare at him until my eyes cross sometimes. There is a small space between his nose and his upper lip, and I swear it is identical to my Mother's.

I watch him as he sleeps with this little look of determination on his face. Bob had a very unique mischievous smile, and I think Cody has the duplicate. Do we really see what we perceive to see? Or do we just long so damn much that we make ourselves see the things we want to? It is a question that only the mourners can answer. I miss my mom and big brother like crazy. I sometimes just can not accept that they will never see Cody, sixteen months old in his little red flannel jammies.

Time to Myself

I am quite grateful I am able to write again. Maybe I am just at a place where there is no blueprint, no pre-ordained map, I will just fill pages. I will be sick with emotions and words to say, and my story will come out like primal throw up of the heart. More friends are in transition, it is both sunny and cold outside, Cody is getting taller and saying more words. Time dribbles on, like a paintbrush pulling my guts out and decorating my environment with all that I have to show. The time is now, and like the saying, it is the best of times, the worst of times...

I know more layers of grief because I have been given time to process. My good friend Pilar has a friend who lost her teenager in a car crash last month. We talked about this a bit on our last walk. She, the Mom I do not know, is obviously having a very difficult time. I am finally at a place where I can just hold someone if needed. I was very anxious to hear how this woman was coping. Pilar told me about her smelling flowers and remarking how vibrant the colors were. This is part of grieving, I am sure. We die, in a very huge way, and for a few months everything feels brand new, like we are seeing it for the first time. My heart has expanded although it is broken. It has more room because it's form has changed. I am humbled.

Maybe it was self-preservation, as I would give until there was nothing left. It zapped me, but I wasn't even aware of it.

I care more about my time and my commitments than what I unconsciously promise to others. I used to do anything to please others, more from a compulsion to heal and mother than to be liked, I think. I like myself more now, I am so much more prudent taking time for myself.

Losing my family has made me a better person in this way, because I have created boundaries. My mother and brother were living their dreams. They will steer my ship now.

It sounds so damn cliché but the truth slaps me in the face, if you don't exercise self-respect, nobody will respect you. People will always be needy, and they will smell a caring person a mile away, testing you to the limits. Saying no will never be easy for me, and like driving in new places, I will have to always take extra precautions and be careful . I know that I am not even mediocre in these departments. So what, really. When I do make plans, or make a commitment, I will know that it is from my heart and that I truly have said yes and not done something out of guilt or to be obligatory. I am a better, more rounded person for it. In my college days, I was at a fair, I think Carina was a young child then. A bearded man with crystal blue eyes told me that I gave too much. I gave him a ten-dollar bill and he read my cards. I remember the simplicity in what he said, how it rang true. He also said something that I will recall easily forever. He gave me the example of those "Etcha-sketches" we played with as kids, where you make a picture by making lines with the knobs, and you can shake the sand tray and it erases. I don't remember his words verbatim, but he told me that it was hard to see my picture because others could take it's shape. I interpreted this to be that I could be wishy-washy, that I say things so softly that I could be easily persuaded. I think of this analogy often as I choose to not wear this dress any longer.

Thinking about how short our time here on this spinning planet really is, and how nothing is promised, really forces me to be careful with my time and energy.

July 2002

I just finished reading the book "Nine Minutes, Twenty Seconds" by Gary Pomerantz. It was very difficult to read. I was forced to re-live a lot of my grief. His fine writing made me feel the airplane seats, visualize the pilot, smell the recycled air and experience the cabin pressure on the doomed flight. I forced myself to finish the whole book. I applaud the writer, and it pleases me that the average person who wouldn't otherwise know how devastating plane crashes are to families can get a lesson. He mentions the repulsive presence of lawyers, as well. Although I have immense respect and terrific rapport with *my* lawyer, it is important to state how much of a business it is when a plane goes down. It's like getting a horrible skin rash and all of the doctors and T.V. stations want to take your picture and talk to you. Then dozens of lawyers want to take you to lunch because your hideous skin will be worth something. Okay, it's just an analogy. But planes going down are a business. I *hate* it too.

I have been in rooms with representatives of the airlines several times. Mostly, I just weep because of the overwhelming sense of feeling victimized." The Other Side," also known as "the plaintiffs," ask me about my family members, if we saw each other much, what we talked about, basically all personal questions. I hate watching them watch me cry, and yet all I have been able to do is tell the truth, paint a picture of who my family was, and have faith in my attorney. I have found that when I feel like a victim, I clam up and lose my power. Jamie always encourages me to elaborate. I tell them I want to find out what really happened. No, I say "I REALLY NEED TO KNOW WHAT HAPPENED."

Waiting for the report of the National Transportation Safety Board goes on forever. It is now two and a half years since the accident. Everything has been pushed back again and again. I feel my jaw hard and set. I feel alert and ugly at times. I don't want to tell everyone what happened again as I have done so many times.

It was hard to go shopping before, as well meaning employees would ask me how my day was going. It was and still is very hard to fake being okay. When a stranger smiles at you, and asks you how your day is, it seems appropriate to smile big and give the predictable answer. But when grief is living in your face, you can't always play by the rules.

Grief comes in waves and usually pops up when you want it to the least. This has been my experience.

Almost seven weeks after the crash I found myself at a previously scheduled doctor's appointment. I didn't know the doctor very well, as I had been healthy as horse. At this time, I was still canceling my Mother and brother's credit cards, cleaning out their houses, hiding from the telephone, bawling in counseling sessions, and basically just putting one foot in front of the other. I think I was able to do one or two errands a day.

This appointment called for a pap smear. I was generally fine with these. With my birthday approaching, I was considering going off of birth control pills, as I kept hearing my brother's voice telling me to have another child. This voice was *not* my imagination. The last few months of his life full of revelations of how parenthood was such a source of joy, and … well… Emily could sure use a little cousin. He said this over and over and over.

I thought I could hold this private thought, but I found myself feeling overly sensitive during the exam. Laying on my back, feet on the cold stirrups, I felt teardrops forming in my eyes.

The Doctor continued with his work. My teardrops got bigger and fell harder. He stopped. He scooted his stool back. He took off his gloves... "Uh, is there something I did or said? Are you okay?" he asked.

I recall needing to take a few minutes to regain the ability to breathe freely again. I was crying uncontrollably. I told him of the crash. He suddenly remembered seeing the local newspapers. HE PUT MY NAME AND FACE TOGETHER.

Again, somebody feeling sorry for my loss. I continued to get what I never asked for.

IT'S INEVITABLE. People feel sorry for me. If I were not me, I would also feel sorry. This has become my new persona.

Being Still, Being Alive

I awoke at 3:52 a.m. this late October morning with the sound of Cody's little voice calling out, "Mommy, MOM-EEEEEEE"! I staggered into his room, lifting my top pajama shirt. This has been our routine for almost 2 years now, if I am not right next to him he calls for me when he is between his dreams.

I lay next to him, and with a tiny amount of light coming through his window; I watch his small, closed eyes while his mouth is sucking away. He is moaning and rubbing his body closer to mine. We are two little mice snuggled together in a cage at a pet store, being still, doing our nightly ritual as our hearts rise and fall in unison, unaware and unaffected by anyone watching or caring. I am learning to be still and content, noticing things which are not moving. There is no direct light or sound beckoning my attention. It is only now that I see the helium balloon moving in tiny circles next to the heater, and the way his shoelaces in his small shoes lie so perfectly waiting for him to wake up and play.

I try to recall my dreams, but I thing it's been a quiet night so far. Trying to conjure up the smells of their hair, or the last joke my brother ever told me, combine with the spiral dreams I have nightly. My writings on the family are so close to me now that it's hard to decipher dream from concrete thought. My two worlds parallel play like the sun and the moon changing shifts of guarding the sky.

As Cody finds me in the night, perhaps my family, now in the stars, can connect with me. I used to ask them to send me a sign when my grief began. A Sage, dressed like a cricket, reminded me that signals were like commercials. I know what I am looking for; I know their spirits dance around me.

Cody came to me before the first anniversary of the plane crash. My house was so quiet and sad. Now he runs in and out of rooms, laughing and carrying his puppies from 101 Dalmatians. His eyebrows, mischievous streak, and climbing abilities are like my brother. His smile and happy little spirit are gifts of my mother. I gage how much I can recall in one day without splitting my heart in half. Longing for parents and your only sibling in the large city of night can be dangerously aggressive. They will not be coming home for me.

I am the brave soldier now, looking for others who are left behind. I clip the toenails of crippled friends. When you feel weak, you must be strong for someone, so I look for birds with broken wings. I have learned to close books when the chapters are too intense.

At night there is a wild buffet, flying dreams, and talking animals. I a m a horse with a bad head cold, breathing through my mouth, aware of my heightened sensations, my acute awareness. I don't have the words for things, it is just a knowing, a remembering. I look at mysteries straight in the eyeballs, sometimes I even outstare cats.

I have come to like the night, looking forward to the still, waiting feeling more and more. What used to be insomnia is now a pleasurable journey, more or less. It is a class I have begun to understand. The memories of a falling snow when others are sleeping, the magic of a creaking dock in the water, even the changing numbers on the clock pacify me. I think I will enjoy death, as I hum with the quietness of the deep darkened corners of night.

Memories, laughter, and then finally stillness touch the edges of my life like a picture being developed in murky water, unaware of the outcome without daylight. A new face is learning how to smile. It is pivoting around. It's scars are there, but it is not afraid to be shattered, and yet whole. I am Raggedy Ann in need of a stitching job. My eyes are still far away, I need help with my buttons, but I know where I came from. I know where I am going. I am not afraid of my insides falling out.

Reunion

Our former neighbors came back, housesat our house, the same one they used to live in, and cared for our cat. Nancy, the mom, wanted to come back and see old friends from Santa Cruz. It seemed to be a perfect trade. Justine, their daughter, soon to be entering the Second Grade, used to have Cody's now bright yellow room.

I like the idea of these people leaving their energy in my home. I've always felt so peaceful in this room. Maybe I am nuts but I can't run from the sensitivity I feel. I was literally thrilled that Justine would be in her former room for a week. Maybe I have my priorities messed up, but the littlest things mean so much.

We booked a trip to Connecticut. We really missed Ashley and Axel. I knew we needed a reunion with my Dad. We decided to stay a few days in New York, and then rent a van and visit the kids.

Cody did well on the plane, and my dad made everyone laugh. We spent some time with Aunt Ruthie and Bill and then left New York City. We drove to Syosset to see cousin Marty, his wife Holly, their daughter Lara, and cousin Norman. It was refreshing to see new scenery, walk around new places and watch my father interact with people. He was fascinating to study. He would listen to people having conversations, hold his hand to his ear, cock his head the way dogs do, and immediately guess where they were from.

He would say, "You're from Haiti, right?" His ear is perfect. He has dialects down to a science.

People found him to be charming, as they often do. Once a conversation went on for a few minutes, he would tell jokes. I would find myself smiling, looking at my father seemingly happy, onstage. He is not always this spontaneous, and I cherished these times..

During the drive to Connecticut, I felt calm and reflective. I sat in the back seat, butted up against Cody's car seat and Carina's bag of magazines and crossword puzzles. My father sat up front with Greg, talking about his experiences in the Prisoner Of War Camps in France, his poor childhood, the schooling he had in Brooklyn.

My dad's French was excellent because his teacher had a wooden leg and threatened to throw it at students if they failed to conjugate verb tenses correctly. Once, he said, she was fed up and threw her leg, hitting a boy. I expect I will never know when my dear father is telling the truth or telling a tall tale. He graduated when he was sixteen, he kept surpassing his peers and they didn't have anything else to teach him. He impresses me with his quick mind. For much of our drive he was talking a mile a minute. Somewhere on the long country road, in between stories, he fell asleep.

We found Ashley and Axel's house with ease. It was a charming, old two-story, right near a lake. As soon as Ashley walked out, I felt teary. I hadn't seen her or my nephew, since their father's memorial service.

At the memorial service, feelings had been running high. Ileana's family had wanted to sit up front, away from my brother's "Ex" the mother of the children from his first marriage. Being the peacemaker in this big extended family, I allowed this to happen. I recall feeling angry about being put in the middle of the decision and looking back, I realize it's impossible to always do" the right thing." I learned that I can't. Someone will always get hurt. I wish I had been able to put the needs of the children first. Instead, my brother's ex-wife Lisa sat at the back of the church with Ashley and Axel. I had trouble forgiving myself for this error in judgement. I felt terrible.

We were all wrecks, we were all in shock. I am relieved that Lisa was able to forgive the role I was asked to fill, and we all lived through it.

Seeing Ashley with her braces off, her cute figure, and her blue eyes like my brother's made me gasp for a moment. She looked just him. Axel came outside and helped us out of the car. My father also couldn't believe how good they looked, how mature they had became.

Lisa was warm and friendly and showed us around. She obviously had done a fantastic job with the kids. They were excited about their summer. Axel was on the best basketball team and Ashley had returned from a camp specializing in boating. She was modest about her beautiful looks, turning heads wherever she went. Axel had my brother's twinkle in his eyes, and laughed at everything that came out of my father's mouth.

We got lost looking for a restaurant, Ashley wasn't sure how to get there from the freeway we were on. We took different exits, only to find ourselves lost again, looking for a chain of restaurants. My father became very agitated, letting out an earsplitting "Jesus Christ!" He claimed we were being unfair to the baby (Cody was perfectly quiet.) His outburst made the van very quiet. I noticed my insides shaking. Suddenly the whole situation became very funny to me. I looked at Ashley. Her hand was over her mouth. She was also shaking. Axel was spitting on his hand, trying hard to contain himself. Carina laughed aloud, and then we all broke loose and ripped out hearty laughs (Except for my dad.) I was carried back in time. Ashley once got in trouble for trying to flush my dad's hat down the toilet. She saw Bob and I constantly trying to throw away the belongings he had that looked as if they belonged in the garbage. My dad is loveable, but easy to tease.

We took the kids out to lunch. My dad was telling the waiter he looked like a cross between Eminem and N'sync. Axel's drink was coming out of his nose. My eighty-three year old father then proceeded to make inappropriate comments about the big-busted woman eating a cheese-burger in front of us, and Axel had to hide under the table. It was embarrassing and delicious. For the first time, I felt I had my family back.

The following day we picked up the kids and headed back to our hotel. Ashley and Axel thought it was cool that nobody made my dad shower. It was day five of vacation. My father does whatever he wants to. Carina, Cody and I took the kids to the shopping center. We decided to walk with the stroller. The kids were so sweet with Cody. It was a long walk and a very hot day. I was so pleased that the four cousins were able to spend good, quality time with each other.

The following day we went to a theme park. I felt a huge void without my brother. I imagined he was on every-body's minds as much as he was on mine. I realized though, that nothing would have made him happier than knowing his children were still a big part of our lives even though we live so far away. Bob was so proud of his kids; he was the most devoted father I have ever known.

That evening we had a nice dinner. My dad kept every-one in stitches again. After dinner we walked through a mall. Axel commented on how he remembered Ileana always smelling so nice. It took me by surprise to hear such a sensitive comment from a Seventh Grade boy.

Suddenly a storm blew in and we lost power. At that point, we'd returned to the hotel. As it turned out, there were no flashlights and my father became very angry, telling the management that this was "an outrage." Again, we all started laughing. I think the laughter kept us sane. My dad told Axel he would get his lawyer Jamie Lebovitz out on the case, that in California, there are *always* back-up flash-lights. This made Axel laugh even harder.

Eventually we got power back and we all forced my dad to take a shower. That night Axel slept in our hotel. I watched him sleep, the covers over half of his head, he looked just like my brother. I had trouble sleeping that night. I recalled driving to Bob's house long before he married Ileana. He'd needed me to watch the kids on New Year's Eve. Carina went everywhere with me, and the kids adored her. She also loved being their big cousin. They were her *only* cousins

Near midnight, I woke the kids up. We stayed up all the rest of the night wrestling, making food, watching movies and being wild.

Now my mind flooded with memories of all of our family picnics, sleepovers and camping adventures together. I felt certain that any minute Bob would burst in the door with his Firefighter uniform on, as always. I felt him and missed him like never before. How could my brother just be *gone? And their stepmother and new baby sister? AND their Grandma and Charlie whom they knew all of their lives?* I tossed and turned, toiling with the demons that changed and challenged everything. It was another seemingly endless night. I kept on looking at Axel, sleeping so peacefully, and wishing I were a super hero with the power to make his and Ashley's lives return to the way they were before.

The following day Lisa, her husband Eric, their two children, and Ashley and Axel hosted a wonderful BBQ on the lake behind their house. We all got along well, and made a pact to stay close. Saying goodbye was very hard.

None of us are big on writing letters or calling on the phone. Our missing link will bind us together. Our time together was precious, a very important experience. The sound of "Aunt Janis" was and still is music to my ears. Witnessing pieces of my brother, seeing him living on in these healthy children made me feel extremely proud.

Writing From A Quiet House

I am visiting Jeanette. I watch the fog roll onto the big trees outside. This house is made of glass and wood. It started out as a sublet for Jeanette, and it turned into a long-term rental. I have always felt so comfortable in this house. Sometimes it is too distracting to write in my own house.

The gnarled tree branches amaze me here. From the table I am writing from, I see only a thicket of old trees and branches. This is a quiet house, a strong house. Jeanette must burn sage every day here. A sweet and ancient aroma permeates the house.

I have been reading about opening up the writer's craft and kicking myself for not writing regularly. Like any discipline, I suppose it's very difficult to execute daily. The irony is, I know what I want to write about, but it hits me the strongest in the middle of the night when I am tossing and turning as if I am watching a movie, not wanting to be distracted.

I wake up at odd hours with the ah-ha's. I feel spirit. It wakes me up. If I pay close attention, I can detect a soothing feeling at the end of the insomniatic ride. I do not do drugs, God as my witness, and I refuse to take any kind of anti-depressant. The good news, if any, is that my movies are organic, un-cut, and self made movies. Perhaps they are giving me my life back; there is a hint of renewal in the air. These are my own, authentic thoughts.

I am not the first or last to suffer, and my suffering may be more or less than others, No matter. It is *my* story, my unique path through these cruel and amazing woods.

Lack of Sleep

I wrote Jamie an e-mail last night. I told him that I needed his promise that the guilty parties to this crash would be punished in ways other than paying out with insurance monies. I also needed a promise that I would get to see my family again.

Jamie is the kindest "professional" I know. He wears a suit and a tie, but you can so easily picture him eating cereal with his children, wearing sweats, and just being a relaxed father. There is such a protective aura about him. Lawyers may not all be honest, but Jamie must have had the kind of good old-fashioned Jewish mama who taught him scruples. Every attorney in America should watch Jamie Lebovitz in action.

Sometimes in the middle of the night I feel so anxious. I want to trust and be in the moment, but I think about the airplane going straight into the ocean like an out of control, iron demon and my eyes don't shut. I listen to my friends all day and I can sort of picture my mom next to me when they talk. I don't think I give advice, but when asked my opinion, I shoot for honesty and I urge people to think highly of themselves and others. Something keeps me going all day.

Lately I feel clear, I make a simple checklist of what I need to do, and I go forward. I even find myself laughing with Cody and chasing him across the house. I feel a sense of accomplishment from folding warm laundry and checking in on my sleeping boy during his nap. It is perhaps a heightened sense of smell and touch and peace that I feel. I keep my nest calm and clean. I function during the day. Work feels like a long time ago. I revel in the luxury of waking up next to my baby boy, free from the pressure of racing to work, my head full of work thoughts on the freeway. I enjoy having my own thoughts now.

"The nights are hard." This is what I say over and over to people who truly want to understand grief. The darkness is difficult and can be relentless. The hours torture me, they destroy me. The nights are a dead animal I must pass on the road. I don't want to look at it, but it gets my full attention and often I can't look away. These are the long nights of mourning.

Pictures

I have been afraid to write. Not afraid, but resistant. I stare into space. I create little snacks in the kitchen. I remember to put the wet clothes in the dryer. I think about what I want to write about . I think of all of the friends who might think I am flaky. Who do I really owe a phone call to? Should I call them or sweep the floor? I have my loved ones, "the fabulous five," above my desk so that I can see them smiling at me when I write. Seeing their faces stirs up my emotions each time. Sometimes I think of theirs as a case that needs to be solved. I see these five beautiful victims, and I am the unofficial detective who will ultimately make their killers accountable. Sometimes I torture myself by staring *into* their faces so much, trying to see how many memories return. Thanksgivings, vacations when I was a kid, what their kitchens looked like, what their inner most fears and fantasies were. Just everything, as much as I can recall. I can still hear their voices so clearly.

August 2002

I am watching my dear friend's children. They go to a private school and begin the following week. School at my site has started, and I am feeling very thankful that I get to stay home. I am desperately trying to get Cody to go to sleep in the crib without me. I did the same thing with Carina at this stage! I loved being close to her, and then I wished that she could just go to sleep independently.

Cody screamed for 45 minutes. I tried to do all of the things I know innately and have read, but his face was drenched in tears and he was breathing super fast. Poor little guy. So I am thinking about what I learned in massage school. I have learned to apply this to my life whenever possible. *Ready?* It is powerful, it is crucial. And *it is imperative that one checks in with their body!*

What is my body saying? What does my spirit need? When I checked in today, I realized that I feel cranky if I don't get time to myself.

When I am with kids, I become very selfless, yes *to a fault.* I try to anticipate and meet their essential needs and before I know it, the kids are happy, but I am depleted. The truth is, kids feed me and teach me more than anything. Once again, I attempt to dance between the two worlds, striving for balance. Too much giving is not healthy, but being a hermit and refraining from helping out friends with childcare is not healthy either.

I resolve continuing to do my good deed for the day, but at the same time, staying committed to checking in with how my body feels a few times a day. I never want to sigh with resentment when a child in my care wants a plate of sliced pickles while I am strumming the guitar or writing. I want to move gracefully and joyfully through my everyday activities, carefully choosing when to cut into my own time. Bottom line, *life is short and we need to be careful with our energy!!!!!*

They Are All Gone

A certain word comes to mind. "Stuck." Yes, "stuck." At different times I have used this word during uncomfortable experiences; the ending of a relationship, the start of a new therapy session. At these times, I bite my lip and rub the fabric contours of a couch. I force a Mona Lisa smile and try to avoid the person seated near me.

"I'm just stuck." it sounds vague and passive. It buys time.

Tonight I am also sick and tired. Not physically sick, but emotionally feeble. I stare at my Mother's picture above me. Okay, I must be a glutton for punishment. I have ALL of their pictures above me, taped onto the desk I write from. I stare at every line of my Mother's face. I have memorized her face, but I still look for more, I want to remember what I may never have noticed.

I try to recall each birthday party she ever threw for me. A swirling image surfaces of Mom putting Band-Aids on me, all in a row, when I would fall off of my bike. The sweet smell of vanilla cake baking from my kitchen and her invitation to lick the beaters. Playing *"Psychologist,"* our noted very favorite game when I was in Kindergarten. We would take turns making up problems and solving them.

I liked school okay, but mostly I looked forward to coming home after school because of the special time we'd spend together. She and my father ran a very sweet gift store/boutique in San Rafael of which I have fond memories. There was a huge iron horse there, as well as soaps, antiques, and unusual things to buy.

As a child, I wished my parents weren't such Bohemian types. I recall being in the "Bluebirds," which was like the Girl Scouts. I would spend the night at friend's houses, and notice they had paintings of landscapes. My parents had nudes. My Mother ate wheat germ and made won ton soup and my friend's mothers made roasts and ate white bread. How I hated those differences then, and love them now.

I remember running around the house with her and dancing wildly to her Jacques Brel record. We would chase each other and laugh and scream. I think I used to pee in my pants because I didn't want to miss even a minute.

I remember one day when I put my head on her stomach, actually my ear, and heard the gurgle of her stomach. It scared me a little, because she was so playful and friendly, but her insides sounded like a mean machine.

I stare at her glistening green eyes in the picture now, and I still hear her voice. That incredibly infamous New York accent I teased her about my whole life. That woman called the operator in New York when we moved to California in 1966 because she was home sick and wanted to hear a New Yorker.

There is a little tiredness in my mother's eyes in this photo, but mostly I just see her blithe spirit, always a playful twinkle lighting her eyes.

I feel angry tonight that all of these trivial things are annoying me. I want to go home and I can't. I want to cry in my Mother's arms and have her call me "Dah-ling" in the way only she could. I want to tell her how hard I have tried to be strong in the past two and a half years, how much I need her and my big brother.

All I want is to return.

I want them to return.

I want that fucking plane to go back to where it came from and be fixed. I want Boeing to put in the right parts and the maintenance department of Alaskan Airlines to follow safety procedures.

I want this to be a bad dream.

A tear slides down my cheek.

They are gone.

They are all gone, poof.

Pictures and memories can't solely sustain me, but that is all I am allowed from here on out. It is a cruel and absolutely accurate realization.

When the little girl inside of me gets overly emotional drowning in the crashing waters of childhood, my adult self lays down these rock-solid boundaries.

I long for the circus, but I am saddled with the dismal five o'clock news..

The angry tiger chews the soft lamb to pieces.

Mid-October 2002

I hear myself trying to make a pretty case for the judge. I have read the grief books. I have sat in therapy sessions both choking on my tears and not having a word to say. I have walked back to my car after sessions both thrilled to have air and freedom from staring at the big clock on the wall to never wanting my 45 minute slot to end. It felt so good to get the demons out. But they never fully leave. Demons always leave their energy behind. I have experienced a new love for life and a strong pulse of excitement that I wasn't on the plane, that I didn't die. Sometimes, I even think I have come a long way in these two and a half years, other times, I am where I was. Sometimes I am more angry and sad than I was in the beginning. Judge, there are no rules to follow, grief is a very tricky class and I don't quite care if I pass the test or not.

The biggest challenge is getting away from the sadness, which takes over. It is leaving the room where the corpse you love lies to rest. It is leaving the flower filled room and the soft music and going back to the noisy city.

It's returning to the bright lights of the grocery store, it's the will to play back the answering machine messages instead of laying in a room watching the day go into night, and being perfectly content not moving. In grief, we stare at ceilings for a long time. Sometimes we don't feel like talking to anybody.

I feel the most like myself when I connect to spirit, when I allow myself to enter into a timeless period of staring at the ceiling and missing what has caused me to grieve.

The world is loud and ego-driven. I am out of place here.

The sweet innocence of my Cody takes my eyes off of the ceiling. I cannot keep him a baby. He is discovering himself and is now a walking and talking toddler. I would do anything humanly possible to have allowed him the opportunity of knowing his Mother's unique family and the love they brought and gave. I can only do this through pictures and stories. It is better than nothing, but sometimes I don't want to accept that this is all. I want to bargain.

ACCEPTANCE IS THE MOST LINGERING AROMA OF GRIEF WORK.

Jobs can be quit, relationships can be ended, but accepting death is final, set in stone, no negotiations.

For some lucky reason, which I have nothing to do with, I do not have addictions. Perhaps I was blessed with the absence of an addictive personality, but I am lucky enough to have friends struggling with addictions. I am lucky to understand it through their eyes, but I can walk away. My Mother used to say that was the same theory as the beauty of being a Grandparent! Anyway, I ask a lot of questions to my friends with addictions.

I am a curious. It is a club I will never join. I know that the fourth step is where one asks for forgiveness to those he/she wronged, and to ask forgiveness for holding grudges. I believe strongly that being self-righteous and holding others wrong is not allowing either party to reach their greatest potential. It holds us hostage, and takes us away from being a human on the quest in that we go to bed and awake with toxic anger.

One friend told me that holding a big grudge is like drinking poison and hoping the other person will die. I think about this quote a lot, it helps me gain perspective...

I have been having so much anguish over the killing of my beloved family, yet there is not one person I can scream at and then ultimately forgive. I feel so much solidarity with the victim's families of the September 11th tragedy. So many family members just like me are outraged and yet it's a blind rage in that it's not a single person to hate, it's nameless and faceless groups of people.

It is such a very detached and unfamiliar realization to feel something as strong as hatred for an organization without knowing their names or faces. This is so strange to own this sense of fantasizing revenge and wanting retribution. I feel it in such a powerful way. The anger lights my candle, as it were, and the reflection from this candle makes me feel like a victim, the mourning family member. In this way, I am powerful and weak at the same time. I think about this dichotomy often. It doesn't propel me nor does it stop me from anything. It lingers, it is always there.

Cody 21 months

Halloween Memories

Today is Halloween. The first Halloween after the crash comes into focus as I pull the file up. I am remembering the first Halloween in 2000. I laid on my side, 5 months pregnant, not pregnant enough to wear huge maternity clothes, but far too big for my own clothes. Pregnant enough that I couldn't lay on my stomach. The elementary school I taught at had a typical parade, and I faked a smile, helping my student's parade around to the "Monster Mash" music. It was sweet and customary, but I was glad when it was time to clock out for the day. I was starting to show, and I felt unusually vulnerable and sensitive to the loud buzz in the air on this Halloween day, the costumes, the honking, the silliness.

Driving home I played a tape a teacher friend had given me. It was made for her mother who had battled with cancer and lost. I hadn't been able to listen to it much because of the sensitive content. As I began listening, I noticed a few people driving around with plastic arms and legs sticking out of their cars. On the tape Jackson Browne was singing, and I was transported back to high school and also to my early twenties, remembering what I was doing when I'd listen to him, and the times I went to see him in concert. I began missing my mom and brother like crazy; music has always helped me to surrender to my emotions. As I witnessed these visuals of body parts sticking out of cars and people laughing and being silly, I felt as if I didn't belong; I missed the joke. I felt like a stranger in a strange land, as the saying goes. I took the Jackson Browne tape out, feeling hot tears dripping down my face. Driving home felt like having to pee like crazy on the freeway without rest stops for miles. It took full control to simply keep both of my hands on the wheel just to make it home. I climbed into bed about 4:30 in the afternoon. I cried myself to sleep.

This was always a time when I felt God or Spirit closest to me. Surprisingly enough, it happened when I would feel the most alone. I felt God crying with me on this Halloween night. I rubbed my small but growing fetus, wishing he could come out and let me hold him.

When you cry so hard that you clutch your insides, you feel like the only person alive while the world goes on, so big and unaffected. My husband took care of the trick-or-treaters. I drifted off to sleep for a short time. The headlights from cars and streetlights cast a soft light into my bedroom. It lit my bedroom, creating the same ambiance I remember seeing as a young girl, waiting all year for the spooky night to come. I remembered how exciting Halloween was, the anticipation, the mystery, the great sugar highs, each year getting better and better. I wanted to be back in the house where I grew up.

One Halloween when I was five or six years old, a family down the street from us set up their garage and rooms in their house with spooky things to touch. I recall this like a favorite kind of field trip. Every sense of mine was put to work, while a witch with a big black hat showed me around. Haunted house music played. We were blindfolded and asked to touch witches' eyeballs. Another touch tank was filled with "guts". Afterwards, I was too excited to sleep, and then my brother told me that the eyeballs were grapes that had been peeled. He thought the guts were cold spaghetti strands. All that I knew or cared about was how cool it was to be a kid at Halloween. I thought about this time in my life for a while, trying to recall what my brother's voice was like, what my room looked like, how much candy I tried to sneak into my little twin size bed. I wanted to return to this time in my life. I missed the voices outside of my room. I missed being the youngest in the family. I missed the comfort, the day-to-day stuff. I didn't want to be a pregnant woman grieving and signing my name to initiate a lawsuit. I didn't want to have to say thank you to people who let me know how much they felt for my loss, I just wanted to be a young trick-or-treater, with red lipstick and a pirate's patch, or bunny ears, or a witch's hat, or whatever I would decide on being that year.

I cried a little more, listening to how sweet my husband sounded from my bedroom. He'd ask the doorbell ringers what they were; they'd thank him, laugh, more footsteps, door opening, closing, candy dropping. When you are really sad or sick, try listening to what people sound like from other rooms. I wanted to shake off my wet coat, drop my broken shell, and smile and pass out candy to the children, but I couldn't stop feeling feeble, overwhelmed and afraid of the darkness, the big world, the realization that bad things happen and people get bloody and die.

The following Halloween got a little easier, maybe even a lot easier. I yawned a lot. I watched the parade from my classroom window. I was only working half of the day, and it was time to go. Filling up with milk (still breast feeding) I just kept yawning. I suppose I was thinking of the long night this time last year.

Cody was born now, houses were cleaned out, my loved ones really weren't coming home. It was a weird, final feeling. I wanted to get into the school spirit, but my life still felt too serious. It is hard to be happy-go-lucky when your heart is still in your mouth. I was a little more present for my daughter, now a sophomore in high school. Although Cody wasn't yet walking, I could expose him to some Halloween fun. I did these things; I did get into Halloween, at least a little bit.

Today is Halloween, the third one. I made Cody oatmeal, we played hide and go seek for a half hour, scaring each other and laughing. We lit a candle and plugged in his jack-o-lantern. I took him to Delaveaga's parade again. He loved watching the kids

That day, I spent half an hour talking with my rock-solid lawyer, Jamie. We both want to see justice. We are feeling positive about the findings and believe that we will make the parties accountable for bringing down the plane. It is still a waiting game. We must be patient. Cody is napping. I am crying less. It has been a few weeks, perhaps a dry season.

Here is what I have learned, I who have so much to learn. I watch more and talk less, trying to stay open as I breathe deeply and take notice. Each season and every holiday it brings finds me still "plugging away." I often feel as if I am going through the motions. Still I pay attention to the people counting on me to notice holidays. I have yet to see a picture where I am beaming, really celebrating and maybe I never will. Little steps are okay; in fact I think they are good and healthy.

The best part of today was being next to Cody, a little round pumpkin, and hearing the happy sounds he made as he opened our front door and dropped candy into children's buckets. Maybe next year I will peel some grapes and blindfold him.

JoVanna

I spoke to Jovanna today. She lost her wonderful son, Jay, in the crash. Although I have only spent a few days with her, I can honestly say that she knows me well. I have thought about her plight so much, that sometimes I too feel as if I have lost a son that I loved incredibly. I have placed Jay's picture with the row of pictures of our five. It seems right that they are together, at least in photographs.

Do we decide who we will die with? Did they have any indication, however miniscule, when they awoke on January 31, 2000, that this would be their last sunrise, their last cup of coffee, their last quick look in the mirror as they were getting ready for the flight home? That they would find themselves together in the end?

I think too much, I know I do. I stare at colors until they become dream-like. I think about the symbolism in language. The flight home, and the flight "home," meaning the spiritual journey toward reunion with God. I think of my mother's face, telling me about a week before their trip about her experience washing dishes. She told me very plainly that she was washing dishes and looking out into her garden, as she always did. Suddenly, her sister Lee, who died unexpectedly a year before, appeared. It was like a daydream, but it was "so real," she said. Lee just turned her face toward her and smiled. A happy smile.

Even though my Mother was very creative in art and music, this sort of story or encounter was uncharacteristic. When she told me about the visit from Lee, I felt that my aunt was telling my Mom she was okay, she was happy, and not to worry. Now though, because I have mulled it over, I can't help but consider the idea that Lee might have been coming for her to give her reassurance that she was not "alone." I do believe that our family members/loved ones come for us. They are our hosts/hostesses, our beacons of light taking us to a place they know and we do not. I have no fear of dying because of this, and it has actually pulled me closer to feeling some excitement about my impending exit. I am not suicidal, I never have been. This is a blessing perhaps, because it helps me know that I am strong, Otherwise, I would not be here. Just as I do not or can not picture myself ever killing another, I could not kill myself. BECAUSE of the crash, I make myself appreciate the gift of life even more. I consciously try to live with more passion.

I advocate talking to people to whom we have no need to explain ourselves. I make it a point not to talk a lot about my grief with most friends and acquaintances . I downplay the feelings, because this seems polite and right. I wrap them quickly and quietly in a blanket. I use commonly acceptable sayings for my "bow" and "ribbon." "I am just taking one day at a time," I say. "I don't cry as much, so I guess I am healing," I offer. "Cody is bringing me so much joy."

M treat is being blatant with the ones who know my darkness, whose eyelids also weigh a few pounds each. JoVanna and I talk on the phone, and I can feel comfort and a bond sizzling through the phone wire. It's like taking off my make-up, it's like how it felt to hug my mom *every* damn time.

One More Thing, Brother

I stare at your eyes in the picture I keep of you above my desk. I muster up enough courage to remind myself that I shall never be able to look at your face again, other than in photos and memories. Whenever I get too sensitive, too dreamy and little girlish, this realistic voice speaks to me. I like to imagine Heaven, the star world, the other side, and then something reminds me that it will take the full extent of my lifetime to even have the chance of seeing you again.

In the spirit world, we may all be spirit. So would we even recognize one another?

My brother's eyes were such a nice blue. I stare at the picture some more.

A year or so ago, I was not able to look closely at any of your pictures, especially yours and Moms.

I say time doesn't heal, we just get used to our losses.

I TRY TO PUT MYSELF IN YOUR SHOES. Perhaps this used to bug you about me, I would work so hard at seeing other's views, and being overly-sensitive to others. You got stuff done, I philosophized and procrastinated.

So I am putting myself in your shoes. What was it like for you? Did you have time to do a life review? I imagine you did your job, what you do so well... trying to save lives. You had your eyes and fast thinking brain on what you could do. Perhaps you tried to calm other's down. Most likely you wanted to know what the hell was happening. Diving out of planes was something you did for sport.

You tried to take care of Ileana, to comfort her, to re-assure crying Emily that the horrible noises and the topsy-turvy sensation of the aircraft would cease.

*Did you get out of your seat and see Mom? At any point did you think this was **it**?*

I can't relate to that. I hydro-planed in a car once, but I knew I would be okay. I can't relate to thinking, let alone knowing that your life is slipping away and in minutes or seconds, your life will be over.

I look at your eyes now, dear brother, and I am sorry that you had to face that.

You were thirty-nine years old in the picture I stare at. Now, I am thirty-nine, too. I wanted to be like you all of my life, but it's different now. The things you loved will be kept alive in my memory, in stories about you. You are not here anymore. I had to accept this. It wasn't easy. When others talk about their siblings, I listen intently, I care, and I want to know, even with stranger's conversations. I wish to keep your candle lit. I want to hold you, wrestle you, laugh with you in the flesh. I miss everything about you, every freckle, every practical joke, every intro-duction. of "This is my big brother Bob." One more thing brother — there a million things I would say to you.

You knew how I loved you. What we both didn't know, what I know now, is how naive I was to count on living my whole life with you. I never imagined we would be cut apart. How cruel, that we are not to see another for the rest of my lifetime.

I am not whole without you. I hope and pray not to be in a room with strangers and be asked innocently if I have brothers and sisters. I miss you brother, in the rain, in the sunshine, in the country, in the city, when I play with my kids, when I weep alone.

Janis & Bob 1999

Synchronicity

Driving back from the bank on this Friday morning, I am listening to a beautiful folk music program on the radio. I feel tremendous peace as I drive, noticing the swirling clouds, getting into the power of the music.

I am feeling tired and vulnerable today, yet my ears perk up like a guard dog's as I take in the words of this song. It is a very melodic, dreamy kind of Irish song.

Suddenly I see the image of my adventurous brother as the plane begins to descend. The imagery in the song takes me to this place, and it is the first time in a long time I feel like being in the moment. I connect with the sad and abandoned feeling. I get a churning mixture of anxiety and inertia. I am so grateful for this music, I realize how much I've had locked up inside. The name of the CD, which I bought the very next day, was Dougie Maclean, "Live From The Corners Of The Earth." Anybody who needs to have an epiphany should listen.

Usually I want to busy myself with cleaning or doing a project when this primal stuff erupts, yet in this moment I want only to be still and feel each nerve ending.

Now as I write this, a song about the passengers on Flight #93 taking over the plane and crashing into Pittsburgh comes on the same radio station. How synchronous to gently be in touch with my pain as a song about a plane crashing plays over the radio.

This is what I love so much about the human experience. If we pay attention, there are lessons and outstanding timings to which we pay little attention.

I realize that I am as ripe as I will ever be.

This is my time to come clean.

I will write to get this monument out of my throat so that I can breathe again.

I will write to retrieve my soul.

I will write about how much I miss my family until I have a new way of expressing that very sentiment.

They say the veil between life and death is thin, that we are not far from the other side. I think it's like a prisoner digging himself out from under the ground, one piece of mud at a time. I think life is one island, and death is another. The great water never allows the other world in too closely.

Larry, Janis and Carina at Graduate
Teacher Celebration June 1990

Another Star In The Sky

Another smiling face taped above my desk,
Another kind face joining the clan of special people
who've crossed over.
Another star in the sky.
Another dead friend, making me cry.
I stare today at Larry, Larry Campbell.
Dear Larry
brown Larry
Infectious laugher
Marvelous piano player
Gourmet Chef
Lover of children
Teacher Larry
Vice-Principal Larry
Class taker, lemon-square maker,
Chicken broiler, creative salad maker,
Gourmet coffee drinker
hugger of children,
World traveler Larry,
Walking, flying, driving all over the street corners
and the magical beaches,
A friend to so many, so many colors, so many ages,
Did you know how many you touched dear Larry, sweet
friend, did you know?
I sat in the front, at your memorial service

next to the friends you and I graduated with,
And I wanted to say something,
but words and sadness choked me,

And I decided "Not to worry" as you always told me, and so I just listened to how much you were loved by so many in our community.

Upon returning home, I wished I had said something. I didn't know you were ill.

Thank you for the candles and the inspiration and for squealing with delight when things cracked you up. Thank you for inviting me to your dinner parties and for reading tarot cards for my daughter when she was young. I adored you and respected you and I am so very sorry you got sick and left this world. Thank you for loving life as you did and for touching so many precious young lives in Watsonville. Thank you for making me feel proud to share your profession as a fellow teacher.

You were selfless, hilarious, flaming, private, ageless, and in my grade book, FLAWLESS.

I only wished we stayed in touch more. I am haunted by special people only staying a short time on this revolving planet.

I peeked only quickly into your casket, as it didn't seem to be you. I had known you a dozen years Larry, I had never seen your mouth closed!

Your famous glasses resting on your peaceful face brought everything to a halt. You never saw Larry without his glasses. This must then, be you Larry.

I was blessed to have known you, and the thought of not bumping into you again really saddens me. To realize how little we actually saw one another and the magnitude of how sad I feel at your passing, I can only imagine how your closest friends are feeling. You are leaving behind a grand legacy, dear Larry.

I heard a saying recently that one's life isn't measured by the breaths one takes, but rather by the things that took one's breath away. To risk sounding cliché, you led a passionate life, Larry Campbell, and I salute you.

Sara and Smith

Smith Weed Dobson III (Papa)

I am sitting in a café writing this while I listen to classical music. The sun is streaming through the windows, even though it is a fall morning. I recall the music at my mom's service, and the absolute kindness on my friends' faces as they filed through the door that winter day almost three years ago. I swallow hard.

Smith Dobson and Sara Poyadue have both passed away since then. Both Smith and Sara played music at the service. Sara and I were taking a music class together and spending time with one another whenever we could. She taught music the first year I taught Kindergarten. She helped me realize that even if I was critical about my singing voice, I loved to sing and so I should. It was very obvious to Sara to do what felt good.

Smith was my dear friend, the father of two amazing kids I used to student teach when I was studying education at the University of California, Santa Cruz. Smith played the most beautiful piano in the world. He was well known all over. Still, he showed up when I needed him, and I never had to ask. He loved my Mom, and played "We Will Meet Again", an old Jazz standard, with his wonderful wife Gail at my Mom's and Charlie's service.

I spent a lot of time with Smith, Gail and their kids,

Sasha and Smith jr. I was at their house soon after he died. Sasha was looking through his dresser. She found he had wrapped up and saved the first tooth she ever lost. Smith was driving home one night from a regular gig when he apparently fell asleep at the wheel. He never made it home. That was April 20, 2001. I was devastated, our whole community was. He called Gail from the gig saying he'd be home soon. Then in the middle of the night, the hospital called, and that was it.

Smith was like a big brother. I miss him so much. I went with Sara to his memorial, we arrived an hour early and there were people lined up all the way down the street. It

Sara and Janis, June 1997

was Smith's farewell concert. I watched Sara as people eulogized Smith and told funny stories about their time with him. Sara was bawling, Sara who had been struggling with cancer for the past 6 years. She knew that she probably wouldn't make it, but she fought like *a stallion*. She got to know Smith when they worked together to put the music together at my Mom's service, and now he was gone in the same immediate way my mom left. I rubbed her back while she cried. I didn't know why she was so affected. But when I tried to imagine, warm tears welled up in my eyes, and I realized at that moment that none of us are immune. People who know they have just a short time are probably more in love and in awe with the everyday stuff. It must be so hard to let go.

Sara waited for her granddaughter Zelda to be born. She died one year later in her home, with her family around her.

Death is a sticky, spiraling web, taking whom it will, when it wants. I don't glorify it, neither am I afraid of it, but *I respect* it. I feel like a paramedic calling in stats when I explain my relationship to death so matter of factly. But I have been forced to take control and give some substance and order to what I do not and can not understand.

Arlene Hamilton

April 2002

⌘

I met Arlene Hamilton in the early 1980's when I was just nineteen years old and attending school at New College of California in San Francisco. She made a huge impact on my life. Arlene was the Vice President's wife, and was extremely friendly and fun to be around. She often invited me to Native American films and ceremonies, as New College was sister schools with D.Q. University, which was an all Native American (Indian) School. We hosted many ceremonies in our school, and I found out very quickly that I had deep empathy and interest with Native Americans.

I worked at the front desk for work-study, and saw Arlene all of the time. She was very dedicated to the Native people of Big Mountain Reservation in Arizona. She spoke out against the Peabody Company when it forced the people to relocate and leave their land. She didn't just whine about unfairness — she led protests, wrote letters, raised money, and these people on the reservations became her extended family. She spent a lot of time on the reservation as well. She had become a stockholder with the companies trying to mine the reservation so that she could have a say. Then she blasted them and was arrested a few times for standing by the elders in an effort to save them from bull-dozers and horrible toxic materials they were exposed to as victims of Peabody's "ammunition." Arlene said over and over again, "My friends will not be relocated, this is their land." Arlene opened my eyes. As we were both North American women, she helped me to see that there were gross politics happening in our names.

I met a refugee from El Salvador taking English classes at our school. We ended up getting married and having a daughter together (Carina). I have fond memories of getting married in our mutual friend Christy's backyard. Arlene led a beautiful wedding circle and burned sage. She wore a dress and big cowboy boots. There was only ever one Arlene.

I struggle to find appropriate words to convey the most spiritual event I have ever experienced. Arlene was with me, along with our mutual friend, Christy. Carina was a year old. I was in the middle of a divorce from her father, and I decided to go to Colorado to be with my dear friend, Kim. I needed time to re-group. At that time, Arlene was doing amazing things with native peoples and Big Mountain. She started a weavers' collective, where people on the reservation made and sold their hand woven rugs. Arlene was helping sell these rugs all over the place. She and Christy were going to rug shows and raising money for the weavers and their families. So Arlene and Christy made plans to come over to see Kim and me in Colorado.

We all went rock climbing and hiking as soon as they arrived. Kim and I made our friends a big dinner that evening. We drank tea and caught up on one another's busy lives. Arlene went outside to the truck. She had hundreds of these hand woven rugs in there, and felt they needed to be secured in the house. We were in awe of these weavings. Gorgeous blues and reds, intricate designs. They were powerful, yet simple. Arlene gave Kim and me two of them. She gave me one made by a blind man. She gave Carina one made by a six-year-old girl. I tried to decline her generous gift, but she wouldn't let me. *That* was Arlene.

I took Carina upstairs to our bedroom, putting her to sleep. Christy and Arlene came upstairs a few minutes later to wish her goodnight. It was about 8:00 pm and we were all relaxed on the big bed, digesting our meal and talking quietly while we took turns rubbing Carina's back.

Our attention was suddenly pulled to the left corner of my bedroom. There we saw a strange light cast on the wall. I closed my curtains, but it was still there. I looked outside the window; it was a warm, quiet night, no wind, just stars and silence. None of us said a word. Carina had fallen asleep on her back.

Arlene, Christy and I sat on the edge of the bed, mesmerized by this light on the wall. It suddenly moved and began spiraling around the whole room. It moved around and around. There was an absolute presence in my room, something I had never experienced before. I wanted to run and get Kim. She was still downstairs. I tried to stand up but there was a feeling of pressure on my chest that preventing me from moving. I could *not* get up, and suddenly it didn't matter. Something magical was happening, and I didn't want to miss anything.

I looked at Arlene and Christy's faces. They reminded me of the movie "E.T." when the little boy sees the alien for the first time. We were small and insignificant, something was bigger than us. We had to stop in our tracks; it was so completely out of our realm, out of our experience. We were all a little teary as well, we were all seeing the same thing, feeling something indescribable. I felt a surge of incredible love and compassion fill my heart. The light continued to spiral, and then split off into different directions. It almost looked like a firefly hovering over Carina's sleeping face. First it moved over to me, and then to Christy. Our eyes became tearier; we couldn't talk. We just whispered and acknowledged that we all were seeing the same kind of light. The main part of the light was right above Arlene's head, moving around her face and around her body, spiraling again and again. This lasted for about half of an hour. The light eventually lost its abundance, as it began to falter and fade away, until it was completely gone. We held on to one another and burned sage and gave thanks. We were not drinking, smoking, nor were we under any kind of influence whatsoever. This visit, or presence, or gift had come out of nowhere.

Carina and I stayed on in this room for another three months or so. I waited every single night for it to return.

That presence so fantastic that I felt if I never believed in aliens, another world, or the light of God before this night; it would all change now. I had to believe because I was a *witness*. I swear to God this happened. I would love to take an oath, or a lie detector test. I will never ever forget the powerful feeling.

This light, with its feeling of love and peace never came back again. We all slept in my room that night, huddled together, but the feeling was gone. Only the memory was alive. We all compared notes and concluded that we had all experienced the exact same thing. I kept telling Arlene that a part of the light split and took turns being above my head, Carina's, and Christy's, but that the big light never left her. She just nodded her head. I had to go to work early the next morning, and Arlene and Christy had plans to head back to Big Mountain in Arizona.

I spoke to Christy some months later since that time I had moved back to California and started graduate school to earn my teaching credential. Christy told me that she and Arlene had told the elders what had happened. They were very pleased. They felt that these rugs brought Spirit, and that all who saw and felt it were blessed. I will take this memory to my grave as one of the most outstanding things I have ever witnessed, next to the birth of my two children.

In April, 2002, I received a call from my old friend Marie with whom I also worked. She explained that Arlene had been driving home from a rug show in New Mexico when her car was struck by another vehicle that had gone out of control. The other driver had lived but Arlene had been thrown from her car and she died instantly.

I hung up the phone numb but riding the shock waves. I had thought of her so many times over the years, wishing we stayed in contact. I felt terribly for her three sons, one who was living on the reservation. Arlene was such an amazing light; she had so much to give.

I thought back, savoring our special experiences in Colorado, trying to recall every detail. I didn't understand how she could leave this world in such a quick but violent way, just like my friend Smith.

I drove for hours to a private ceremony honoring her in Cazadero, California. Jeanette rode up with me, helping me out with Cody. We picked up Marie along the way in San Francisco.

Two elders from Big Mountain spoke in their Native tongue. A translator helped us understand their message. One elder named Roberta said Arlene was "perfect," she felt she had "lost a daughter." Other people came up to the stage, surrounded by trees and beautiful nature, and shared their stories. More than anything, the common thread weaving every story and testimony was that Arlene was passionate about service. She lived. She had fun.

I spoke to Christy for a while. Christy had basically put this service together; she and Arlene had been best friends always. I knew it probably wasn't the right time or place, but I had to ask her one more time if this event I remembered in Colorado so well had really happened. She hugged me tight. "Yes", she said. She and Arlene talked about it a lot. In fact, it had happened again to them.

I felt Arlene so close to me. Jeanette and I had a heavy talk driving home. We bought some coffee in Santa Rosa, talking a mile a minute. Arlene had left us a legacy of inspiration. We became excited to live our lives, to find more meaning, to make a difference as she had done. We saw how intensely she loved and lived what she died for. She fought for justice all of her life.

Sometimes I see myself as a butterfly, staying in different places for just a short time, then moving on. I feel passionately about a lot of things. But when Arlene sits on my shoulder and I am honest with myself, I see that I too must find the *most important thing*, then stick to it. I know it will involve helping children. I am searching inside myself and out everyday.

Christmas 2002

There are more crosses to bear, strange and painful moods continuing to surface, flashbacks flooding my mind. I feel as if I am riding a wild river in a storm. I am different from the rest. It is nearly impossible to be at peace, to sit still, to relax on a couch and watch TV. The images constantly reappear on my mental screen.

I want to move on, but as the saying goes, *"what you resist persists..."*

And so, I laugh when jokes are delivered, I pretend to be in the holiday spirit, calmly confirming that three years have almost passed. Perhaps honesty is better off withheld. I am still not okay.

I stare at their pictures extra closely these days, wondering when the pain will ease up another notch. True, the tears are less intense and not as frequent, but the gaping whole in my heart has not closed or even shrunk a little.

A report from the National Transportation Safety Board has just arrived. I am digesting the disturbing data. How can people be so careless with loved ones? It's like loading a class of pre-schoolers into a big truck with a drunk driver at the wheel. My insides are reeling, churning with bewilderment and disbelief. Anger is the blade that turns these feelings, tossing glass around my throat.

I do not understand the absence of jail time for greedy corporate officers. The time that has elapsed since the plane crashed violently into the cold Pacific waters bares no relevance. My vista hold only one vast sky in the daylight and one quiet moon in the evening; I stand on a little piece of the world missing my family, lost at sea, lost in space.

Janis and Bob 1966

Revenge

I have the urge to detach, to restlessly abandon all.
If I were a smoker, I would exaggerate exhalations smoke.
If I were a painter I would throw
gray and black paint on a canvas.
If I had a boat I would go
very far into the dark waves at night.
Usually I explain my actions and I am apologetic and polite
to everyone
but today I will say nothing, I will go into my own fire and
not care
who is looking.
I don't want to be kissed today.
I don't want to be missed by anyone or make plans
with people on the phone because
I don't want to go anywhere and I don't want company.
No food or drink or distraction appeals to me.
(I haven't rolled my eyes like this in a while.)
Something lingers in my throat, it smells like old soup left
out for too long.
My jaw is tight, the world is loud and careless. People laugh
and drink coffee, they steer big cars
with polished fingernails. They make superficial plans
on their cell phones. I hate seeing this.
I watched an airplane landing
slowly

near San Francisco today
feeling sorry for myself that those people
will have a homecoming
and my family never came home.
Then I felt sick
and tired of having a reaction
to an innocent plane and probably very nice passengers.
The world is mundane and colorless today.
I am angry and alone,
Tired and ready to give someone a long cold stare.
I want to hit someone and fall to the ground with them.
They will cry and I will cry, while some kind of lesson is
being learned.

Janis, Jean and Bob 1967

2003

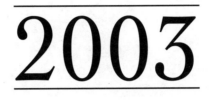

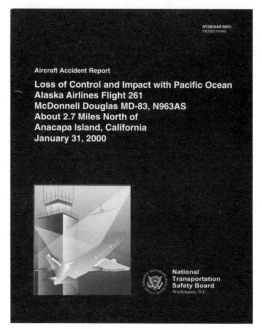

Cover of Aircraft Accident Report

Zone/Area		Generating Item 24627000			No. of Men	Skill
41	*Alaska Airlines* MIG-4 NON-ROUTINE WORK CARD	Work Order No. 02525	Insp. No. 71	Date 9-27-97	Station OAK	Est. M. Hrs

IRF	LOG NO.	N° 423 374	A/C NO. 963	FLT or CHECK SC	ORIGINATING EMPLOYEE 6 545 1	ATA CODE 27 40

Discrepancy:

HORIZONTAL STAB - ACME SCREW AND NUT HAS
MAXIMUM ALLOWABLE END PLAY LIMIT (.040 IN.)

Planned Action: Replace nut and perform E.O. 8-55-70-01 R# 9/30/97
Re-evaluate Test per wc 24627000
Authorized by: RB 49462

IRO 27 40	EMPLOYEE NO. 52 471	Enter "Y" for correction or code for deferral (obtain code from SEA M.C.) Y	DAY OAK	MO 30	MONTH SEA	Partial work on back ☐

Corrective Action: Rechecked Acme screw & Nut end play per. WC
24627000. Found end play to be within limits .033 for
step 11 and .001 for step 12. Rechecked five times with
same result.

Corrected By: Ron ___   Reviewed by: R___ 5945

Final Inspection Buy Back	☐ MIG-85 S/N		to		attached.		Enter rotable change information below.
		TRACKING NO. ON	ASA S/N OFF	2 TRACKING NO. ON	ASA S/N ON	3 TRACKING NO. ON	ASA S/N OFF
14983	Were rotables changed due to:	(c) Convenience ☐	(s) Scheduled ☐	(u) Unscheduled ☐		Check if ARCTIC entry required ☐	Entered in ARCTIC
	REMOVE ONLY	ASA P/N		(or) Installed only ASA tracking no.			

MIG-4 (Rev. 9/94) ASA# 0-0410-3-0204

Nonroutine work card (MIG-4) generated on September 27, 1997

3. Conclusion

3.1 Findings

1. The flight crewmembers on Alaska Airlines flight 261 were properly certificated and qualified and had received the training and off-duty time prescribed by Federal regulations. No evidence indicated any preexisting medical or other condition that might have adversely affected the flight crew's performance during the accident flight.

2. The airplane was dispatched in accordance with Federal Aviation Administration regulations and approved Alaska Airlines procedures. The weight and balance of the airplane were within limits for dispatch, takeoff, climb, and cruise.

3. Weather was not a factor in the accident.

4. There was no evidence of a fire or of impact with birds or any other foreign object.

5. No evidence indicated that the airplane experienced any preimpact structural or system failures, other than those associated with the longitudinal trim control system, the horizontal stabilizer, and its surrounding structure.

6. Both engines were operating normally before the final dive.

7. Air traffic control personnel involved with the accident flight were properly certificated and qualified for their assigned duty stations.

8. The longitudinal trim control system on the accident airplane was functioning normally during the initial phase of the accident flight.

9. The horizontal stabilizer stopped responding to autopilot and pilot commands after the airplane passed through 23,400 feet. The pilots recognized that the longitudinal trim control system was jammed, but neither they not the Alaska Airlines maintenance personnel could determine the cause of the jam.

10. The worn threads inside the horizontal stabilizer acme nut were incrementally sheared off by the acme screw and were completely sheared off during the accident flight. As the airplane passed through 23,400 feet, the acme screw

and nut jammed, preventing further movement of the horizontal stabilizer until the initial dive.

11. The accident airplane's initial dive from 31,050 feet began when the jam between the acme screw and nut was overcome as a result of operation of the primary trim motor. Release of the jam allowed the acme screw to pull up through the acme nut, causing the horizontal stabilizer leading edge to move upward, thus causing the airplane to pitch rapidly downward.

12. The acme screw did not completely separate from the acme nut during the initial dive because the screw's lower mechanical stop was restrained by the lower surface of the acme nut until just before the second and final dive about 10 minutes later.

13. The cause of the final dive was the low-cycle fatigue fracture of the torque tube, followed by the failure of the vertical stabilizer tip fairing brackets, which allowed the horizontal stabilizer leading edge to move upward significantly beyond what is permitted by a normally operating jackscrew assembly. The resulting upward movement of the horizontal stabilizer leading edge created an excessive upward aerodynamic tail load, which caused an uncontrollable downward pitching of the airplane from which recovery was not possible.

14. In light of the absence of a checklist requirement to land as soon as possible and the circumstances confronting the flight crew, the flight crew's decision not to return to Lic Gustavo Diaz Ordaz International Airport, Puerto Vallarta, Mexico, immediately after recognizing the horizontal stabilizer trim system malfunction was understandable.

15. The flight crew's decision to divert the flight to Los Angeles International Airport, Los Angeles, California, rather than continue to San Francisco International Airport, San Francisco, California, as originally planned was prudent and appropriate.

16. Alaska Airlines dispatch personnel appear to have attempted to influence the flight crew to continue to San Francisco International Airport, San Francisco, California, instead of diverting to Los Angeles International Airport, Los Angeles, California.

17. The flight crew's use of the autopilot while the horizontal

stabilizer was jammed was not appropriate.

18. Flight crews dealing with and in-flight control problem should maintain any configuration change that would aid in accomplishing a safe approach and landing, unless that configuration change adversely affect the airplane's controllability.

19. Without clearer guidance to flight crews regarding which actions are appropriate and which are inappropriate in the event of an inoperative or malfunctioning flight control system, pilots may experiment with improvised troubleshooting measures that could inadvertently worsen the condition of a controllable airplane.

20. The acme nut threads on the accident airplane's horizontal stabilizer jackscrew assembly wore at an excessive rate.

21. Alaska Airlines' use of Aeroshell 33 for lubrication of the jackscrew assembly, acme screw thread surface finish, foreign debris, and abnormal loading of the acme nut threads were not factors in the excessive wear of the accident acme nut threads.

22. There was no effective lubrication on the acme screw and nut interface at the time of the Alaska Airlines flight 261 accident.

23. The excessive and accelerated wear of the accident jackscrew assembly acme nut threads was the result of insufficient lubrication, which was directly causal to the Alaska Airlines flight 261 accident.

24. Alaska Airlines' extensions of its lubrication interval for it McDonnell Douglas MD-80 horizontal stabilizer components and the Federal Aviation Administration's approval of these extensions, the last of which was based on Boeing's extension of the recommended lubrication interval, increased the likelihood that a missed or inadequate lubrication would result in excessive wear of jackscrew assembly acme nut threads and, therefore, as a direct cause of the excessive wear and contributed to the Alaska Airlines flight 261 accident.

25. When lubricating the jackscrew assembly, removal of used grease from the acme screw before application of fresh grease will increase the effectiveness of the lubrication.

26. A larger access panel would facilitate the proper accom-

plishment of the jackscrew assembly lubrication task.

27. If the jackscrew assembly lubrication procedure were a required inspection item for which an inspector's signoff is needed, the potential for unperformed or improperly performed lubrications would be reduced.

28. Alaska Airlines' extension of the end play check interval and the Federal Aviation Administration's approval of theat extension allowed the accident acme nut threads to wear to failure without the opportunity for detection and, therefore, as a direct cause of the excessive wear and contributed to the Alaska Airlines flight 261 accident.

29. Alaska Airlines' end play check interval extension should have been, but was not, supported by adequate technical data to demonstrate that the extension would not present a potential hazard.

30. The existing process by which manufacturers revise recommended maintenance task interval s and by which airlines establish and revise these intervals does not include task-by-task engineering analysis and justification and, therefore, allows for the possibility of inappropriate interval extensions for potentially critical maintenance tasks.

31. Because of the possibility that higher-than-expected wear could cause excessive wear in less than 2,000 flight hours and the additional possibility that an end play check could be not performed or improperly performed, the current 2,000-flight-hour end play check interval specified in Airworthiness Directive 2000-15-15 may be inadequate to ensure the safety of the Douglas DC-9, McDonnell douglas MD-80/90, and Boeing 717 fleet.

32. The continued collection and analysis of end play data are critical to monitoring acme nut thread wear and identifying excessive or unexpected wear rates, trends, or anomalies.

33. Until August 2000, Alaska Airlines used a fabricated restraining fixture that did not meet Boeing specification; however, the Safety Board could not determine whether the use of this noncompliant fixture generated an inaccurate end play measurement during the last end play check or whether the use of this fixture contributed to the accident.

34. The on-wing end play check procedure, as currently practiced, has not been validated and has low reliability.

35. Deficiencies in the overhaul process increase the likelihood that jackscrew assemblies may be improperly overhauled.

36. The absence of a requirement to record or inform customers of the end play measurement of an overhauled jackscrew assembly could result in an operator unknowingly returning a jackscrew assembly to service with a higher-than-expected end play measurement.

37. Operators will maximize the usefulness of end play measurements and wear rate calculations by recording on-wing end play measurements whenever a jackscrew assembly is replaced on an airplane.

38. Because the jackscrew assembly is an integral and essential part of the horizontal stabilizer trim system, a critical flight system, it is important to ensure that maintenance facilities authorized to overhaul these assemblies possess the proper qualifications, equipment, and documentation.

39. The dual-thread design of the acme screw and nut does not provide redundancy with regard to wear.

40. The design of the Douglas DC-9, McDonnell Douglas MD-80/90, and Boeing 717 horizontal stabilizer jackscrew assembly did not account for the loss of the acme nut threads as a catastrophic single-point failure mode. The absence of a fail-safe mechanism to prevent the catastrophic effects of total acme nut thread loss contributed to the Alaska Airlines flight 261 accident.

41. When a single failure could have catastrophic results and there is a practicable design alternative that could eliminate the catastrophic effects of the failure mode, it is not appropriate to rely solely on maintenance and inspection intervention to prevent the failure from occurring; if a practicable design alternative does not exist, a comprehensive systemic maintenance and inspection process is necessary.

42. Transport-category airplanes should be modified, if practicable, to ensure that horizontal stabilizer trim system failures do not preclude continued safe flight and landing.

43. Catastrophic single-point failure modes should be prohibited in the design of all future airplanes with horizontal stabilizer trim systems, regardless of whether any element of that system is considered structure rather than system or is otherwise considered exempt from certification standards

for systems.

44. The certification requirements applicable to transport-category airplanes should full consider and address the consequences of failures resulting from wear.

45. At the time of the flight 261 accident, Alaska Airlines' maintenance program had widespread systemic deficiencies.

46. The Federal Aviation Administration (FAA) did not fulfill its responsibility to properly oversee the maintenance operations at Alaska Airlines, and at the time of the Alaska Airlines flight 261 accident, FAA surveillance of Alaska Airlines had been deficient for at least several years.

Santa Cruz Sentinel January 2003

Recognize whistleblower

Time magazine has recently honored three "whistle-blowers" and deservedly so. I believe they left out the most important one, however — John Liotine, formerly chief mechanic with Alaskan Airlines. Mr. Liotine revealed that his employer was sending up aircraft deficient in lubrication, being in dire need of replacement. He also reported this to the FAA, as Alaskan Airlines was showing a definite culture of putting profit before safety. Mechanics were accused of "gold-lining" the aircraft when in fact this was everyday maintenance. He was ignored and his work orders crossed out.

John Liotine couldn't live with going against what he knew to be safe and right, and he was ousted from his job. His findings were seconded by the Dec. 10 hearing of the National Safety Transportation Board in Washington, D.C. This report issued scathing findings on the doomed Alaskan Airlines Flight 261, which crashed into the Pacific Ocean near Los Angeles on Jan. 31, 2000.

I salute John Liotine, wishing the whole world knew how the acts of bravery could bring solace to families, giving a little hope for mankind. My family was killed in this plane crash, and it is only now that government agencies are looking into aviation safety and tougher regulations. My pain and bitterness only ceases slightly when I remember that John Liotine tried to prevent this catastrophe by speaking up. What an example to set. What a good man in a den of greedy tigers.

John Liotine should absolutely be on the cover of next year's Time magazine as the most outstanding citizen/whistleblower. Better yet, employ him with our homeland security problem.

JANIS FORD
SANTA CRUZ

Third Year Anniversary

Port Hueneme, California

The drive to Southern California is quite lovely. Cody talks about puppies, Cruela De Vil, and names some of his friends on the way. He has such a delightful high-pitched voice; it is very soothing to whiz down the highway, listening to this uninhibited two year old. We stop off at a Sizzler after a few hours, sharing food and taking advantage of Carina's favorite all-you-can-eat salad bar. As I watch both of my kids dipping fried dinosaur shaped nuggets into sauce and sharing ice cream, I make a firm decision to enjoy this trip.

There are times when I catch a certain look from my savvy sixteen year old, immediately alerting me that I am displaying my "overcooked grief". I call it this, because she gives me this icy stare when my sadness becomes overwhelming. I am aware my spiraling down, of dark emotions and images taking me over. Admitting to myself that I am overcooked means I must turn off the heat, open some windows, and let my emotions cool down. I am not afraid of the pain anymore, as I always come out the other side. I am becoming more and more comfortable with accepting death, with longing, with intense missing but Carina doesn't like it when I get into my grief too much, not that I can blame her.

When Cody gets a little older, I will volunteer with

Hospice and sit with dying people. I used to do quite a lot of massage/body work, many of my clients close to death. Personally, it was a gift to be near these people. I really like the quietness of it all, tapping into the transition period between two worlds.

When Cody takes his nap, Carina is at school, and Greg is working, I light candles and play soothing music, going inside very deeply. Perhaps this is a form of informal meditation. It has become very clear to me that when I deprive myself of this inward time, I become cranky, overwhelmed with everything, and depressed. I used to be such a social creature, now I crave opportunities to find the exit door. I look forward to breaking away by myself. Once I insist on having a little time alone, I can function. My introspection subsides when I am able to decide the kind of company and stimulation I want. The company may be my own, equipped with a few bags of fresh produce for making soup. I may need to be in my water aerobics class, watching others interact as I do my routine exercises, noticing others while remaining inside my center.

I think of the people who matter in my life, and I imagine seeing a nice matinee with one, drinking coffee with another, taking a brisk walk with another. I have learned that people who are calm in their core are the only ones I strive to be around. As much as I have adored various people who've continued to stumble through life year after year, I have begun to question how I honestly feel around them. Sometimes it is similar to sitting in a bar and hearing the same story told over and over by a likeable alcoholic. I become bored, irritated, anxious, feeling as if my internal clock is ticking, telling me I need to be productive. Never one to preach or act like a "goody two shoes," I think this new feeling stems from the realization that life is a fast trip. The accident has been a sobering wake up call. Now I want to be inspired by people, not play the part of a caretaker waiting in the recovery room. Whether this seems a little judgmental, selfish, or makes me come off a bit hardened, I absolutely crave the company of healthy friends. Once I am around people I admire, I automatically tone down the intensity of my feelings. I can see the crash in perspective *almost* knowing, that I am not totally broken, I can still live my life with some joy. Healthy people remind me that I will slowly get up and dance again, the way that they do. It isn't what they say; it's how they live.

At this stage, I am acquiring a sense of accomplishment. For one, I have made time for myself. I now allow myself to "clock out" when feelings are too elusive and fleeting to name. Two, I treat myself gently as if I were a child having brand new experiences with sorrow. Three, I am getting to know what I feel as I become entangled with the emotions as they surface. This has taken me to a different level, my fear is gone because it has been fully experienced. I have paid in full for my pain.

In my psyche there is a big wooden door, left ajar. Inside loom terrifying screams, broken skulls, blood and water. I am kneeling at the water's edge, trying to rescue my family.

This gruesome scene transforms to a photo album filled with images of everyone smiling and laughing. I see a shelf in this room bearing sacred artifacts and only the best of memories of each person. I squint my eyes, watching myself look at these items while I am feeling the presence of each loved one. Suddenly I am filled up with their love, with their kindness and gentleness.

These days I can walk away from the first door, keeping this gift of resolve, acceptance, redemption, peace in my heart. It is true that my mind frequently wanders back to the grotesque images of the crash and my anger toward the guilty parties. I am still not so strong that the darkness leaves me alone entirely. I continue looking forward, striving for the calm acceptance. But I will fight until the end, and I will never fully forgive what has happened. The only real control I have is over myself, I want to make the best out of what my family taught me. Spreading kindness through deeds and examples, keeping the memory of them alive, that is all I can do. I look through a Kahlil Gibran book my mother gave me when I was ten years old. "Your pain is the breaking of the shell that encloses your understanding," it tells me.

I would like to be able to know for certain that I am dialed into my family so much that I can tune into them to judge myself through their eyes. I hear them reminding me that my spirit is very dark. I am not living my life passionately, and I haven't for three years. My head falls down slowly in a lukewarm bath of shame. My ears become hot and red. There is nobody I can point my finger at. This is my doing. I will be ashamed of myself if I live the rest of my years not being a passionate and joyful woman. As much as this crash was a horrific, unjust, life altering event, I am still able bodied and have a strong will and working brain. I realize I have a choice. Now I imagine my family saluting a grand jury as it looks into the accountability of the airlines, assigning responsibility so that they would not have died in vain. Perhaps broadcasting news of this crash will help eliminate sloppiness, greed, and gross negligence.

This is my first long road trip with my kids. It is my hope that we will all remember how, one sunny day in January, we drove far, sang, and laughed at silly things. And on the day of the third memorial, how Mom let her tears out without any interruptions. That we headed out to take part in a memorial dedicated to my fallen family, and to look at a prospective college for Carina. Not all sad reasons to be together as a family.

Carina had been wanting to see Woodbury University in Burbank for quite some time, so we've made a plan to visit it before going to the memorial. I feel more stable and mature than usual as I am able to navigate both my children's needs and my own.

Cody is missing his dad and is sick of being in the car seat. This happens at the same time as I merge onto the LA freeways, looking desperately for signs as Carina reads the map. My mother always told me she couldn't stand having to make split second decisions on the freeway, and I have inherited this hatred. The freeing part of this, the great ending is that I simply chew gum, feel like a good driver, and we make it! Carina and I are cracking up as we finally exit and find we have no idea where we are. We look for our hotel while we take turns rubbing Cody's knee in the backseat, singing him the theme song from "101 Dalmatians". We find the hotel eventually, as Carina comments about it looking like a throw-back from the 1950's. She has this vision of Frank Sinatra sunbathing on the upstairs patio.

Carina looks so mature and beautiful to me at this moment. She keeps me present, and this is the best gift I could receive at this time. I always get a little crazy around the anniversary of the crash. She teaches me to put my feet up a little, clean later, and watch Dr. Phil and Oprah with her. I can't believe she is almost grown up, that we are actually at this funny hotel near Woodbury University. She tells me she wants to have a lot of gay male friends in college. I feel a familiar tickle in my throat, as I was exactly the same way at her age.

We take Cody on a carousel ride at the Burbank mall and Carina handles his meltdown gracefully as I pick out some cheap sushi. He is being a stubborn "stick-man" child, not wanting to move his legs or listen. A few minutes later, she has him laughing and peeling the rice around his sushi rolls, his eyelashes still wet, but he is wearing a rhinoceros smile.

We go back to our hotel a little later and watch singers being showcased on American Idol. I complain about the lack of pillows and can't understand what I am told when I call the office, asking for extras. We are pinning each other down and throwing things at one another in fits of laughter, when suddenly there is a knock on the door. We laugh so hard we can't unlock the bolted door. The man from "housekeeping" stands there, looking confused as Cody in his diapers opens the door. Here is this half-naked toddler, a teenager, and a middle-aged mother, each in their own worlds, enjoying the moment and ordering extra pillows. I want to write this line down again until it penetrates into my DNA. I am *enjoying* the moment. I am really having a good time. I am laughing and enjoying the heck out of my kids and my life.

The next day Carina has an appointment to tour the school and meet with an admissions counselor. It is a gloriously warm day. Cody and I hang out at the fountain, as Carina meets with her designated admissions counselor. I watch attractive people look over drawings and talk intimately over their cups of coffee. These 18-25 year olds could be her, and possibly will be her in a year or so.

Cody is touching blades of grass and singing little songs to himself. I am so grateful for this picture in my mind, for this lasting memory. Whether I am a good mother or a very sad woman or neither or both, my children are thriving. They are going to make it, so I am going to make it, too.

After the admissions meeting, Carina is extremely excited. She talks about the likely possibility of being a Freshman in 2004 as we drive all the way back to Port Hueneme. I begin to feel very small and vulnerable as we approach our destination. Reading the signs brings me back to places I don't want to re-visit. Ventura signs reminded me of the coroner's letters and final death certificates. Point Hueneme is the closest place to the crash site, a place where a wonderful community of caring people live. They came forward with flowers and prayers when the plane came down, and now this monument, a sun-dial dolphin, will be in their backyard on the beach. I like the thought of it being there forever.

We find the hotel easily and see a Wendy's restaurant across the street. It means a clean bathroom, inexpensive salads, and a free toy for Cody. Across from our table is a group of people. Something about their posture tells me they might be a part of the convergence of families tied to the crash. I look closely at a familiar looking woman. She looks as if she's been out in the sun a little, she looks younger and softer than what I remember. I think she may be Earlene, a wonderful widow I had met in Seattle at the family group a year and a half ago. I walk up to her and meekly say "Earlene?" She stares at me, not knowing for a minute how the heck I know her name. I tell her, and in less than a second, we are embracing. I feel my mother in her hug.

There is nothing better in the world than getting a bear hug from a petite woman. When it happens, I like to pretend it is my mother. It is, at the very least, a tangible incarnation of what meant so much to me. In a warm, safe hug from a trusted person, I can close my eyes and go back to a very special time.

The gratifying embrace is soon over, and it's time to come back to reality. It is wonderful to see Earlene in this brightly lit Wendy's; we had been in touch a lot recently via e-mails. She lost her husband Donald in the crash. I read his bio in the passenger memorial book and realized he would have been the best Principal to work for. They say you could hear him listening, he did it so well. She described him as being a most romantic husband as well, so every Valentines Day I think of what this unknown man would have planned for his wife. It just kills me; he was in Puerta Vallarta looking for a retirement vacation home for them.

We chat about the upcoming events of the monument unveiling in which she has been completely involved. I admire her tireless spirit.

Is the pain the same if the one you lost, the one killed in the air was your spouse, sibling, parent, child or close relative? I believe it is, but the hardest eyes for me to look into are those who have lost their children. Perhaps this is my biggest bias. I feel guilt when I hold my children close to me while I am next to a survivor who has lost a child. Earlene sends Carina, Cody and me down the street looking for a K-Mart because I want to take Cody in the hotel pool and he needs "Swimmies" (a special diaper to wear in the water.)

I am thinking about what Earlene's house looks like, and if she has her husband's pictures all over the bedroom dresser. I think about sweet Claire and wonder what she is doing on this day, the 30th of January, the day before the big bad day. My active imagination is in full swing. I go back to my Kindergarten year when I stepped on a dead bird near the creek behind my house. I was horrified, and I couldn't get over the sensation of a cold, lifeless thing which used to have a beating heart. I can't get this bird out of my mind. Do sensitive people torture themselves on purpose, or do we just have trouble turning off our minds?

Carina interrupts my mind with a complaint that we've been walking too long and that there is still no K-Mart in sight. We look at each other sharing a moment of confusion when a very nice gardener asks us where we are headed; he points out that the walk to K-Mart is another 25 minutes or so. Luckily we stumble into a funny little store, which oddly enough, carries Swimmies. We make our purchase and head back to the hotel.

We walk slowly, enjoying the peaceful quality of Port Hueneme. Cody gets excited about seeing the hotel pool, so we ride down the elevator. Simple pleasures delight my son. Carina stays in the room, wanting to look over her college papers. It is good to occasionally separate from one another. We get along the best when we take little breaks. I take Cody in the hot tub, holding him close to me. There is nothing quite like the feel of his head on my shoulder, or the way he conforms to my body. I notice some people on lawn chairs out on the patio talking. I try not to stare, but there is a man with sadness on his mustache, I know his mustache, I know his face, I've studied it.

He smiles at Cody, as people usually do. I introduce myself to him, and sure enough, I'd seen him in LA right after the crash. We were part of the small family group getting status reports at the hotel. He lost his daughter and her fiancé. I marvel at my brain's ability to recall, even in intense grieving, a sad mustached face I'd seen no more than once.

After Cody and I dry off, people begin convening in the patio/bar area near the pool. Earlene is there with her family; other familiar people are eating popcorn and pulling chairs together. I am busy holding a cup of cranberry juice upright for Cody. A mother always knows when her children will spill and they are generally a split second too slow to catch it. Cody throws his towel down and sits on his knees eating popcorn and making funny faces at people. When people come up and ask his name, he wants to run with his plate of popcorn, teasing anyone interested in pursuing this game. I find it cute for a minute, but am suddenly hit with the sobering thought of these people, all connected to Flight # 261 like me, I don't want to be chasing a two year old any longer. By the fourth or fifth time I scoop him up spilling cranberry juice, while nervously picking up his popcorn trail, I realize it is best to go upstairs.

My back aches from twisting and turning, and I want to sit with adults. I feel teary and alone upon entering the hotel room. Carina asks me about dinner plans. I am supposed to meet with the President of NADA (National Air Disaster Alliance) but I feel anything but cheerful and friendly. It's getting dark, and the looming anniversary date is slowly crawling up my legs like a slithering snake, illuminating a pain I wish to keep private.

We eat sushi out, come home and light a candle. Cody is in a good mood and plays with a bag of toys we've brought from home, occasionally asking us to read him a book. Carina becomes fascinated with a local story on the television news involving a high-speed chase. I settle on top of our king size bed next to her. After two hours, the drunken father behind the wheel has surrendered to the police. I surrender to exhaustion. Cody falls asleep and Carina makes sure that we blow out the candles before we close our eyes.

In the darkness, I listen to the strange sounds of the ice machine down the hall. I take a deep whiff of Cody's hair, Johnson's *No More Tears* mixed with sweat and boyish bouncing. Carina's mouth drops open ever so little, revealing a glint of metal from her braces. Her face even in sleep, bears a look of determination, just like her Grandmothers.

One of Carina's grandmothers' spirit has taken flight just a few miles away, in the Pacific Ocean near the Channel Islands. The other grandmother she has never met. She lives in El Salvador, where Carina's picture hangs on the wall of a poor but clean apartment in San Salvador. I hoped both grandmothers can steer my daughter in beautiful directions from where they reside.

I think of all of our family group, and where they all might be on this evening, waiting for the 31st to roll around. No matter where I end up on any given January 30th, I want to light a candle and have my children near enough to smell their hair. I ask only that I wake up next to them in order to face the thirty-first day of that winter month.

I toss and turn a lot during the night, but wake up quickly as the sun rises. I want to go to the beach and find the monument, but I decided instead to attend the church service, Carina reminds me that she will watch Cody in the morning, but definitely does not want to go to church.

As I blow my hair dry, I give myself a strong maternal stare in the mirror. I look older and more tired. What do I really want to do or accomplish today, on this most sacred and dreaded day? After a long exhalation, I catch the reflection of Cody pulling something long and white behind him into the hotel room doorway. He is pulling the toilet paper as he walks. By the time I pick him up, he is wrapped inside the paper, not wanting to be interrupted.

I feel a sudden loss of patience. I am claustrophobic, bored, snappy. I don't want to be in a hotel room with a two year old. Hell, I want to be at home. But home means phones ringing and people at the door and what I would do on this day anyway? Let helium balloons go again? Scream?

Cry? Reflect? I do that all the time anyway! No solution solves this dilemma of what to do. Poor Cody is only being an inquisitive, healthy two year old. I have no right to be annoyed, to feel boxed-in and tired of saying no; "No" to the hundredth time he tries to pick up the hotel telephone or sticks a pen in the air conditioner.

Tears of frustration form in my eyes, and I don't want Carina to see. I flash back to the first week staying in a hotel room after the crash, how I put a towel under the door and over my face to muffle my crying noises. Here I am three years later, still trying to hide tears from my daughter. Same characters, same problems, and three long years later, we are still in hotel rooms with the same holes in our broken hearts.

I put on a dress, surprised at how warm the day is already, so early in the morning. The sun streams in through the window, and I am relieved I am able to make a decision. I call Paige, my dear comrade from Seattle. She had e-mailed me her cell phone number so we could get together. She answers on the first ring, saying of course, she'd love to take me with her to the church service. I kiss the kids goodbye, give Carina a ten-dollar bill and head down to the lobby. This is my first moment alone. Proudly, I wear my family buttons, all five, and somehow am surprised by how incredibly vulnerable I feel without Cody. Cody, has been my buffer from the world. How easy it has become to face people when they tell me how lucky I am to have such a cute little child. Much better than having everyone feeling sorry for me. As much as I need my breaks, I miss Cody the second he is out of my view.

As I stand in the lobby, it overwhelms me to view all of these people in different colors, sizes and ages wearing their mourner's buttons. We learn to wear on the outside what drives us from the inside. I never thought I would be wearing a button as a tribute to my lovely and humble little family.

Paige gives me a great big familiar hug. Everything stops for a second. It doesn't matter where we are. When pain meets pain, it holds and connects, and whatever else is around temporarily freezes. Nothing matters except the shared feelings in that embrace.

I sit in the back of Paige's car with her cello rolling around on me everytime we go around curves. It is really nice to meet Steve, her new husband. They are newly married. Paige has worked like a tireless warrior with the preparation for this memorial. We first met in San Francisco as attending our first Flight 261 family meeting. I have been continually impressed with her seemingly innate ability to put emotion into action; all along she has encouraged all of us on the west coast to meet regularly and network our resources.

On the way to the church, Paige and I catch up on one another's busy lives. She's very devoted to her new husband and has grown softer and happier since our last encounter in Seattle. Her sadness is obviously still there, but there she wears a big smile I have not witnessed before.

We pull into the church parking lot, one car in this big caravan of cars. As I walk up the to the entrance of the church, a familiar scent of incense takes over. This was the old church in Mexico I knew as a visitor, and the aroma of mass and funeral services of Catholic services. I walk in with Paige, and Steve, and Paige's one hundred pound cello. Paige looks for the music director. A sweet quietness reigns in this church. To my left and right are huge poster boards bearing the airplane victim's pictures. In front of me is a table with pretty, smiling women looking at a list and handing out white carnations.

I look across the vast church and see Paige, now sitting near the podium. She softly begins playing her cello.

I wish for a minute that I had a job and a talent like hers, to simply *play*. I do not feel like looking at the pictures of everyone and finding their names on this list. I remind myself that I am here to pay respect, that it is okay to be a welcomed mourner, a taker if you will. I don't have to make coffee and clean up anyone's mess. For once, Cody isn't under my feet or in my arms. This is the time I've been needing. I feel my resistance as well as my tears of redemption and grace. I walk up to the carnation table. "Good morning ma'am, who are you here to represent?"

"Well, there are actually five, Jean Permison, Robert Ost, and on I went with my list. A beautiful mouthful I can say without taking a breath. Over the last year, I have perfected this monologue of names without my voice breaking. The women hands me my five carnations with their names typed neatly on pieces of attached paper." "I am so sorry" she says, looking straight at me, touching my arm gently.

I walk with Steve towards the front of the church. As I ease into my chair, I simply take notice of things – a huge wooden Jesus suspended in the air, stained glass, cathedral ceilings, and an unmistakable presence of peace.

The tears surface, slowly they fall. A warm salty tear falls into my mouth. My mouth and chin began to twitch, as I look around this filled cathedral, knowing how loved our eighty eight angels were. The man with the big mustache I saw at the pool area the day before not only lost his daughter, but his son was killed in a motorcycle accident five years prior. Paige told me this during our ride to the church, and I was stunned and numb. He walks up to the podium with his wife to read a scripture, and I weep for the unfairness in this couple's life. The aromatic incense permeates the congregation, and the pastor speaks of the pain we all share, but gently reminds us that the passengers are home now. I feel it. I know it. I cry for my longing for all of them, for their unfinished lives, for the wreckage and debris and broken innocent lives all over the ocean. I cry also for the pain that never goes away.

As a pregnant woman in her ninth month will automatically go into a certain position and simply give birth under the right circumstances, I truly believe that grief will spill out and beautifully take you to where you need to be. As you are moved forward, you stand still in the moment of vulnerability and redemption, like a chosen handful of sand in the slack tide.

Sitting in a church, a place I do not frequent anymore, I feel like a tiny child sitting amongst big walls and pillars. The church is foreign to me, as is the city and neighborhood

I am in. The one familiar part is that I felt the presence of something greater than myself, it is finally okay to absolutely sob and shake and squeeze my insides with the emptiness of grand loss. The fact that this is the third anniversary is only an added coincidence. I have entered the present moment, and in this moment nothing feels safer or more natural or free flowing than pools of tears. And so they keep flowing.

At one point the organ player sings a song of hope where each victim's name is mentioned. He sings "On Eagle's Wings" with another woman from the church, as I reach complete nirvana. I realize that although my heart will be broken for the rest of my life, this moment has brought me enough peace to face acceptance. This realization comes to me in a flash. It may change at any time. My anger will never subside, but at last I am witnessing the coming of peace with this horrible situation I cannot change.

The Prasad family, an extremely close family from the Fiji Islands, come forth with a basket of pictures of the passengers. Paige and I walk up together with our sentimental photos and place them, too, in the basket. A special candle is lit and then 88 small white candles are also passed out and immediately lit. The entire congregation comes to the front of the church and holds hands. From where I stand, I can see a cluster of smiles peering out of this basket. It has been left so simply on the altar, but there is a richness and stillness emanating from the basket like sacred smoke. I see a little piece of Emily's face covered by Paige's parents in a vacation picture while a picture of another couple kissing lies proudly on top of a gray haired smiling lady. They were our families, flying together, dying together. They had very little in common, they had everything in common.

As I look around the church, I see, hear, and feel an enormous surge of love, yet in the same breath I cannot look away from the sorrow. The bodies in this basket of photographs, these empty shells, can no longer voice joy or sorrow or hope. They will never laugh or cry again. We have a sobering responsibility to keep their dreams and their spirits alive. The debt we've inherited is to be compassionate people who live passionately. I know my five angels lived just that way, and the wonderful people I have met through all of is have all directly or indirectly informed me that their loved ones also were joyful and loved their lives. They were all doing incredibly "well" on the day of the crash. They all seemed to be on a mission of doing good things for the world and achieving personal goals. They were the kind of people who were quietly very hard on themselves, as they had so much to accomplish. They were modest but confident, always striving to do more, to live life even to a fuller level. So there you have it. The depth of grief and loss is so overwhelmingly powerful and strong during this memorial service, but that is only the logical consequence of their leaving us- we miss them, we need them, there is a infinite void without them.

It is not clear as to why I am able to cry in a way I haven't in a long time during this service. It is for all that I mentioned and for all of the emotions I struggle to find words to describe. It is for the horrific way in which my loved ones met their death. I cry for the mountain thick barrier I cannot cross, knowing I will never see them again. I had told them I loved them before they left but the words do not seem enough. I weep for the hugs I will not feel again. I weep for the advice I will not hear, the new memories not to come. The sadness swirls around my body until a piece of anger separates from my core and begins to wake up my senses. It is for the unfairness and gross negligence, which took their last breaths. I feel as if I am in a foreign country and cannot speak the language to argue for justice. How can innocent lives be taken and nobody goes to jail? How can a rich multi-million dollar corporation send well-dressed men into a room with me and offer an amount of money as a settlement? How will getting a check make my pain go away? How can any person or business put a price tag on another person's life? Conversely, how will forgiving them and refusing money as compensation defuse my rage? Who can assure me that another plane will not go down because of improper maintenance and corner cutting? Either way, there are no winners. We are all losers. As I said during a mediation meeting last March, we've all lost. Alaskan Airlines lost their plane, crew, co-pilot and pilot, along with the confidence of hundreds of thousands.

The music becomes more euphoric and then Paige plays her cello again. I cry because somewhere in me, I feel that there is more to life than ultimate death. I can almost feel my five angels around me as well as the eighty-three others. I feel everybody who has ever loved me simply holding me, nodding their heads respectfully. I feel forgiveness for things I have said or not said in my lifetime, things which hurt others. I feel my two children being born, and I see my parents and Bob smiling at me. I feel my insides shaking and a sensation of weakness, of being orphaned runs through my body. My candle had a small but steady flicker when I realize that the congregation is now moving outside to the big patio entrance.

After the last candle goes out, our service ends. Paige talks to a reporter, and I choose to remain private. I walk back in to the church to get my purse and collect the pictures in the basket. Passing the poster boards, I see my mother's big sunshine face. I don't want to get up close to it. I pick up my belongings and realize that very few people are inside, I can pay my respects to the pictures without people taking notice. As I touch the names on my five carnations, I pick my head up. I didn't have any coffee in the morning and now I feel a little headache coming on. My eyes hurt from crying. It is that heaviness in the upper lids I remember from when the pain takes over your throbbing head. I look at my mom's smiling eyes from six inches away, then Bob's, Emily's and Ileana's. My body begins to shake and a very masculine sounding moan comes out from my diaphragm. I feel both of my eyes shut and all I can do is release this torn up prisoner from within.

Somebody begins to stroke my back; a woman with light hair, visibly upset as well. I am not ready to open my eyes and see just yet; I see only the figure of her body. She asks me who I am mourning for, and I am only able to touch their faces and their names. We manage to look at each other, and she nods her head when I tell her Bob was my brother. "I lost mine too," she says. "His name was Wil." I realize immediately who Wil was. He was the man traveling with Jay. We hold one another as I tell her how JoVanna was so important to me. We have learned about one another through her. It is a powerful moment. I want to tell her how surreal the loss of a sibling is, I want to know if he comes to her in dreams, if she thinks about their childhood a lot, if they fought in restaurants and teased waitresses if they didn't bring extra whip cream on their hot chocolates. All that I can squeak out are mumblings about JoVanna. My eyes are burning and she doesn't look very happy either. I find Paige and Steve and we walk silently back to the car, holding the poster boards to carry back to the beach service. I wonder if I can do this kind of purging again in few hours. The song "On Eagle's Wings" keeps going around and around my head. I feel God, or Spirit, or the presence of something very grand in the core of my being.

The sun warms me in the backseat driving home from the service. I admit to Paige and Steve that I didn't expect to have the strong reaction I did. I feel like a kid who took a bad fall from the playground. I am just getting cleaned up, catching my breath.

We wonder about accountability on the part of the airlines and the manufacturer of the plane. We talk about keeping our anger and staying vocal about preventing another crash, but at the same time trying to enjoy our lives. I suppose that means finding peace again. I suppose it's that damn balancing act we are supposed to do everyday. I suppose after three years we should be getting it close to right.

I hate the time frames associated with healing so much that I have become incredibly sarcastic about them. As we drive quietly, I notice all of the billboards and strip malls in the distance, I think of John Liotine being in Florida with his family. As I am new to this area, John and his family are also new to theirs, getting to know schools, strip malls and parks, I assume. I think of how difficult it must be to be in a new state, to be looking for work. I think of how heroic it was for him to risk personal and professional attack for doing the right thing. I recall the old Crosby, Stills, Nash, and Young song, "Ohio", about the killing of protesters of Vietnam at Kent State. Steven Stills sings a line that reminds me of John. "How can you run when you know?"

John couldn't be thanked enough if each victim's surviving family member telephoned or wrote to him every single day. I wish I had money, even a little money, to secretly put in his bank account. No warning, no fanfare, just a thank you note and some money to make his life a little easier. One day I will make sure this happens. I will make this transfer on the way to my volunteer job with Hospice, or to elementary schools where I can help students with sudden loss. But for now, I am lighting my candles for John Liotine. His being thanked must be coming in another form, in another time. I still can't believe that he was the *only* mechanic to come forward and challenge a working condition, one which has no regard to safety, prevention and the sanctity of human life. How could these people at Alaskan Airlines live with themselves?

Sometimes going to church causes me to see things in very black and white terms. There are very good people and very bad people. I can't stop thinking about John Liotine trying to save our families' plane. If Mother Teresa had a son, he would be John. I have always believed in the law of karma. It bothers me that John's employers lied about him, and that they probably have big bank accounts. Those criminals didn't have to relocate and move in with their in-laws. As far as I know, today John and his wife Debbie are substitute teaching in Florida trying to raise four children with a substitute teaching salary. This is no reward for integrity.

Paige and I get cups of coffee to go upon returning, we arrange to meet at the memorial site. Carina and Cody have had a nice morning together. They are sandy and excited. They've been swimming and are in good spirits. We head downstairs and drive to the beach. It's just a short drive, but we take the car because I want to be sure Cody has all of his necessary paraphernalia.

There is plastic around the monument, but through it, the beautiful curves, color, and flow of the dolphins are vaguely visible. The sundial stands twelve feet high, looking bold and proud in this southern California afternoon sun. People walking around it, touching the nameplates very slowly and carefully.

We stand in a long line and get some boxed lunches. Every time I look at my watch, I become more uneasy. It's approaching 3:00, and the ceremony is set to begin soon. Cody seems very hungry and sleepy, so I push him in the stroller, leaving Carina with some friends. Earlene has offered to let her family members take roses up for our designated five if nobody else from our family shows up (I am expecting Charlie's daughters, but things may have changed at the last minute. I am uncertain they'll arrive before the ceremony begins). Each of the eighty-eight chairs has a sticker bearing the name of the crash victim. Each has a red rose sitting in the middle of the seat. I take this in and decide to walk Cody in the stroller down the pier. I am feeling nervous. My eyes are very swollen from the morning. I turn around to see hundreds of people behind me. As proud as I feel of wearing my button representing all five, I feel a twinge of wanting to hide. I do not want to show them off. My loss suddenly feels like a topic I have obsessed over too much. I think maybe I should talk about it less.

I stroll Cody over to a fish market restaurant with a fast food window. It is now a few minutes after 3:00. I order him a piece of fish and fantasize living here in Port Hueneme. I would be a regular mom walking my kid on the pier. I would have my parents and family nearby and, my husband would have his; our lives would be simple and easy. There would be no fights with the airlines, no loss to agonize over in the middle of the night. It is a very quick but satisfying daydream.

I stared down at my button showing Mom and Charlie looking delightful at a dinner party with a bottle of wine.

Bob, Ileana, and baby Emily smile brightly during their first Christmas as a family of three. In a moment I must march back to the crowd of hundreds and walk a rose proudly to each of their nameplates on the monument. I must stand up and be counted so that they may also be counted. Looking at my watch, I quickly make my way back through the crowd navigating Cody safely through the sea of legs. Before long, the music begins, speeches are made by the family members who've spent time and energy planning and executing the reality of this monument. What strikes me most is how many chairs make up the space of eighty-eight missing people. What strikes me more is the ashen look of so many mourners just like me. Even with make-up, lipstick, the sunshine, and camera's flashing, we all seemed to own the same pallor, suffer from the same rash, the same disease, the same rotten secret.

The sound system is terrible, but the powerful sentiment and the flow of the service marking this third anniversary are healing and good. But Cody grows a bit restless and begins calling me "Janis", chanting my name over and over. I catch myself sighing and wanting to be alone. The Hall family who has lost their daughter tolls a bell after each name is called out. The moment between the names and the sound of this holy bell is both timeless and gigantic. I wonder for a split second whether I should walk up with Cody when Bob's name is called, or if I should deliver his rose alone. By the time my mind registers his name being spoken, I am up and walking. It is a weighty and stiff walk. I feel my mouth and chin tremble. Damn it, everything is just coming out today. The monument artist, Bud Bottoms, has placed each victim/passenger with their families, so our five are placed next to one another. Somehow seeing five red long stemmed roses and the three with the name "Ost" I grew up with makes me feel terribly cursed. I looked around me, there is a moment of silence at 4:22 and then we slowly file out to the beach.

In a blind fury of tears, I notice a man in uniform. "Ma'am, did you see the rainbow?' he asks excitedly. All that I can do is nod my head. As he opens his mouth to speak of this incredible beauty in the sky, I have, in the same moment, noticed a full on rainbow. But there had been no rain. I am surprised by how sunny and bright the day is. I am wearing a sleeveless dress and it has stayed warm all day.

A small part of me feels embarrassed by my tears. I am in awe of this multi-colored phenomenon. Either this is a "sign" from the other side or a brilliant coincidence. Either way, I want to smile; I want to appreciate the beauty and peace of the day; yet the miserable abandoned sensation takes over again. As I walk a few feet to the shore, helicopters fly overhead and bagpipers play "Amazing Grace". I compose myself and surrender to a peaceful feeling.

Charlie's son-in-law is holding Cody, and I am able to be a woman in touch with her senses as opposed to being a needed mother.

A friendly red haired man approaches me. He's a local, and was on a nearby island when the plane went down. Once in the military, he wears a nametag that tells me his name is Kevin. He says that these days he installs and maintains phone wires on San Nicholas Island (where the book "Island Of the Blue Dolphins" takes place). He wants me to know he did everything he could to assist with the search and rescue of flight 261. He was part of the Coast Guard, and wishes to God he could have done more. His face becomes a grimace, as he appears to mentally recall the scene. The surge of compassion floods his face. He goes on to tell me that he's been burning sage and making prayers regularly for our families when he walks on the beach. He points out the exact spot the plane went down.

I immediately feel gratitude towards this stranger. As tired as I am, as heavy as my eyelids have grown; I want to hug this good citizen. He gives me his card and asks me to contact him if I think of anything he might be able to do to ease my pain. I ask him to continue his prayers and ask if he will please visit this monument often. He walks to his truck to retrieve an abalone shell he wants to pass on for smudging sage. I get caught up talking to other people, suddenly feeling emotionally exhausted. Cody now seems overtired, covered in sand; the scene depicts the expression "enough already."

I turn around to see if Kevin is returning to the parking area with his shell, but I can see only a mound of hugging people and it dawns on me that I need to slip away. I fold the stroller up, tuck it in the car, and promise Carina we'll take it easy for the rest of the day. I look at my watch; it is close to 6:00 pm. The sun is quickly disappearing. As I signal to leave the parking lot, I take a final glance at the dolphin statue, feeling utterly connected to it.

We return to the hotel room, where I feel homesick and want a hot bubble bath. I draw one, and feel Cody and I sink into it, as I recount the day in my mind. My tears are complete, I am tired, yet pleased that there have been both blessings and cathartic moments. Cody falls asleep on the bed a few minutes later. Charlie's daughters come to the door, but we decide to get together the following day, going out again would be too much for us. I look up nearby restaurants that will deliver to our hotel room, feeling quite thrilled that I won't have to face any more people. As infrequently as I get in touch with this feeling, I am appreciative of the ability to know when others' company will be an overload. I am realizing that it's okay to say, "no thank you."

The warm aroma of Italian food fills our room within half an hour or so, and my beautiful daughter and I eat together in silence. A yellow candle flickers gently above the TV we we are ignoring. Cody wakes a few hours later, eats some ravioli, and gets his second wind. Carina and I take turns pulling him back off the night table, putting the hotel phone back on the hook, and running interference between objects he wants to hold, and safety. At one point we look at each other, and almost at the same time, and say, "Cody needs a drive, let's get out of here!"

We recall Earlene's infamous information of the whereabouts of K-Mart, and figure we'll take a drive there, allowing Cody to run off some excess energy. I cannot remember Carina ever being so bouncy. We stroll the aisles of K-Mart, spending a chunk of time in the messy toy section. My eyes are now burning, and I feel uncomfortable from overeating the Italian food. I miss the comforts of home, wishing it were the morning and we could hit the freeway. We find an inexpensive toy cash register with play food and money; needless to say Cody is thrilled and wants to play with it. We drive back to the hotel, and Cody is very excited to try out his new goods. Carina asks me if I can give her some free time, so I take Cody and his new grocery store paraphernalia.

Paige is speaking to the receptionist up front. I find her and invite her to join me for a conversation near the fireplace, in the lounge. Cody plays with his new toy while we talk about sadness being an everyday part of our lives. We share our disgust for criminal activities conducted by the airlines and the anger that prevails in our hearts as a result. We talk about Paige's new niece, excited at the thought of Paige and Steve being blessed with a child. Cody gathers pamphlets from the hotel lobby advertising places to visit and he begins passing them out to people. He runs down the hallway, or up the stairs, and it's difficult to finish a conversation. Eventually we give up. Cody has one, but his presence has proved our point. I walk Paige to her car, and spend a little time with Fred Miller, a very kind man whose daughter Abigail was on the plane. He assures me that his suit of armor is on, as he was prepared for the big "fight" in June. Our jury is set to begin on June 3rd. Fred shares some candy from his pocket with Cody. Cody sits in his arms, laughing at a trick Fred would pull, offering him candy and then hiding it. I see the love and compassion in this father, and suffer a sudden bout of sadness as I realize he will never have grandchildren from his departed daughter. I pray he has other children who may one day make him a grandfather. We say goodnight and hope to stay in touch via e-mail. He makes me miss my own father. I know all the reasons why my father simply can't be at these functions, and still I wish he could be less stubborn and more like me. I guess this shows my own stubbornness! I wish I could have speak more with Fred, but Cody is getting a little too excited, and I know it's time to wrap things up and go to bed.

Sometime in the middle of the night, I put my nose as close as I can to Cody's hair, inhaling the strong scent of Johnson's Baby Shampoo. I stroke his cheeks, cover Carina with more blankets, and sigh. I feel the anguish of the tens of thousands of people feeling especially torn up tonight as we reflect on the murders of our parents, grandparents, children, siblings, cousins, aunts, uncles, nieces, nephews, husbands, wives, lovers, co-workers, friends, neighbors, fellow human beings. As sad as I felt during this day, I now have my children in bed with me, and this alone gives me courage to inhale, exhale, trust, and go to sleep. Cody's hair has never smelled so sweet.

Carina & Cody

292

Inspirational People

My father is inspirational to me because he keeps on going. He doesn't bullshit anybody about where he stands. He has become more liberal as he gets older, which goes against the norm. He identifies most with people of color and those who struggle. He wears old clothes and refuses to learn how to use a computer. He has a bunch of old typewriters and bottles of White Out, this is what he knows and where he stays.

His letters to the editor are printed in the local paper a few times a week; he is notorious among his neighbors and friends for his leftist politics and disgust for current affairs, the waging of an unjust war, and corrupt politicians. He tells dirty jokes, yet encourages people to have self-respect. When we were kids he let my brother and I call him "Arthur" instead of "Dad." My father is a study in complexity, yet he can be a calming presence. This is Arthur.

He was our family clown, the butt of our jokes, the topic of conversation. He chained himself to the Lincoln Memorial when he was a young man because a black man was framed. The press didn't come. He fell off of a ten speed bike when Bob and I were kids because he refused to listen to us when we informed him that ten speeds have hand brakes. (This wasn't an old fashioned bike from the 1940's, he would *have* to listen to us.) He got stitches and still grumbled that nobody told him he couldn't stop the bike with his feet.

Bob and I used to take turns throwing out his old holey hats, he would then find them in dumpsters and wear them the next day. Even today, he works out at the gym and then goes directly to Taco Bell. He has his own way of doing things.

Arthur misses my brother, Ileana and baby Emily and talks to people about them often. The only way he is surviving is by fooling himself into thinking they are still on their vacation. When he comes over, he has to remain sitting in his car for a few minutes, recovering from the curvy trip through the Santa Cruz Mountains. The older he gets, the harder and longer the trip seems to be. Eventually he comes into the house where he slowly sips diet Pepsi and says, "Oy-vay" for the next hour or so. His suitcase is old and broken; it carries a few toiletries, ripped trousers, a jar of Tylenol and mis-matched socks. He brings unusual food items, becoming excited about the prospect of getting me to make his instant mashed potatoes, or try his Israeli cereal. God only knows where he finds these things.

He gives rubber band balls and dollars to the young ones, free advice and Dr. Phil kind of "Think-more-of-yourself" lectures to the rest of us. He speaks fast and loud, in as New York accent. He does crossword puzzles, everyday. He leaves a trail of tissues wherever he goes. My father knows he makes me crazy with this, but I almost look forward to finding them, which translates to finding which room he is in. His idiosyncratic routines are unchanging. He makes me take him to buy lotto tickets (he still hasn't won even though he blows five dollars every Wednesday and Saturday). He sleeps for a while, talks about politics, and then is ready to eat.

When I make his bed in the morning, I find candy wrappers and little pieces of candy stuck to the pillow case. I lecture him about choking. He turns into my little boy, somehow. Since nobody cooks for him, it feels good to bake him some chicken and pour him a glass of wine. Bob gets brought up consciously and unconsciously during his visits, and Arthur looks at me in the eye (but only for a second) and says, "I miss Bobby." I know he also misses the only woman he ever loved.

My father's life has not been easy. I really don't know his dreams, but they are interchangeable with service. What is Arthur Ost passionate about? Civil rights and fair politics. Everybody having food and shelter. An abolishment of prejudice and racism. He loves his grandchildren, limericks, and showing off his ability to speak in five languages fluently. He loves helping people. This keeps him alive.

Arthur talks about going to France, but I can't see him missing his Second Harvest Food Bank volunteer days or checking in to see if his neighbors need anything. I have bothered him about moving closer since the Bob's death, but he is unable to make a decision about moving. He claims he is in the process of getting rid of things, sorting through papers, etc. But I am certain that he is stuck. Nobody goes into his house, into his world. There is a "commons" or recreation room in his apartment building, and that is the only place he will meet us these days. He knows I want to help, but he will not accept help in this way. His car is messy, and so is his crowded apartment, at least it was the last time I saw it, many years ago. We had an extra room built in our house in case he ever wants to live with us, but I have to remember my father has lived alone for over twenty years. We get on his nerves when we occasionally vacuum, which he can't seem to understand.

I worry about Arthur driving over Highway 17, but more than that, I worry that he won't be alive forever. I am terrified of his leaving. He picks at his fingers and his bald and brilliant head all of the time. He is eccentric and simple, independent and tortured at the same time.

What inspires me is that he is a fighter. What makes me smile is the fact that he is his own, authentic person. He is so young at heart, full of mischief and questions. I don't think he has ever lifted the hood of his car or replaced batteries in anything. He is a poet and a feminist, a gentleman and an enigma.

I used to wish he lived neater, or knew how to nurture me the way my mother did, but this is not him. I've wished he golfed or collected art and thus he would find positive things to do in his old age. At eighty-three years old, he still participates in marches to end wars or gain health care for farm workers. He seems to enjoy complaining, not letting up on issues that are important to him. Occasionally he enjoys rock concerts, and recently, he let me introduce him to sushi. I love this ageless, sarcastic, perfect speller more than he can ever know. God bless his funny habits, his tenacity to be himself, this stamina he has to keep on getting up everyday.

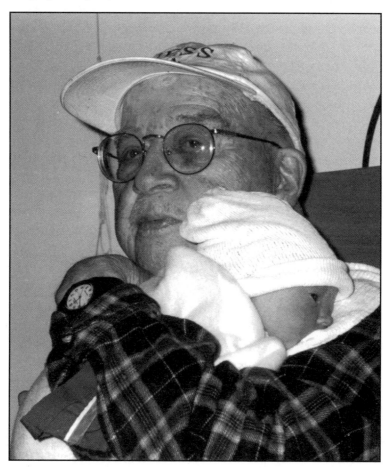

Grandpa Arthur & Cody

Dan Adragna

Dan Adragna was dating a good friend, Georgina, with whom I used to teach. After years of persistence, I finally convinced her to answer a personal ad. She met Dan and had been going out with him for all of a few weeks. I was very interested in this courtship; she had been filling me in. Georgina had been raising her daughter alone for years. She and Dan took things slowly, but there was definite potential.

It was Christmas, 1995. Georgina and I planned to double date over Christmas break, and we were very excited. But Dan had caught the flue and he wasn't recovering. He was diabetic, but he had never had any episodes. He went to the doctor, and they told him to go home and drink fluids. After a few days, he was like a zombie and his son drove him to emergency. He went into a coma. When I met him, he was completely knocked out, in another zone, breathing through a machine. He looked like he'd been in a wreck of some kind. Although I had never met him before, I was tearing up in his closed-eyed presence. I remember hanging out with his parents and Georgina in the hospital waiting room, periodically hearing updates on his progress which looked very dismal.

At that time I was teaching Kindergarten, it was my first full-time teaching position. I figured I would be spending a lot of time decorating my classroom and just enjoying Christmas break, but I was deeply affected by Dan's situation. He was only a few years older than me, it just wasn't fair that this seemingly nice and recently healthy man was fighting for his life. I would call Georgina or she would call me and we would just sit with Dan while he was in the coma, in this white hospital room, without saying a word. He could roll his eyes a little. His hair was matted, his nose was black and blue from tubes and oxygen tanks, but he had these amazing happy and dancing Italian eyes which glistened from his confused face. He had so many friends coming by; there were big poster boards with pictures of Dan in different places with various people.

In him, I saw a vibrant man wrestling with a very sick man. After several weeks, doctors told Dan's family to prepare for death. Dan's legs had been amputated right below the knees due to gangrene that had set in because his blood wasn't circulating. Georgina and I continued to visit him regularly; I brought him a sucker once, as he wasn't eating. He smiled so big and pumpkin like. He wasn't talking, but he sure could acknowledge people and let them know he knew what was going on.

Dan came home from this hospital after this horrible ordeal a few months later. He and Georgina stayed friends, and then eventually drifted apart, as he was too sick to really carry on a new relationship. He moved back to his parent's house in San Jose to be rehabilitated. I will always idolize Dan Adragna for his ability to hang so tough. He ended up giving up his house and profession as an electrician since he was no longer able to perform the same physical labor. He got prosthetics, and amazingly he learned to walk again, slowly gaining upper body strength. What struck me was his glowing smile and spirit, like he was the proudest person alive. He said he was *"with God"* a lot, going through some very powerful interactions. Dan spoke about it openly in his church. I went to hear him speak several times, sitting in the back of the church alone, reminiscing the impact he had on my life. Once I brought a plant to the church, and gave him a card explaining he wouldn't remember me because we had never been formally introduced since our contact had occurred when he had been in a coma. Although he is a very devout Christian, Dan has always respected where I come from. He has told me if and when I was ready to hear how close God was, he would tell me.

I bump into Dan at strange times in my life, and he still impresses the heck out of me. He volunteered one day to be with my students and help them with math. Due to his many operations, his larynx was cut and thus he has a very throaty voice, which took my students by surprise a little. Once my students got past this difference, they fought for his attention. He showed them shortcuts with their math and encouraged them to go to college. It was a really neat visit for everyone.

When I bought a hot tub a few months after the crash, I called Dan to ask him about wiring it. He drove right over, climbed up on the counter and came up with this creative but practical rig job. Yes, it worked perfectly.

I gave him a massage once, and was completely humbled by his comfortable attitude toward his new body. Dan has been a hero to me, and last summer I attended his wedding. He found a sweet, young bride from the Midwest, who, interestingly enough, works with people with disabilities. I sat in the back of the church, as Dan knows I always do, holding Cody in my arms, as my friend walked down the aisle. The pastor was cracking jokes about Dan not having a leg to stand on, and people were laughing. All of us had been through Dan's hardships over the years, and his pastor was very close to him so it was okay to make fun in a loving way. Dan's ability to laugh at his own predicament gives further testimony to the extent he has truly healed.

I used to joke with him about the way women always loved him, no matter what. When he first went back to junior college to re-learn a profession, women in his classes wouldn't leave him alone. I believe his spirit is so good and strong it's become a magnet for people. He and his young wife are going to try to have kids (his are grown). I tell everybody my Dan story. He could have given up, feeling really sorry for himself. Something humbled him; in his loss he was forced to re-define himself. I am like a child at the ocean, wanting to be close to the water, but suddenly feeling afraid when I ask Dan about his conversations with God. His new life is a miracle in the same way that Cody is a miracle. Both of our stories affirm life. We both somehow are making the best out of lousy situations. Where we are different though, is that Dan doesn't feel sorry for himself. He believes in God enough to let him take over.

I still struggle with feeling sorry for my situation, and I want to be independent enough to recovery without believing in anything too much. I often think of the time I found

Dan sitting in front of my house when I returned from Southern California right after the crash. He was just sitting in his car on my quiet cul-de-sac. We both somehow found each other during the worst times of our lives. The best memory, the real story, was holding Cody in the chapel while Dan and Melynda got married, watching Dan glide down the aisle on his beautiful man-made legs.

Fred

My mother was constantly taking me on walks. We lived on a quiet, residential street in San Rafael, California. We lived across the street from a small body of water. If you stood directly in front of the water, you could see Richmond. Basically, there was this vast bay and big rocks. I used to climb on these rocks with my brother. My mom and dad taught me to ride my bike in front of the fire station, which was right down the street. A childhood memory that stands out the most for me involves meeting Fred. I met Fred when I entered Kindergarten. This would have been 1968. Fred was already an old man who lived between my house and the Elementary School. Perhaps I thought he lived in his garage; the door was always open as he greeted children before and after school. There was a chair he always sat in, it was the only thing I recall in the garage. I had never know my own grandfathers, and I had only met one grandmother, she lived in Brooklyn, and she died while I was in the First Grade.

Fred had white whiskers and was missing some bottom teeth. He lived with his sister. Fred's back was bent over; he must have been taller than he looked. He smiled joyfully when my mother and I passed his house on the way to and from school. My mother told me he'd never had kids, and encouraged me to draw him pictures. He was the first person to witness my trees with the big circles on the top, representing apples. He wore long sweaters and I remember seeing that he had bruises on his old, skinny hands. His sister repeated things to him when he couldn't hear. She was one of those people who didn't really know how to talk to kids, the kind that doesn't really leave a lasting impression. The kind whose voice goes up an octave or two in order to sound sweet.

I thought of Fred all of the time. I wanted him to come visit our house, but he couldn't walk much, so the only place to see him was in his garage, where he would eagerly await us in his chair. Fred had a very popular candy dish, giving our neighborhood candy everyday. My parents were health food nuts, but out of politeness, they always allowed me to take one candy after lunch.

I have some fond memories of Kindergarten and enjoyed some of the songs we sang, but mostly I remember the joy of seeing Fred. One day on the way to school, I saw that Fred's garage was closed. My feet went on strike, I remember not wanting to go to school that day. My mother kept on pulling my arm, but I was stunned to see Fred's "office" closed down.

Reluctantly, I entered a noisy classroom. There were blocks all over the place. I had trouble with my left and right, and recall crying a few times when the teacher seemed frustrated with me. This was perhaps a defining moment for me, realizing I was a sensitive kid. I am sure I enjoyed Fred's candy like the rest of the kids, but there was something that pulled me into his spirit; I knew innately that I was very attached. A few more days passed and Fred was still not to be seen. The garage remained closed, and Kindergarten felt very loud to me. I missed having this beautiful old face break out into delightful noises as I'd explain my newest painting or picture.

I am not certain how much time elapsed, but one day the garage was open and Fred's sister, whose name was not important enough for me to recall, was sweeping. She motioned for my mother and I to come in. She whispered something to my mom, and handed her a piece of paper.

Fred was in a convalescent hospital after taking a serious fall. My parents drove me out to see him. The place smelled bad. Fred had tubes in his nose and didn't say hello to me. He looked up at the ceiling. I remember his mouth being wide open. I looked inside. His sister told him loudly that I was there, no response.

On the drive home, I stared at the dots on the roof of my parent's Volkswagen. My parents were talking quietly in the front seat, it seemed important. This was the first time I recall having real tears, touching them, getting into the sensation of wetness coming out of my young eyes.

I never saw Fred again.

It was very difficult to walk in front of his house, the path I took everyday. Some neighborhood kids were talking about missing the candy, but I hated not seeing Fred's face, smelling his smell, not passing him twice a day. I missed the attention, the companionship.

Fred died, and I grew up. I recently took my 16-year-old daughter and my toddler son to the old neighborhood. It was all so different. But my memories remain perfect. When I grew up, only nice old men gave out candy. There were no perverts or murderers. The sweet memory of Fred visits me regularly. Even in my high school years, when I wanted to be tough, I was quickly reminded of Fred when I read the infamous "Catcher In The Rye." As Holden Caulfied caught people, Fred also held out his hands for people, or at least caught me, woke me up, introduced me to loving and losing. Fred's impeccable and venerable face was the first wonderful image I recall in my life, aside from my parents. I can't see my Kindergarten teacher's face, but I do see Fred's. I am eternally grateful.

As far back as I can remember, I have tried to learn a little bit from every inspirational relationship. I have watched people closely. Everybody I know has given me an opportunity to grow. I remember in massage school back in the early 1990's, my instructor Larry told us that the person on the table is getting the same effect of the massage whether they are awake and alert or asleep. His words still bring me solace; they help me to relax. It means that connections with others are still penetrating us and leaving marks even when we are not aware of it. The cheerful person making you a latte in the morning is still in your psyche, if even just a little, long after you finish your drink and go about your day. I must admit that the world is still turning me on, there are too many people to name whom I like, love, and then simultaneously become inspired by.

When I feel alone, I contemplate people and their words. I see them as little children, the people I like the most. I imagine each of their gifts and passions in different jars on shelves. I dust them and hold them respectfully. I smile, and laugh about things, and treasure their sayings. My dear friend Charles Capone says, "No means no, maybe means no, yes means a check." I quickly remember he told me this when he was teaching me about business and selling things at garage sales. I have recycled his saying over and over, applying it to so many aspects of people, promises, and life. He also invented "Teach me how to be wonderful." If you say this to difficult people, it shuts them up right away and they can go on thinking they have won you over.

A friend named Kalvis, with whom I have lost touch, told me to "hold my head up and be graceful and slow" when I doubt myself. Is this not beautiful? I carry these instructions with me.

We are all here for special reasons. Some of us deliver messages, some wake others up, some lead, follow, befriend, make big mistakes, and discover things. The people we have weeded out of our lives are also incredibly inspirational because having had negative encounters, we will avoid others like them. We will remember the lessons we learned in humility and cherish the gift of not wasting time.

I am inspired by those who look deeply and try to love others the same way they did when they were little. I am inspired by my daughter who is self-motivated in school. She claims she will be well known and very successful. While those attributes mean little to me, I believe her, and I know that she will fulfill her purpose in life. I love her focus, her self respect.

I am inspired by my mother-in-law, Naida, who doesn't gossip, who doesn't ask or tell personal things. She lives alone and shows up.

I am inspired by my girlfriend Loel who is mourning her twenty-two year old cat that died recently. I am watching Loel now through a sliding glass door, laughing as she tickles Jeanette's cat's stomach. I know Loel will love another cat.

I am inspired by Jeanette's quest to find joy and meet new people. I am inspired by my stepson Ben's completion of training in the Navy. The more I think of it, I am in awe of the human spirit, of determination. I love people getting out of their comfort zones and making slow, steady progress in a vulnerable and authentic way.

Jenni Smead, thirty years old

Jenni Smead

Jenni is thirty years old. She is the daughter of my teaching colleague and good friend John Smead. John talks about his darling daughter very often in the staff room at school.

I am intrigued with Jenni, and have found that nobody hugs like her. She has Down's Syndrome. She stutters, but with time, she expresses herself just fine. She lives in the moment. She plays solitaire, watches wrestling and cooking shows, and has pretend friends. Her room is filled with Disney movies. She reads at a First grade level, but looks at or "reads" the bible and novels every day. She can find a lot of high frequency words like "it", "I", "the", etc. Mostly, Jenni is a dancer. She practices every day and has "recitals" often. She has taken lessons since she was 3 years old.

I notice that Jenni doesn't have any worry lines on her face. She has beautiful young skin and long blonde hair. She has no worries. Again, she lives in the moment and knows Mom and Dad will help her brush her teeth, fix her meals, read to her, help her cross the street.

I adore Jenni and her simplicity. She is pure and good. I feel absolute joy when she is around. We enjoy eating together. Once I took her to a happy hour function celebrating our school's high-test scores. She devoured the appetizers and giggled after a few sips of her wine. The waitress couldn't believe she was even close to twenty-one years old. This is the beauty of Jenni. She doesn't fit in any category; she lives without fear. I feel ageless and protected when we play. She is my sweet friend.

Jamie Lebovitz

To Jamie Lebovitz, my attorney and champion, I want to say these things. I have a hunch your mother taught you well. I think you climbed upon your parent's bed in dinosaur pajamas and lay sleeping between safety and love. I think you put puzzles together effortlessly. I think you looked at maps and brushed your teeth carefully. I think you smiled brightly as you blew out each birthday candle.

I think you helped elderly people across the street and amused your chemistry teacher with your questions. I think you had a social conscience at a young age. I think you wished everything could be fair.

I imagine you were pulled aside as a young man by leaders who told you that you too could lead. I think you had an insatiable appetite for wanting to understand.

Whatever brought you to this table is unknown to me. When courageous people are asked why they commit acts of bravery, they look blankly at the person presenting the question. They see nothing more than common sense as the driving factor, or maybe good morals. I would not ask you why you make others feel safe, and why you fight for the underdogs. You might give me a blank stare. Like a child interested in holding a shell next to his ear, like an opera singer hitting a perfect pitch- certain things just are the way they are.

You have stayed next to me, watching me weep uncontrollably. You've told me that sitting in offices with insurance carriers working with the airline would not be comfortable. That answering questions about my relationship with my ghost family would haunt me. You don't say this, but you let me know they are not sincere like we are. It is not their job to welcome me. There will be no chicken soup or art books on the table that we might discuss. They don't care that Cody loves "101 Dalmatians" and can pronounce the name "Cruela." They will not care. but you do.

When we sit in a meeting with these insurance company negotiators the problem gets very clear. My family was needlessly killed because of mistakes made by men and machine. These men in suits seem robotic to me; they want me to sign a paper, so they can hand me a check and send us back to the different world we come from.

You know I cannot do this. Mentally, physically, spiritually, morally, at this time I am frozen. I look to you, at you, in these moments of panic. You give me a Kleenex, waiting for my tears to form words. You don't look at your watch at these moments. Your briefcase is firmly planted on the tile floor. You are tall and stoic and you believe in me, in my plight, in our struggle for justice. You are not chasing ambulances or covering bad news in modern cities. You are on my ruthless playground, helping me face the bullies, allowing me to stand up and spit the dirt out of my teary mouth.

This is the first time in my life I have ever felt so afraid, because I feel *hatred*. They may just be men in suits, but I don't like who they work for. I don't support big corporations who think safety is just a slogan. Something bad happened out here, and you are my advocate.

I have a hunch your mother taught you well, Jamie. When the calendar pages flip to July, our partnership on paper will officially come to a close. We will send e-mails only to stay in touch; in our later years, we may be smaller and smaller in each other's lives, like the view from a window seat on a plane. Ah, we will remember one another when we think of planes. That is inevitable.

I am afraid for the time to come when you are no longer a requirement in my life. If this were a fairy tale, you would be the perfect lawyer, and I would be the devastated daughter, sister, Auntie. We would befriend one another, working side by side to fulfill our purpose. But this story is my life, it is as real as a truck hitting and killing a deer. Nothing can repair the damage. I do not expect you to remove your mask. It will not come off, because it is your skin. Your professionalism and compassion are not of this world, they are far too great. Thank you for sticking up for me, for looking at my family pictures, and for knowing how much I love and miss them. Thank you for being someone who allowed his mother to teach him so well...

What Has Helped Me

The company of oldest and dearest friends.
Taking hot tubs outside.
Hot bubble baths, when you fist sink in and then turn off
the water, hearing silence and feeling the warmth.
Windows to look out of.
Silence.
Keith Greeninger music.
Neil Young music.
Native American sweats.
Lighting candles at night.
Lighting candles during the day.
Staying in touch with family members who have suffered
the loss of loved ones on Flight # 261.
Having a baby.
Working in a very supportive work industry (elementary
education).
People who look you straight in the eyeballs and ask you
how you are feeling.
At times, being able to laugh.
Sunshine.
Healthy food.
Rest.
The sensation of being able to taste food again.
Staring at the sky, no matter what the season is, and totally
appreciating the beauty.

Knowing in my heart of hearts that I was at complete peace with my family at the time they were killed, and that they knew I loved them unconditionally.
Being able to help others. Trying to do at least ONE random act of kindness a day.
Seeing movies, which help me to get out of my head ("I am Sam" was particularly delightful).
Occasionally getting a massage and a pedicure.
Being around emotionally stable people.
Working out at the gym, slow and deliberate on some machines, very aggressively on others- depending on my mood.
Water aerobics.
Making plans.
Breaking plans if I didn't feel like being with people.
Playing hide and go seek with my kids. (Once, while pregnant, I hid in my daughter's closet for a few minutes, watching her look for me.
She came back into her room, and still didn't see me. I jumped out at her, and scared her big time, where as we both laughed uncontrollably. It was the best feeling I think I had in a year.)
Driving around holding my husband's hand, saying nothing.
Brushing a horse's mane.
Eating sushi with just enough wasabi that my eyes water.
Spending time with Jenni, my dear friend with Down's syndrome, and getting a very meaningful hug from her.
Chewing gum.
Going to the toy store with Cody. Reading to Cody.
Nursing Cody.
Writing my truths down.
Making food for people I care about.
Being in bookstores.
Walking on the beach.
Getting acupuncture for grief.

What Hurts

Loud Noises
Too many people
Over planning my day
Bad dreams
Holidays
Seeing the logo of the Eskimo on Alaskan Airlines
airplanes
When people didn't know what to say to me, and said
nothing after the crash.
Ringing telephones
Messes to clean
People fighting around me
Caring about people who have not talked to family
members due to grievances.
Pushy people, greedy people, loud people.
Bible pushers vs. good listeners
Fraudulent "mediums" or want-to-be-psychics,
capitalizing on vulnerable people after losses.
The idea of anti-depressants vs. feeling the feelings if at all
possible.
Long, long nights when horrible visuals of violent deaths
take over.
Staring for hours at my loved ones' pictures and knowing
I will never hold them again.

The anger and absolute disgust that big corporations like The Airline Industry would jeopardize safety for profit.
Seeing laughing women my age with their mothers.
Seeing adult brothers and sisters play fighting the way my brother and I did.
Knowing that my elderly father will carry pain for his lost son for the rest of time.
Realizing my big fear-that the loss of my family will torment me for all of my life and that I will never be fully happy again. That my heart will never be full again, and thus I won't live the life I would have.

My Hope

I pray often that if I do obsess over what happened , that it won't show in an obvious way. I met Melody Beattie briefly last summer after a book signing of her new book, "Choices." She also wrote "Co-dependent No More", and has been a huge inspiration to me. She lost her sixteen year old son, Shane in a skiing accident. My good friend, Tori insisted I listen to the book she wrote about her loss called, "Lessons In Love" on tape soon after the crash. I wanted to read the book, but found that the estate responsibilities and working just wiped me out. I had no time or energy to read for awhile. I ended up listening to this book read by the author as I would drive to work in Watsonville.

The greatest joy I derived from this experience was getting that the author really did live and heal, that she kept on, at least for the sake of her daughter. After I found out I was pregnant and it was a boy, I realized how wonderful and joyful a little baby boy would be. The story, the power, the promise of healing actually carried me through for a few months. It was like my travel I.V.

When I saw Melody at her book signing, I felt that I knew her. I figured the best thing I could do was to tell her how much her story and her courage inspired me. The worst thing I could do was to say nothing to her as she signed my book.

When the situation presents itself, I try to reassure

people in my own quiet way that they will recover slowly. When I was in my lowest, darkest and deepest cave of despair, hearing that I would recover, slowly but surely, gave me hope. Talking to me must have been like talking to someone in a coma. You can't be sure they can hear. Grief can be coma-like, but somewhere in there, a little device is recording the promise and one day the message will reach the person's consciousness.

I wish I could recall verbatim what Melody said about the grieving stages, but I think she said there were really two more stages. One happens when mourners obsess over what happened, and the other is when they glorifying the recently departed in a obsessive way. Again, I can't quote her, but this is what I heard her say. What's more, I think she is entirely right. I find myself glorifying my lost family members, making them better than mortal beings, and thinking about how they died, what it was like, where they are, if they are still together, if they can feel my love still…etc.

I don't mind if people who know me well notice when I do this a little. I just don't want to ever be a bore, an immobilized glob of "Why me?" This was, after all, their death, their departure, not mine.

I MADE A CONSCIOUS DECISION TO WRITE AS A MEANS OF UNDERSTANDING AND HEAL-ING, SO I MUST WALK AN HONEST PATH. I AM WRITING FOR MYSELF FIRST AND FOREMOST. AND I KNOW I AM FAR FROM BEING ALONE.

People die suddenly and unexpectedly all of the time. It would be my greatest triumph if even one sentence in this writing journey could help somebody else who has been left behind to feel less alone and more hopeful.

Three A Day

I was sitting in the bathtub one evening thinking about balance.

Familiar words entered my mind. I could not trace the origin of these words, but I kept hearing "Do something you don't like and then reward yourself." It would be an honor to imagine I made that idea up, but I honestly do not know who told me or if it just landed in my head one day.

After the crash, my whole life became about cleaning up messes and being an administrator. I knew nothing about this kind of role, and I was in deep mourning. I spent my days teaching, and my weekends organizing my brother's files, my mother's as well, paying bills, calling insurance companies, talking with the coroners, dealing with real estate and probate law, and rarely sleeping. My life was entirely out of whack. Being completely focused and self-less allowed me to get a lot of needed work done. I learned I could take care of business.

What I didn't do was take care of myself. I had emergency acupuncture when shock and grief overtook me, and then I pretty much ignored my needs except for going to pre-natal appointments. I was adamant about trying to have Cody V-BAC (Vaginal birth after c-section) and so I went back to my acupuncturist, Phil Caylor. He did amazing work and Cody came out fine. (Phil gently reminds me when I see him around town that I haven't been in the office for a long time.) I still neglect taking special care of myself, nurturing my spirit. I want to do this more. What I have discovered is that we can look at balancing three important pieces each day. I will refrain from putting them in any significant order because they are all equally important. There is no "triage" to perform here, only balance to achieve. When we get comfortable with this, we know that each day will be different as we give more energy to certain areas.

It's good to be mindful about doing something you don't like to do. Take care of something you are putting off and resisting. It can be correcting an inaccurate insurance bill. It can be returning a phone call to someone you'd rather avoid. It can be taking your closet apart and giving half of your clothes to charity because they don't fit you anymore. The key is being honest with yourself and tackling something that annoys you everyday. Alleviating pressure from a nagging challenge definitely improves my sense of balance.

Next, after you make that call, go to the dump, re-do your filing system or whatever, decide on what you can do to take care of yourself. Maybe go to a bookstore/café and order a nice hot drink. Look through an aisle of interesting books. Go for a walk. Call someone you haven't spoken to but want to. Cook yourself a nice meal, or if you can afford it, take yourself out. Bring a friend, or go alone. Go see a movie. Go to a pet store and watch exotic fish. Follow your breath, look deep within and try to tap into what your mind or body is asking for. Make it happen. Love yourself enough to know that you have needs and deserve kindness.

The other piece to find wholeness, as I see it, is being of service. This step has helped me the most to heal. I try to do at least one spontaneous act of kindness a day. It can be simple. It will have an immediate effect on you and the person or group of people you are being kind to. I have always drawn strength from giving to others, during my time of grief, I found this habit to be rewarding, even healing. In the last two years, I began cutting my neighbor's nails. He has M.S. and is one of my very dearest friends. I try to do this regularly for him, and I think I am benefiting the most by this. I try to send people unexpected cards. I cook extra food and drop it off at friend's houses. I try to be a listener; this is probably the area of service the most needed in our hectic and over-done society. I try to read to children or listen to children's stories. I try to pamper people in a light and non-patronizing fashion. I try to be a good friend, I try to invite new people to events and check in on friends who may be struggling or feeling alone. I try to reach out to at least one person a day and let them know I appreciate them.

If I manage to achieve these three "balancing acts" a day, I am so much happier and more fulfilled. I hope this list makes getting in balance a little easier for you, too.

Words from Paige Stockley-Lerner

What has helped in coping with my grief has been to have something to DO. Since I was powerless in the face of the airplane crash, this created a feeling of impotence, that I was unable to save my parents in their moment of need. I had a dream once that I was hiding in the bushes, and saw my parents inside a barbed wire concentration camp. I was able to master-mind their escape, and succeeded in saving their lives.

Since the crash I feel as if I have been a crusader against evil, and have relentlessly fought against the corporations whose merciless greed led to deaths of 88 people. This has helped combat my feelings of helplessness. I have also poured energy into monument projects, and in reaching out to fellow survivors.

My father has come to me in several dreams, and he also appeared to my sister in a dream on the night of the crash. She was walking down the basement stairs at my grandmother's house in her dream, going to check on the wine cellar. My father was waiting for her and said, "Everything is going to be OK kiddo," he said, "Don't worry."

Later, I had a dream that my father arrived home from a trip and I greeted him at the airport. He and my mother were coming home, and everyone knew that they had a terminal illness, and wouldn't be here for very long. My father came to me first as I waited in the crowd, handing me a

323

sprig of rosemary (for remembrance) and hugged me for a very long time, meaningfully. He said, "We can't stay long, but we will be with you for awhile, as long as you need us."

The other visitation in dreams I had from my dad was a long talk, just the two of us, as he helped me sort out the business issues we were grappling with in the wake of the crash. He appeared younger and thinner, in a leather bomber's jacket, about the age of 40. My mother has not appeared to me in dreams, but I know she is surrounding me, mostly in the form of flowers. One of my worst days, a few months after the crash when I could not stop crying or get out of bed, an enormous floral bouquet arrived. I had not received flowers from anyone in months, and this bouquet happened to arrive on the first day of Spring. My friend Polly in NY had sent them, not even realizing it was the first day of Spring.

I knew that my mother was trying to comfort me. The other day, as I was driving, worried about something at work, a rainbow appeared in the sky. I knew again that it was my parents' telling me not to worry.

Paige lost her mother, Peggy Stockley and her father Tom Stockley on flight #261.

Earlene Shaw's Comments

By Earlene Shaw, Wife of Donald Shaw

I would love to share a couple of thoughts about Don... We met in 1961 for the first time... at the student housing on the campus of Western Washington University. We were both married to other people and had families, he with two children and me with three... all very little. We were all good friends in the married housing unit... wonderful time, great friends. After graduation everyone went their own way with their careers and some eighteen years later, Don and I ran into each other again. He had been divorced for about eight years and I had divorced nine years earlier... coincidentally, our last two children were in colleges in the area. After three incredible years of getting to know each other on this different level we married... never looking back to wonder if this was the right thing... it was soooo right!!! We were married 15 and 1/2 years when he died.

What helped me get through these three plus years? The family group of #261 in this area and the incredible constant support of my sister and kids... it was almost easier with them grieving almost as much as me because they never tried to talk me out of it with promises of how it "will be better in time"... "all things happen for a reason"... on and on... they let me build my "shrine" to Don in our home and cry everyday for two years, rant and write letters, go to

Washington, DC to raise as much hell as I could... these are the things that kept me somewhat sane. My future had been erased with Don's death... I still am searching to re-define myself without him.

Yes, I do dream about Don once in a while... they are usually very simple, loving contacts... sometimes intimate. I have had nightmares but they are not of the crash and don't have Don in them... just unusual dreams for me.

If I were to say anything else about Don and me it would have to be that we had the most profound love for each other... like none I have ever had or heard of... for this I try to be thankful... too many people never have it. However, corporate greed and neglect took that away from us and that is *wrong*. I don't hate these people. I would rather be me than them... I can live with my actions.

Musings of A Grieving Mother

By JoVanna Luque, Mother of Jay Luque

On April 1, 2000, I retired from Hospice of San Francisco and moved to Olympia Washington. It was my plan after getting settled and taking a rest to become involved in advocacy related to the lack of availability and lack of quality Health Care in this country for too many people and especially for Seniors. I did not know at this time that soon I would be attempting to take on the Airline Industry and trying to make them accountable for caring more about their bottom line than about the safety of their passengers.

On January 31, 2000, my life changed so drastically that just to breathe and think clearly became an effort. For on that day, Alaska flight 261 crashed into the Pacific Ocean while returning from Puerta Vallarta, Mexico. Our son Jay and 87 others perished.

First came disbelief. "No he was not on the plane, he caught a later plane." Then the need to pace the floor with a heart pounding so fiercely against my breast that I thought my life would end right then. And in fact my life did change – it only felt like it was ending on June 31, 2000. A roller coaster of emotions was to be my life for a long time and on an hourly, daily basis.

It is now three years later. I am still surviving. I have

327

gone through rage at those who chose bottom line profits over passenger safety, rage so intense that at a point in time, I had to give it up because it was consuming me and isolating me from family and friends. It became apparent to me that appropriately directed anger and action would serve a better purpose. I needed to try and find a way that would make sense of this terrible accident. I needed to learn to breathe easily again.

One has to find the path back to sanity. Each one of us affected by that day struggled to find ways to regain a sense of balance. Even in my own family we all approached our grief differently. Some like me raged, some withdrew, some I believe actually died sooner then they would have, affected in such a cruel way by their grief.

I found others who I felt safe with, to whom I did not have to explain every word and feeling. Those who were not intimidated by my consuming grief. Such empathic souls are not easy to come by. Because they had their own grief to deal with and nothing to give back, they were just trying to make it through a day. But fate brought them to me... some of the other family members who lost loved ones on that plane. Our paths crossed and these people created some of the few positive experiences to come out of this terrible day that Jay died. They too had their grief, but we were able to support each other through the insanity of so many deaths on that day. We had a connection. We were emotionally and spiritually connected by that crash in a way that is very hard to describe.

My dreams sometimes are of Jay, his presence, his face and smile. They are fleeting, they never last long enough. Sometimes during my waking hours I see a rainbow, hear a song, or get a feeling that he is watching, listening and guiding me until he feels I can go on with some quality in my life. In the beginning there were nightmares of what he and others were experiencing as that plane went nose down into the Pacific Ocean. I could not prevent his fear and pain. Those were terrible nights. His sister, after three years still does not sleep well because of the nightmares.

There is no rhythm or reason to why some days now are better than others. Bouts of grief and missing him can be triggered by seeing someone while shopping who looks like him. Hearing the music he loved. A rainbow, a sunset or sunrise, a movie. Grief and fond memories can come and be a part of me all at once. Colliding and sharing a place in my heart.

I have been very involved with a group that promotes airline safety called National Air Disaster Alliance / NADA. Some of the people I met there have helped me through to this point. They too have lost loved ones in other plane crashes. They have given me emotional support and guidance.

I have written letters to the government agencies over-seeing this case, I have spoken and written to the FBI investigating the case, allowed myself to be interview by the press, spoken with people all over the country who in some way are tied to or affected by a lack of oversight of the Airline industry. Has it made a difference? Who knows, maybe in some way that I may never experience. But in the end after all is said and done, my son Jay and eighty-seven other people are still dead.

It has occurred to me recently that the time has come to accept that this journey will continue, I have choices on how I make the journey. I can no longer give over to rage as that gives those responsible for this crash too much power over my life. They have taken too much from me already, and I no longer wish to allow them to take more from me. I need to give energy to living my life with quality. Too much of my energy has been given to those who caused this crash.

329

Claire, Coriander and Blake Barnett-Clemetson

Claire's Article

*By Claire Barnett, Mother of
Coriander and Blake Barnett-Clemetson
Her daughters were ages 6 and 8.*

People keep asking me "Is it getting a little easier?" They worry that the anniversary of the crash must be especially hard. They so much want time to be helping me, they want things to be getting better. The questions and thoughts are well intended but they profoundly miss the realities of my experience and in doing that deeply echo the loneliness of this place I am in. I want to explain something to people. I want to help people understand why time doesn't heal this wound, and why hoping that it does only makes those with this kind of loss feel even emptier.

January 31st marks the 3rd year since the plane crashed. It was and is a big black horrible dark, dark day – the realities of the crash are unbearable. What it must have been like on the plane. The violence, the fear, and the destruction. The blood and death pounded into the ocean. My beautiful perfect babies. Blake torn into partial pieces. Cori shattered into so many pieces that they never identified her body, not even with DNA analysis. No body was found whole. All of us, the ones left here, have had to face such gruesome facts. The identification process alone took over a year. We are told how much of someone is found. We have had to make unacceptable decisions about unacceptable facts. What do you do with partial remains? What do I do? I have Blake's ashes, some of David's but nothing of Cori. What do I do with this? All the conversations around this are so unacceptable to my heart that the ashes sit in a box David and Miles made together, by my bed, waiting for me to someday have some clear thought about this unthinkable reality.

And the list of horrors goes on and on when dealing with a plane crash. There were false paternity suits showing the most despicable faces of human nature. The "unassociated belongings" – everything found in the wreckage that was not clearly identified to a passenger, was cataloged in a book and we are to pour over it, looking for a familiar T-shirt, socks, book, underwear, hair band... Anything from the trivial to the most meaningful. Looking through that book, at page after page of unidentified clothing and belongings, shoe after shoe, each with its own story, is in itself a horror hard to imagine getting over. The legal system betraying us at every turn, forcing us to argue things like how much they suffered while they died, instead of allowing us to show the clear facts that Alaska Airlines gross negligence, blatant disregard for safety and maintenance and corporate greed murdered these 88 people.

Everyday on the radio, on TV, in the paper, we are forced to see ads by Alaska Airlines, smiling, encouraging people to fly them. It shocks me every time. Alaska Airlines recklessly killed my daughters, destroyed so many lives, and yet somehow that smiling face of its logo is allowed to continue promoting itself. How is it that they are allowed to go on and on? It mocks my reality. A shock every time. They are supposed to be in jail, not cheerfully expanding and cutting fares. Then there is the NTSB investigation. Just finally completed. This big government agency full of smart and dedicated aeronautical experts that have spent the last three years fully investigating every aspect of the crash and finally proving without a doubt that basically Alaska Airlines did not maintain, did not lubricate one of the most critical parts of its airplane. There was no grease on the jackscrew. This was a completely preventable and criminal crash. We have known it for a long time, but to hear just last month the public report of the despicable maintenance and corporate greed that fostered it is staggering.

The list goes on. Selling homes, packing belongings, sorting through the financial and personal details of people. More plane crashes bringing it all back. September 11th. On and on. So much has happened and had to be dealt with over these last three years.

So, the point of all this is that three years ago there was the destruction and horror of the plane crashing and their broken destroyed bodies. For the last three years there have been ongoing "details" that have continued to increase the trauma and magnify the horror of this experience. What time has there been to heal anything? The realities of a plane crash make it something that goes on and on.

I do believe, however, that someday this event, the "crash", will be over. It will not be in the newspaper or on the radio anymore. There won't be any more news or findings or discoveries. And time, at that point, will hopefully help lessen the pain. I hope that the "post traumatic stress" will gradually become more manageable. Then, maybe, time will help heal the wounds of the event of that day, January 31st, 2000. I will be grateful if this happens, but it will be insignificant to the real wound, the big wound, the ongoing relentless wound.

This is my important point. Not to minimize the trauma of the plane crash and its aftermath, because that is in itself an unspeakable horror, but it is nothing compared to the "trauma" of living each day without my daughters. Any mother will understand this. Imagine a day without your children, then imagine a week. Just gone. Disappeared. Away. Day after day without them. Now imagine you have missed them for a year. It only gets worse. The "trauma", the horrible event, is living each day without my daughters. And each day it gets bigger and bigger. Each day the number of days it has been grows larger. Unrelenting. Why would anyone, if he actually thought about it, ask if being prevented from holding, smelling loving, kissing, touching your own precious child for three years had become more bearable after one day, one week, one year? It makes no sense and denies this brutal truth. It is living without my daughters that is the "trauma", that is the unbearable thing. And their absence grows each day. Every day it has been longer since I have held them. And since today seems more painful than I can bear, I can't let myself think about tomorrow. I know it will be harder than today. Today is harder than yesterday. And yesterday was too much. How can anyone think that time helps?

The thing that I have realized, in some sick torturous way, is that I get stronger each day. It is as if each day I have to climb a mountain with a pile of stones on my back, and each day I can carry the weight of yet another stone. I get stronger each day. I am incredibly strong now, stronger than I could ever have imagined, but that is because each day I am asked to do more, live with more pain, more longing, more sadness. The only way I survive is to live in this present moment. I ask myself over and over again through the day, "Can you handle this exact moment?" And so far, I have been able to. It is too much to even look at the day as a whole, to look at the mountain and the rocks I am carrying. I see the three year pile of stones. It daunts me beyond belief, even though I carried almost all of it yesterday. I can't let myself imagine what that pile will look like in five years, ten years. I just go step by step. It is how I don't kill myself, which is really the only way out of this situation, but that would only pass on this burden of pain tho those who love me, those who stand by me each day, wishing they could help, could carry a stone for me. But they can't. No one can. I am alone in this journey. So I go on, step by step, with this heavy load growing heavier each day, up the mountain. I am somehow managing. I do it because there is no way not to. This is the truth of this story. This is what it is like to live when your children have been killed. But don't tell me time will help... each day just adds another stone.

Epilogue

I am very apprehensive about turning forty this April. Some of my reasons were typical; it meant admitting it might be time to say farewell to my youth. There was an immediate association with middle age I felt entering a new decade. Even though I work out at the gym, Cody becomes increasingly more difficult to catch up with. My body is changing; there are definite lines on my face. But facing my birthday this year is a different animal to encounter. It is difficult in a new way, miles and miles from being at all superficial. I believe it has to do with reaching a milestone without my familiar tribe, without the cheering and teasing from my section, without my loved ones. I am realizing my life is now at the middle mark; my glass is half full and half empty.

Digging deeper, I am still waking up and going to bed with my head inside of the airplane, as it were. I have to admit that I still have not shaken this horrific event off. I still feel deprived and ripped off, and mostly I want to hug and laugh with my family once again. Each morning I wake up, I have to gently remind myself that I may not call them, They are not in this world in physical forms anymore.

I find myself eager to talk to people in mourning, and I offer (when asked) sound advice, but rarely do I take heed of my own words. Prescribing exercise and talking to friends about needed support, I sit in front of windows and

335

experience self-pity and inertia. Those two (the pity and inertia) are never a good combination and should be separated from each other whenever possible. Some good friends ask me about planning a party to celebrate my birthday, and nothing seems right. I need to be private about my birthday, and certainly don't want to ruin anybody's good intentions.

Taking this year off from teaching has been enlightening and scary. I am the same person, but I have changed. I welcome the silence I get when Cody is at his neighborhood pre-school a few hours a week, and then I miss his asking names of items, his requests to watch Spiderman again, or the re-filling of his bottomless bottle. I weaned him right before he turned two, and then had times of not feeling needed enough by him. I push my husband away even though I want and crave to be held and loved.

Am I different from others, or just healing? I don't know and I will never know really. My drive and passion as a human being has been damaged, or at least challenged. I thought it would be easy to stay in pajamas until late morning and not go to work. I thought if I set up my house in a child-centered way, Cody would co-exist with me naturally and easily. We could eat healthy lunches together and I would write when he was sleeping. I would ignore the phone and focus on my writing. Few days ended up like this. Yet, we are still thriving, still breathing, having meltdowns and good laughs. We are both seemingly new in this world. We care for each other, spend a lot of time lying down together, touching each other's ears and communicating and trusting each other without words.

I don't know what I would do without my children. Claire's losses seem absolutely insurmountable to me. My heart aches for her, knowing she has lost her greatest source of joy and comfort, her two precious daughters. I was also deeply affected by the murder of Laci Peterson and her unborn son last Christmas Eve.

I watched Laci Peterson's mother give a heart-wrenching press conference yesterday on the television. Her inno-

cent 27 year old daughter and unborn son were found float-
ing in the water near the Oakland marina almost four
months after they disappeared. This has gained national
coverage, as the husband of Laci was arrested, accused of
being the murderer. To hear and see the pain of this poor
mother and the rest of her family was powerful, gut
wrenching, and all too familiar. Her face scrunched up with
screaming tears as she pleaded that her daughter and her
unborn Grandson did not deserve to die in a watery grave.
She wanted the killer (without mentioning his name) to
hear her daughter's desperate cry and the cry for her
unborn son ringing in his ears forever.

I think the war of grief has given me a hand at predict-
ing how this will go. Neither time, nor the fact that her son-
in-law will sit behind bars or get the death penalty will ease
Laci's mother's pain or still her pounding heart in the middle of the night. As much as she tries to conjure up sweet
memories of her daughter, her mind will imagine what her
poor daughter looked like in the ocean, how she was murdered, she will wonder how terrified she was and how long
she stayed conscious. She will hate having these bloody
images as she tries to piece together the worst mystery
imaginable, but she will have nights and nights of being tortured.

My good friend JoVanna suggested that I still need to
hold my own grief at arm's length. I asked her to read this
epilogue. I told her I didn't know how to end this book. She
wasn't sure why I brought up my sorrow over Laci
Peterson murder as I was ending my book. This book, after
all, is about my own journey with grief.

Nobody stares inside of my guts like JoVanna. Her fifteen years working as the volunteer coordinator with
Hospice shows. I can hear the humming of the refrigerator
as she studies my face and waits ever so patiently for me to
find words. Often there are no words in the English language, that fit. I think JoVanna just wants me to be aware,
to notice.

I slowly find words to express that it is a natural instinct for me to re-live my shock and pain as if it were brand new. When Laci Peterson's mother, or other new faces on the news react to sudden death, murders, plane and car wrecks, random shootings, disappearances happen, I fall down again. I feel the scrapes – the raw scraping on asphalt. When these innocent newcomers, the families, get their phone calls, I feel so sensitive to it that I project my own agony on all grievers, knowing that we all get involuntarily sucked down into the basement of shock and disbelief. It wasn't so long ago, January 31, 2000. I have come a little way, but still have a long way to go. I want to take new griever's hands, sit with them, listen to them, and mostly be present. This is *all* I can do.

Every time I get together with JoVanna we talk about our real feelings and processes. We share how it truly feels to be the same people, when we *know* we have changed as much as our lives have.

I think there is a part of me so connected to the deceased that when a new tragedy occurs, I force myself to see the whole picture, to uncover every single detail. The not knowing is the worst. I identify so much with Mrs. Rocha because there are no witnesses to either of our tragedies, and the autopsy reports could only be read while throwing up in the bathroom. She may sleep better or feel the Lord or Great Spirit beside her more over the weeks and months and years, but it is more about becoming accustomed to having a gaping hole in one's heart. She will feel the love and support and unconditional sympathy from the world, but the journey is hers, alone. I feel terrible for her, and for the parents whose children will never be found. I feel sick for the Iraqi children who lost their families in this stupid war. I weep for the thousands affected by the deaths of those killed in the September 11th tragedy. I still mourn for those innocent kids and teachers at Columbine High School. I want to say goodbye to Arlene Hamilton and talk about our mystical experience in Colorado. Easter just passed, and happened to fall on April 20th, the second anniversary of the passing of my friend, Smith Dobson.

There are so many long nights when I place myself in his wife Gail's shoes empathizing with their children, Smith Jr. and Sasha. I can fall back so easily; right to the place of shock and terror of learning that our loved ones left this world in a horrible way.

I rehearse what I would want to say to the airlines, behind closed doors. How I want to yell and kick the husbands who would murder their neighbors' wives and unborn children. When motherhood gives me especially sweet days, (recently Cody tells me he loves me "much"), I sometimes feel the need to reach out to JoVanna or Claire, to give away this joy as if I am not deserving of the love of my own child.

I can't always feel it coming on, but I know when the obsessive spiraling down images of those killed begins to take me over. At times I become too uncomfortable to remain complacent. This is when I realize I want to be a wise forty year old and not a former thirty-nine year old living in the past. I want to make a transition, to shed my old skin.

There will always be some very long nights of mourning, and other nights I can sleep more peacefully. My doctor prescribed Klonopin for the times I can't shut off my mind. Usually it's the unpleasant images, that sing the loudest. I had terrible dreams when the bodies of Laci Peterson and her fetus were found in the bay. I had nightmares when I learned that the criminal investigation of Flight # 261 had been re-opened. I was excited, but my mind bubbled over with imagining what might be uncovered.

Now I want control, I want to lead and be a hero of some kind so that accidents will be prevented. I want to settle the pending lawsuits in conjunction with my father, but I want to *hold on* and wait for a jury to decide how to punish the airlines. I can see it in the eyes of my friends. This has gone on too long.

A big part of me never wants to settle because I don't want to ever give the airlines the false idea that things are even or will *ever* be fair. I know that CEO's don't go to jail, and I know that big corporations will always be protected. As much as I am a broken record about the murders of these innocent travelers, these eight-eight people, there will be more unfairness and tragedy in this world. I think, as a culture, we are overcooked. Done. We can be so powerful, yet in truth, we are still *powerless*. I never knew how excruciating it could be to lose the family I loved so dearly because I never saw it coming. That is the whole puzzle about sudden death, we just don't know. Nobody ever told me what it was like because *I never asked*.

As my life was going so well three years ago, others might also recite my alibi, that death took their loved ones away so quickly and unexpectedly. They may also admit they are torn and broken, that their spirit is broken and they can't function. This experience of loss is larger than any one or any twenty-one of us. The losses come from all corners. I protested this current war in Iraq like so may others, and it happened anyway. This is my opportunity to say three things. The first is *love your family and friends unconditionally*. Tell them you love them every chance you get. Get over resentments and arguments with them, because you never know when and if you will see them again. Keep olive branches in your pockets at all times, laugh at your faults and shortcomings and forgive others for theirs.

Second, know this. *You will survive.* You will get through this darkness and someday you will be able to sleep again. You will get used to your suffering and find that you are alone, but *not* alone. Your life will never be the same and the holidays will always be the worst. But so will the cold nights and bright mornings and the pre and post anniversaries. What I am saying is that grief is timeless and can't be regulated with a time release capsule you choose to take. It will knock you on your ass when you least expect it, and sometimes you may be pleasantly surprised by your own resilience.

Third, the best medicine is to love yourself and love others. Try to volunteer. Be of service. Look at the person for whom you grieve so heavily and try to be inside of them by allowing yourself to enter their soul. What were they passionate about in this life? What can you pass on for them? Tell one more person one more time who they were and what they lived for. Do this whenever the grief builds up inside. Like ice, it can prevent swelling, just a little.

And finally, demand that airlines maintain their planes. Insist that planes be made and kept safe. Remind your friends to use seatbelts in their cars. Do whatever you can to keep yourself and the ones you love safe. Do not forget that bad stuff can happen, but remember babies are also being born every minute, flowers are blooming, and we are all capable of having resurrections. Ones that keep us here on earth but see us changed for the better and wiser. Our time here is so short; make a good life. Be gentle with yourself and with others. I believe our loved ones are never too far away. They want us to find the balance between remembering them deeply and privately, dancing for them, and for ourselves.

The past can can feel like broken glass. We'll cut ourselves very badly on the jagged pieces if we hold them too tightly. It's best for us to seek our reflections in these shards, piece together our shattered lives into the glorious mosaics they are, and dance with them slowly, holding them lightly and close to our hearts, careful not to let the blood stain the new clothes we have just changed into.

Janis Ost Ford
Santa Cruz, California
April 22, 2003

Glad You're Here – Keith Greeninger
www.keithgreeninger.com

There comes a time when you can't run any more
A time to face the wind
When all the years have taken their toll
And all the pain must be set free
And all this talk about destiny
All these endless questions about fate
Each child's born into some unknown situation
With an open mind and an instinct to survive

I don't know where you've been
But I sure am glad you're here
You've seen your share of pain
Lord it's written on your face
I don't know why it has to be this way, but it is
At the mercy of our past we all move towards another day
And we hang onto one another
And try to help each other's pain go away

Everybody's carrying a masterpiece
Everybody's got their secrets to tell
I'm just looking for a hand to hold onto in the darkness
Give me some kind of reason to believe in myself
You and I we were lovers
I swear we touched each other's soul
But don't it seem strange
No matter how close we get to one another
There come these times in our lives
When we're always alone

I don't know where you've been
But I sure am glad you're here
You've seen your share of pain
Lord it's written on your face
I don't know why it has to be this way, but it is

At the mercy of our past we all move

Towards another day
And we hang onto one another
And try to help each other's pain go away

River Banks – lyrics by Niki Leeman, sung by Keith Greeninger

God I believe that I don't believe
You're anything I can conceive
You're a liar, you're a prop
I am a thief, you are a cop
I am a tiny grain of sand
You are a puddle in my hand
Drag my nails across my chest
You bleed red like all the rest
Come on God confess
You're crippled fragile and helpless
Tell 'em you don't have a clue
We're on our own and so are you

We'll go down to the river banks
Confess our sins and give our thanks
Drop down upon our knees
C'mon God just you and me
I gather flowers in the park
I drop them in your rainbow heart
They blossom in your raven hair
Each one a tiny colored prayer
Each one exploding in my eyes
Each one taking me by surprise
That something so lovely and new
Is just a still life painting of you

As I let go of your hand
A fragment naked in the sand
I crumble gently to the shore
Nothing is as it was before
I now remember my own name

I am Abel, I am Cain
Spend my love stitching up the rain
I quench my thirst drinking your pain

Someday when you're by the sea
Your undressed heart will think of me
I'll be the tiny grain of sand
That you let slip right through your hand
You'll go down to the river banks
Confess your sins and give your thanks
You'll drop down upon your knees
Right there, love, you will find me

Underneath this forgiving moon
I lay my weapons down with you
We are no longer on trial
I take my place with the orphan child
Remake myself in this holy fire
Add my voice to the orphan's choir
Re-find my family once again
Rejoin my gypsy caravan

Moon Is Shining – Keith Greeninger

Moon is shining,
Moon is shining through the storm clouds
Moon is shining,
Moon is shining through the storm clouds
And the rain that was falling
Ain't gonna fall no more

Stop your crying,
Wipe those tears from your weary eyes
That old moon is shining,
Soon your sun it will be on the rise
And all the pain you were feeling
Ain't gonna hurt no more.

The Other Side – lyrics by Niki Leeman
vocals- Niki Leeman

Time is a tomb the shape of a prayer
An unpolished stone
An old creaking chair
The caretaker moans,
The Goddess, she sighs
I'm so alone
The great compromise

Chorus:
The water is high
The river is wide
I'll meet you someday
On the other side

My sister, my silence
My sweet salvation
My shipwreck my sorrow
My beautiful one
You in my arms
In the carnival light
Is the closest I've come
To feeling alright

Chorus

My tidal wave brother
My old buddy boy
When we were young
We made a whole lot of noise
We banged on our drum
Though I know that we tried
We never did get
The mud from our eyes

Chorus

And we will awake
On a fine day in Spring
With the eyes of a saint
And an unclaimed blessing
And almost forget
Each time that we died
And how far it seemed
To the other side.

Light Up the Sky – by Jessica Baron Turner
Vocals by Jessica Baron Turner

1. I heard you laugh close to the end,
When all your good-byes were forever
Welcoming fate into your arms,
and holding her close as if she were your lover

Chorus:
Long after the stars go out,
Long after they die
Long after the stars go out,
They light up the sky

2. Places in town are all closing down,
except for the weary survivors
But the music you made remains in our hearts.
We're listening now, we will listen forever.

Chorus:
Long after the stars go out,
Long after they die
Long after the stars go out,
They light up the sky

3. Now you are gone, and we've all moved on,
But every last friend still remembers
The joy in your voice, that spark in your eyes,
You're lighting the past like some eternal ember.
Final 2 Choruses